Henry William Tytler

The Works of Callimachus, Translated Into English Verse

The hymns and epigrams from the Greek; with the Coma Berenices from the Latin

of Catallus: with the original text, and notes carefully selected from former

commentators, and additional observat

Henry William Tytler

The Works of Callimachus, Translated Into English Verse
The hymns and epigrams from the Greek; with the Coma Berenices from the Latin of Catallus: with the original text, and notes carefully selected from former commentators, and additional observat

ISBN/EAN: 9783337082857

Printed in Europe, USA, Canada, Australia, Japan

Cover: Foto ©Thomas Meinert / pixelio.de

More available books at **www.hansebooks.com**

THE
WORKS
OF
CALLIMACHUS,

TRANSLATED INTO ENGLISH VERSE.

THE

HYMNS AND EPIGRAMS

FROM THE GREEK;

WITH THE

COMA BERENICES

FROM THE LATIN OF CATULLUS:

WITH THE

ORIGINAL TEXT,

AND NOTES CAREFULLY SELECTED FROM FORMER COMMENTATORS,

AND ADDITIONAL OBSERVATIONS,

By H. W. TYTLER, M.D.

INTER CALLIMACHI SAT ERIT PLACUISSE LIBELLOS,
ET CECINISSE MODIS, PURE POETA, TUIS.   PROPERT.

———————

LONDON:
PRINTED BY T. DAVISON,
AND SOLD BY CHARLES DILLY, BOOKSELLER, IN THE POULTRY.
M.DCC.XCIII.

PREFACE.

EARL OF BUCHAN.

HAVING endeavoured from my earlieſt youth (though ſecluded from the honours of the ſtate and the brilliant ſituations incident to my rank) to imitate the example of that rare and famous Engliſh character *, in whom every compatriot of extraordinary merit found a friend without hire, and a common rendezvous of worth; I had the honour to receive from the unfortunate Author of the following tranſlations an early notification of his intention to offer them to the public, and afterwards the peruſal of the MS. which met with my ſincere appro-bation.

† Sir Philip Sidney.

Dr.

Dr. Tytler was a man of indefatigable induſtry in literary reſearch, to which were added the rare accompaniments of Genius, Taſte, and Imagination.

Scotland though ſufficiently eminent in Philoſophy, Arms and Arts, has been defective till of late in claſſical taſte and erudition. The tranſlations now offered to the public are the firſt from a Greek Poet that have been publiſhed by a native of Scotland in the Engliſh language.

In the tranſlations of Dr. Tytler there will be found in transfuſion of ſentiment, correctneſs of poetry and ſtyle; and in felicity of expreſſion, a ſuperior degree of merit to thoſe publiſhed by the unfortunate Dr. Dodd in the year 1755; and upon the whole an agreeable acceſſion to an Engliſh Claſſical Library.

The tranſlation of ancient Epigram is a difficult taſk. The genius of the Greek or Roman muſt be preſerved, and the point of ſatire or novelty of thought muſt not be hid by the flippancy of a modern dreſs, nor that dignity and ſimplicity abated which belongs to the ages of antiquity, when the Poet was not diſtracted by the multitude of figures connected with artificial refinements.

With

With a view to prepare himself for the tranflation of Callimachus, Dr. Tytler compared every line of the Iliad with Mr. Pope's tranflation, whereby he put himfelf in a congenial train for undertaking to do juftice to Callimachus, and meditating a tranflation of Lucretius; he meant to have done the fame by the Georgics of Virgil and Mr. Dryden.

Whatever may be faid upon thefe fubjects, it is evident to every perfon of learning and tafte, that the ftyle of ancient, is greatly fuperior to that of modern, poetry ; and that thofe who can enable the unlearned to tafte of the beauties of the Greek and Roman poets of eminence in modern languages, are entitled to no vulgar praife.

With refpect to Callimachus himfelf, every man of learning knows, that he was one of the keepers of the Alexandrian Library, and a favourite of Ptolemy Phila-delphus King of Egypt, whofe praifes he celebrates in a beautiful Hymn which almoft infinitely degrades our mo-dern " Joys to great Cæfar;" not on account of its fuperior veracity, but the beauty and fimplicity of its conftruc-tion, devoid of that cumberfome and naufeous machinery of extravagant encomium ; on account of which a

modern

modern man of taſte cannot help wiſhing to fall down and bury the Laureates and the Laurelled in obſcurity. Indeed Voltaire's ſpecimen of an Ode, in the addreſs to the proud man in Zadig, contains an ever-laſting model for the inſtruction of Laureates in the com-poſition of their vile madrigals to Princes :

> Que ſon merite eſt extrême,
> Que des Graces que des Grandeurs,
> ——Ah ! combien Monſeigneur,
> Doit etre content de lui même.

THE FIRST HYMN

OF

CALLIMACHUS

TO JUPITER.

WHILST we to Jove immortal and divine,
Perform the rites, and pour the ruddy wine;

ZHNOΣ εοι τι κεν αλλο παρα σπονδησιν αειδειν

Hymn to Jupiter.] As hymns to the deities were inconteſtibly the moſt ancient ſpecies of poetry, ſo many modern Mythologiſts are of opinion that theſe hymns refer in ſome meaſure to the creation of the world, though wrapt up in fable, and covered with miſt and obſcurity. Without entering into a minute diſcuſſion of this intricate ſubject, it may be obſerved that the beginning of the preſent hymn, the whole of the fourth, and ſeveral paſſages of the ſecond and ſixth, ſeem to favour this hypotheſis. And from the remaining fragments of Orpheus, the writings of Homer, Heſiod, and indeed all the ancient poets, we are well aſſured that the firſt inhabitants of Greece and Egypt acknowledged one ſupreme Being, under various names and with many wonderful, attributes. Sometimes he was called Bacchus, ſometimes Apollo, Pan, Rhea, Diana, or whatever name was moſt agreeable to the fancy of his worſhippers, or more commonly of thoſe poets who celebrated him in their hymns; the poets being the firſt divines as well as hiſtori-

B

Whom fhall the Mufe, with facred rapture fing,
But Jove th' almighty and eternal king,

Λωιον, η Θεον αυτον, αει μεγαν, αιεν ανακτα ;

ans *. At length the fovereignty was given to Jupiter, whom all the nations of Greece
adored as King and Lord of the Univerfe ; and he was fuppofed to be the fource of power,
law and juftice, as we may learn from this hymn of Callimachus, and many paffages of
Homer. Nay fome fragments of orphic poetry, ftill remaining, have defcribed him as
Omnipotent, Omniprefent, and the Creator of the Univerfe.

Ζιυς ωυθμην γαιης τι και ηρανη αςιροοιτος †,
Ζιυς ωοιτυ ριζα, Ζιυς Ηλιος ηδι σιληνη ;
Ζιυς βασιλιυς, Ζιυς αυτος απαντων αρχιγενιθλος;,
Παντα γαρ εν Ζηνος μεγαλω ταδι σωματι κειται
Εν κρατος, εις Δαιμων, γινεται μεγας αρχος απαντων.
Εις Ζιυς, εις Αιδης, εις Ηλιος, εις Διονυσος,
Εις Θεος εν ωαντεσσι ‡.

" Jupiter, the foundation of the earth and the ftarry heaven ; Jupiter the fountain of
" the fea ; Jupiter, the Sun and Moon ; Jupiter the King ; Jupiter the firft progenitor
" of all. For all things are within the great body of Jupiter. One Lord, one deity, and
" the great fource of all."

" Jupiter, Pluto, Bacchus and the Sun are one deity in all."

But when the firft traditions were loft by various events happening in a long fucceffion
of ages ; when it became the cuftom to worfhip the feveral appearances of nature under
different names, and to deify kings and great men after their deaths, human actions were
afcribed to the fupreme Being. Hence the multiplicity of Gods, the ridiculous attributes
they were thought to poffefs, and the many fables about their birth, life and death. A
King of Crete, and an Arcadian prince had been called Jupiter ; the tomb of the firft
was ftill remaining in the time of Callimachus, and the laft was remembered by tradition.

---

* Bryant's Mythol. Vol. I. p. 306, and feq.

† Orphic. Fragm. 6. p. 366. Edit. Gefner, from Proclus on Plato's Alcibiades.

‡ Orphic. Fragm. 4. Edit. Gefner.

Thus

Who from high heav'n, with burſting thunder, hurl'd　　　　5
The ſons of earth, and awes th' ætherial world!

Πηλογονων ελατηρα, δικασπολον ουρανιδητι;

Thus both nations contended for the honour of the birth of Jupiter, and had many diſputes concerning it. But ſtill they ſuppoſed that he muſt have been born at a very remote
period, when the face of things was different, the world but thinly peopled, and mankind
lived uncomfortably. The blending of ſo many ſtories together neceſſarily introduced
much confuſion in the worſhip and celebration of the deities. Callimachus took theſe
ſtories as they were handed down to him, no doubt adding fictions of his own to make
them the more poetical, and ſeldom forgetting to celebrate his great patron Ptolemy
Philadelphus, whoſe power he derives immediately from Jupiter. In the hymn before us,
this Deity is repreſented under three different characters; firſt as the Air; ſecond as a
Man; third as the Sovereign of heaven and earth, all which will be taken notice of in
the following notes.

The Greek Ζευς is derived either from ζη, vivere; becauſe Air was thought to be the
principle of life; or from δυω, to moiſten with ſhowers; becauſe rain falls from the
heavens*. As for the Latin name Jupiter, it is ſo plain a compound of the two Greek
words Ζευ πατηρ that I need not trouble my readers with arguments to prove the de-
rivation of it.

V. 2. Perform the rites and pour the ruddy wine] The hymns to the deities were
ſung while the prieſts performed the ſacred rites, and poured out the libations. They
were ſometimes accompanied with dancing, but always with inſtrumental muſic either
from the flute or harp, as we read in Proclus and the Scholiaſt on Euripides, Spanheim.
It is not a little ſurpriſing that Mr. Prior ſhould have deviated ſo much from his
original in the very firſt line, as to tranſlate it in this manner:

" While we to Jove ſelect the holy victim."

For the hymns began with the libations, but never with the chooſing of the victim,
which muſt have been ſelected at a diſtance from the temple, and ſometime before the
commencement of the ſacrifices.

* Tobias Damm in verb Ζευς.

But fay, thou firft and greateft pow'r above!
Shall I Dictæan or Lycæan Jove

Πως και ιν, Δικταιον αεισομεν, ηε Λυκαιον;

V. 3. Whom fhall the Mufe, with facred rapture fing] There is a great beauty in the
beginning of this hymn. The Poet feems to be at once tranfported and awed with the
grandeur of his fubject. He is impatient to begin, but, ftruck with the thought of
celebrating the king of Gods and Men, he makes a paufe, and doubts if his poems are
equal to the tafk. Horace begins one of his fineft Odes in the fame manner.

> Quem virum aut heroa lyra vel acri
> Tibia fumes celebrare, Clio ?
> Quem Deum *?
> What man, what hero, on the tuneful lyre,
> Or harp-ton'd flute will Clio choofe to raife
> Deathlefs to flame ? What God ?——FRANCIS.

V. 5. Who from high heav'n, with burfting thunder hurl'd
     The fons of earth, and awes th' ætherial world]

The Commentators and Mythologifts differ very much about the expulfion of the
Giants, the moft famous action afcribed to Jupiter. Frifchlinus tells us that they were
called the Sons of the earth, on account of their obfcure and uncertain original, but
gives no authority to fupport his opinion. The name ωπλογοιοι fignifies the offspring of
flime or mud, and may as well refer to the formation of man in general, as to any particular race of mankind, whatever their fize might be. Frifchlinus offers four different
fignifications of this fable ; 1ft. That it fignifies the fall of the Angels. 2d. The fall of
Man. 3d. The difperfion of Mankind at the building of Babel. And 4th. That this
fable contains an obfcure tradition of the deluge : which opinion feems the moft probable ; and is confirmed by the ftory in Homer, that Thetis affifted Jupiter in his war with
the Giants. Or, in other words, that the Sea received the waters of the deluge in part,
after they began to fubfide, and thus contributed to difperfe the thick clouds and noxious

* Hor. lib. i. ode 12.

vapours

Attempt to fing? ... Who knows thy mighty line?
And who can tell, except by pow'r divine, 10
If Ida's hills thy facred birth may claim,
Or far Arcadia boaft an equal fame?

Εν δοιη μαλα θυμος· επει γενος αμφηριςον. 5
Ζευ, σε μεν Ιδαιοισιν εν ουρεσι, φασι γενεσθαι,
Ζευ, σε δ' εν Αρκαδιη· ποτεροι, πατερ, εψευσαντο;

vapours that darkened the fky, and rendered the air unwholefome*. The Abbé Banier, who has almoft entirely banifhed Allegory from the Mythological fyftem, and laboured to give a connected hiftory of ages in which no hiftory exifted, affures us that the Titans and the Giants were very different perfons; that the former inhabited Spain and Italy, but that the latter were a Set of Banditti whom Jupiter king of Crete deftroyed in an expedition to the Continent of Greece†. And by joining the traditions concerning the deluge with the laft mentioned hiftorical fact, we have the moft probable account of the war with the Giants. At the fame time I muft obferve that Mr. Pope makes this fable allude to the confufion of the elements before they were brought into their natural order‡. But events happening at a period fo remote could fcarce have been handed down by tradition; and if what the Abbé Banier fays be true, namely, that no proof remains of the Pagans having been acquainted with the building of Babel §; it is not likely that they could know much about the war of the elements before the foundation of the world. Befides this idea of fighting elements bears a nearer refemblance to the philofophy of Lucretius, than to the Mofaic account of the Creation.

V. 12. Or fair Arcadia boaft an equal fame] It is to be obferved that all the prayers and addreffes to Jupiter and the fubordinate Deities, fo frequent among the ancient poets, are wonderfully grand and folemn: but the defcription of their lives and actions is always trifling and puerile. This, no doubt, proceeds from confounding them with

* Hom. Il. v. 396. and feq.   † Banier's Mythol. vol. II. p. 205.
‡ Note on Pope's Iliad Book I. v. 514.   § Banier's Mythol. vol. II. p. 307.

real

The Cretans, prone to falſehood, vaunt in vain,
And impious! built thy tomb on Dicte's plain;

Κρητες αει ψευται. και γαρ ταφον, ω ανα, σειο

real men, whoſe hiſtory in the firſt ages of the world, and before the invention of letters, could be known only from tradition. Callimachus after a ſolemn invocation to Jupiter, as the King of Gods and Men, immediately degrades him to a mere Mortal, by telling us that he was born either on the mountain of Dicte in Crete, or of Lycæus in Arcadia; and endeavours to ſettle the diſpute betwixt the two nations by giving his birth to the one, and his education to the other. We are infoimed by Cicero that the ancient Theologiſts enumerated three Jupiters, the firſt and ſecond born in Arcadia, and the third in Crete, where his Monument was ſtill to be ſeen in the time of that Author*. To give a particular account of any of theſe would far exceed the bounds of a Note; and the ancient Poets differ very much with regard to the birth of even the Cretan Jupiter. The reader deſirous of information on this ſubject may have his curioſity fully gratified by conſulting Banier. Beſides the three mentioned above, we are told by Euſebius that almoſt every nation had a Jupiter of their own, whom they worſhipped under various names, and whom they ſuppoſed to have been born in their country†. This confirms what was ſaid in the beginning, that in times of groſſeſt idolatry all Mankind acknowledged one Supreme Being; and it was then as uncommon to doubt the exiſtence of a Deity, as it is with ſome modern Philoſophers to believe it.

V. 14. And impious! built thy tomb on Dicte's plain] The Greeks and Romans aſcribed no property to their deities not belonging to mankind except Immortality, an opinion admirably ridiculed by Lucian in his moſt humourous dialogue entitled Πρασις Σιων, or the Sale of Lives. And it ſeems the Cretans, denied even this to the greateſt of their Gods, for which they were cenſured by the poet Epimenides in that celebrated ſaying Κρητες αει ψευται, "the Cretans always Liars." This was become a proverb long before the time of Callimachus, and he reproaches them in the words of their own poet for having built a tomb to a deity who muſt neceſſarily live for ever. The ſame proverb is

* Cic. de Nat. Deor. Lib. III. cap. 21.   † Euſeb. Lib. III. Evangelic. Præparat.

quoted

For Jove, th' immortal king, fhall never die,   15
But reign o'er men and Gods above the fky.
 In high Parrhafia Rhea bore the God,
Where gloomy forefts on the mountains nod ;

Κρητες ετεκτηνανῖο. συ δ' ου θανες· εσσι γαρ αιει.
Εν δε σε Παρρασιη Ρειη τεκεν, ἡχι μαλιᵴα   10

quoted by St. Paul Titus I. 12. and we are informed by Erafmus that St. Jerom found
this line in a poem of Epimenides exactly as it ftands in the New Teftament, where it
makes a complete Hexameter verfe.†

   Κρητες αει ψευται, κακα θηρια, γαϛερις αργαι.
   " The Cretans always Liars, evil Beafts, flow Bellies."
The Greek Scholiaft endeavours to remove the firft part of this imputation from them,
and tells us that the infcription upon the tomb originally runs thus, Μινως τε Διος ταφος,
" The tomb of Minos the Son of Jupiter." And that the two firft words being effaced
by time there remained only Διος ταφος, " The tomb of Jupiter," which gave rife to the
ftory. But fince it is allowed by all Hiftorians that a king, named Jupiter, once reigned
in Crete, died and was buired there, the account given by Suidas feems the moft probable ; namely, that the words of the infcription were, ενθαδε κειται θανων Πηκος ὁ Ζιυς, " Here
" lies Pecus (or according to Kufter) Picus who was called Jupiter."† Banier cites this
paffage of Suidas, but, for I know not what reafon, tranflates the infcription given by
Porphyry in place of it. " Here lies Zan who was called Jupiter."‡ This tomb was
fituated near the city of Gnoffus, below the mountain of Dicte. But the very learned
and ingenious Mr Bryant, who has ftudied ancient Mythology with more diligence than
any native of Great Britain, affures us that thefe ταφοι were not tombs, but λοφοι μετεωδεις,
" Conical mounds of earth," on which in the firft ages Offerings were made by fire.
Vide Bryant's Mythology, Vol. I. p. 449 and feq. where the Reader will find an accurate
and entertaining difcuffion of this fubject.

 * Erafm. in Chiliad. † Suid. in verb Πηκος. ‡ Dan. Mythol. vol. II. p. 177.

                 Ver. 26.

And hence such awful horror guards the grove,

Made holy by the glorious birth of Jove,   20

That now no teeming female dares presume

To bear her young amid the hallowed gloom :

Nor beast nor insect shall approach the shade,

Nor matron chaste invoke Lucina's aid

Within the dark recess, still known to fame,   25

And Rheas ancient bed th' Arcadians name.

     Soon as her womb discharged the mighty load,

She sought a spring to bath the new-born God,

Εσκεν ορος Θαμνοισι περισκεπες. ενθεν ὁ χωρος

Ιερος. ύδε τι μιν κεχρημενον Ειλειθυιης

Ερπετον, ύδε γυνη επινισσεται. αλλα ἑ Ρειης

Ωγυγιον καλεουσι λεχωιον Απιδανηες.

Ενθα σ᾽ επει μητηρ μεγαλων απεθηκατο κολπων,   15

V. 26. And Rhea's ancient bed th' Arcadians name] All the former translators of the hymn of Jupiter have omitted this line, although it relates to a piece of ancient history preserved by Pausanias, namely, that no person durst enter the cave on the top of mount Lycæus, in which Rhea was supposed to have brought forth Jupiter, except the priestesses of that Goddess. Upon one of the Summits stood a temple sacred to Jupiter Lycæus, which men were forbidden to enter; and on another an altar, where sacred rites were performed to this deity.*   Arcadia was called Parrhasia from Parrhasus one of the sons of Lycaon. Mount Lycæus and the Olympus of Arcadia are the same.

* Pausanias in Arcadic.

Ver. 40.

But in Parrhafia yet no ftream appears,
Tho' fam'd for num'rous rills in after-years ;   30
And when the Pow'r ungirt her fpacious breaft,
The dufty fields difplayed a barren wafte.
Nor yet broad Ladon flow'd, the plains to lave,
Nor Erymanthus pour'd his limpid wave ;
Wide branching oaks Iafus' channel fhade,   35
And chariots roll on Mela's fandy bed :
Unnumbered favage beafts fecurely throng,
Where now deep Carion fwiftly glides along ;
A thirfty fwain amid the wilds might go
Where chryftal Cratis and Metopè flow,   40

Αυτικα διζητο ροον υδατος, ῳ κε τοκοιο
Λυματα χυτλωσαιτο, τεον δ᾽ ενι χρωτα λοεσσαι.
Λαδων αλλ᾽ ουπω μεγας ερρεεν, ουδ᾽ Ερυμανθος
Λευκοτατος ποταμων. ετι δ᾽ αβροχος ηεν απασα
Αρκαδιη᾽ μελλεν δε μαλ᾽ ευυδρος καλεεσθαι   20
Αυτις. επει τημοσδε Ρεη οτ᾽ ελυσατο μιτρην,
Η πολλας εφυπερθε σαρωνιδας υγρος Ιαων
Ηειρεν, πολλας δε Μελας ωχησεν αμαξας.
Πολλα δε Καριωνος ανω, διερῃ περ εοντος,
Ιλυους εβαλοντο κινωπετα, νισσετο δ᾽ ανηρ   25
Πεζος υπερ Κραθιν τε, πολυςεισν τε Μετωπην

V. 40. Where chryftal (or literally ftoney) Crathis and Metopè flow] All the rivers
enumerated by Callimachus are mentioned by ancient Geographers, particularly by
Dionyfius, Pliny, Solinus and Strabo.——Frifchlinus.

C

Nor find a fpring ; but ftill, with wonder, hear
Th' imprifon'd water murm'ring on his ear.

The venerable Goddefs, thus diftrefs'd,
With awful voice the pregnant earth addrefs'd ;
Slight are thy pangs, O friendly Pow'r, fhe faid,   45
Bring forth like me to give thy fuppliant aid :
She rais'd her mighty arm as thus fhe fpoke,
And with her fceptre, ftruck the folid rock ;
Wide at the blow, the yawning mountain rent,
The floods impetuous iffued from the vent,   50
And pour'd along the ground in fwelling ftreams,
Where foon fhe bath'd Jove's beauteous infant-limbs.
Thy body cleans'd, and wrapt in purple bands,
She gave the precious pledge to Neda's hands,

Διψαλεος. το δε πολλον ὑδωρ ὑπο ποσσιν εκειτο.
Και ῥ ὑπ᾽ αμηχανιης σχομενη φατο ποτνια Ρειη,
Γαια φιλη, τεκε ϰ συ. τεαι δ᾽ ωδινες ελαφραι.
Ειπε, ϰ ανταννσασα θεα μεγαν ὑψοθι πηχυν,   30
Πληξεν ορος σκηπ῀ρω. το δε οι διχα πουλυ διεϛη,
Εκ δ᾽ εχεεν μεγα χευμα. τοθι χροα φαιδρυνασα,
Ωνα, τεον σπειρωσε. Νεδη δε σε δωκε κομισσαι

V. 44. With awful voice the pregnant Earth addrefs'd] Dr. Dodd has reduced the
great Mother of the Gods to a whining girl by tranflating this paffage as follows ;
" Diftreft the Goddefs heav'd a feeble Sigh."

V. 53. Thy body cleans'd and wrapt in purple bands] The Greeks had feveral
methods of managing new-born infants. The Athenians plunged them in cold water
(a cuftom

And much enjoin'd her, with a mother's care, 55
To feek the Cretan cave and hide thee there.
For fhe was firft-born of the beauteous maids
That nurs'd the Thund'rer in the gloomy fhades,
Save Styx and Philyrè; from whence fhe gain'd
More high rewards than virgin e'er obtain'd : 60
For Neda's name the grateful Goddefs gave
To this moft ancient ftream, whofe rolling wave

Κευθμον εσω Κρηταιον, (ινα κρυφα παιδευοιο)
Πρεσβυτατη νυμφεων αι μιν τοτε μαιωσαντο, 35
Πρωτιζη γενεη, μετα τε Στυγα, Φιλυρην τε.
Ουδ' αλιην απετισε θεη χαριν, αλλα το χευμα
Κεινο Νεδην ονομηνε. το μεν ποθι πουλυ κα]' αυτο

(a cuftom ftill followed in many countries), and the Lacedæmonians in wine, to give
health and vigour to their bodies, and likewife to try their future Conftitutions. For
they fuppofed that ftrong children would bear the bath eafily ; but that thofe of a more
weakly frame would immediately faint or fall into fits. The nurfe then divided the
Umbilical Cord, and wrapt the child in fwaddling bands ; but thefe were never ufed by
the Spartans, who thought that they confined the body too much, and did not allow the
free motion of the limbs. At Athens the new-born infant was wrapped in a Cloth, on
which was reprefented the Gorgon's head, in imitation of the Shield of Minerva, to
fhew that the child was entrufted to the care of the Goddefs of Wifdom. If a boy, he
was laid on a buckler, as an omen of his future valour ; and it was a common practice
among perfons of quality at Athens, to place their infants on dragons of gold ; a cuftom
thought to have been inftituted by Minerva, in memory of King Erichthonius, who had
feet like a Serpent, and being expofed when an infant, the Goddefs gave him in charge
to two dragons. The Reader will find a particular account of all thefe ceremonies in
Potter's Antiquities, Vol. II. p. 325 and feq. where the learned Bifhop refers to this
hymn of Callimachus.

                V. 70.

With force impetuous pours along the plain,
And near the walls of Leprium meets the main;
The fons of Arcas hear the waters roar,   65
And drink the facred flood, and crowd the fhore.

   Thee, mighty Jove, the nymph to Thenæ bore,
And thence to Gnoſſus on the Cretan fhore,
But firſt at Thenæ, cur'd thy recent wound;
Cydonians hence Omphalè nam'd the ground.   70

Καυκωνων π]ολιεθρον, ο Λεπριον πεφατιςαι,
Συμφερεται Νηρηϊ παλαιοτατον δε μιν υδωρ   40
Υιωνοι πινουσι Λυκαονιης αρκ]οιο.

Ευτε Θενας απελειπεν, επι Κρωσσοιο φερουσα,
Ζευ πατερ, η νυμφη σε· (Θεναι δ᾽ εσαν εγγυθι Κνωσσου)
Τουτακι τοι πεσε, δαιμον, απ᾽ ομφαλος· ενθεν εκεινο
Ομφαλιον μετεπειτα πεδον καλεουσι Κυδωνες.   45

V. 70. Cydonians hence Omphalè named the ground] Neither Mr. Prior, Mr. Pitt,
nor Dr. Dodd have thought proper to give this paſſage in Engliſh, although it alludes to
a very curious piece of ancient fuperſtition. They had probably been deterred by the
difficulty of tranſlating the verſe,

          Τουτακι τοι πεσι, Δαιμον, απ ομφαλος· ——
          Ibi tum decidit tibi, Deus, omphalus, vel umbilicus:
But though fuch phrafes tranſlated literally may feem grofs or indelicate to the ears of a
modern Reader, I apprehend they cannot, with propriety be altogether omitted, when
they relate either to an ancient cuſtom or an hiſtorical fact.

   In the dark ages of idolatry and fuperſtition, mankind erected altars to the deities on
the tops of mountains, and repaired with much veneration to rocks and caverns, whence
the Gods were fuppofed to deliver their oracles, called by the Phœnicians Omphi, and
by the Greeks ομφαι, or voices. In the fame manner the mountain of Delphi was
                                                          named

The nymphs of Dictè with encircling arms,
Embrac'd thee blooming in immortal charms;

Ζευ, σε δε Κυρβαντων εταραι προσεπηχυναν]ο

named Omphi-el, or the oracle of the fun; and the Greeks, endeavouring to find a word of a fimilar found in their own language, immediately thought of ὀμφαλος, *Omphalus, a navel*; which by a ftrange perverfion they fubftituted in its place *. And hence Delphi, being the moft celebrated oracle, was thought to be the middle or umbilicus of the whole earth, as Sophocles calls it †. By degrees, the fame appellation was beftowed on every place famous for the refponfes of an oracle, or the refidence of a deity. Thus, in the firft book of the Odyffey, Homer tells us that the ifland of Calypfo was the Omphalos, or Umbilicus of the fea:

Νησω ἐν ἀμφιρυτη ὁθι τ' ὀμφαλος ἐστι θαλασσης,
Νησος διδηνισσα ‡.
Amidft an ifle, around whofe rocky fhore
The forefts murmur, and the furges roar.   Pope.

Every reader muft obferve that the original idea is entirely loft in Mr. Pope's tranflation, which does not give the leaft hint of this ifland being the Omphalus of the fea, and we are only informed that Calypfo lived in the middle of an ifland. At Enna in Sicily was another place of the fame name, probably becaufe that was thought to be the fcene of the rape of Proferpine. It is therefore no wonder that Callimachus, finding a place in Crete named Omphalos or the navel, fhould pretend that it was fo called becaufe the Umbilical Cord of young Jupiter was there fuppofed to have dropped from his body. But it is furely a little ftrange that Diodorus Siculus fhould gravely prefent his readers with the fame ftory, as an hiftorical fact, and tell them that this famous Umbilicus dropped into the river Triton, "from which accident the place", fays he, "was called Omphalos or the navel §". A ftriking inftance of the blindnefs and credulity of the Greeks in relation to religion and mythology. In all other matters, as Mr. Bryant well

---

* Bryant's Mythol. vol. I. p. 240.   † Oedip. Tyrann. v. 487.
‡ Hom. Odyff. Lib. I. v. 50.   § Diodor. Sicul. Lib. V. p. 337.

observes,

The fair Adraste next thy care began,
And laid thy Godhead in a golden van.
On Ida's hills the goat Amalthea bred,   75
There gave thee suck; and mountain-honey fed,
From bees that o'er the cliffs, appear in swarms,
Prepare their waxen domes with hoarse alarms,
Collect the sweets of every fragrant flow'r,
And on thy lips distil th' ambrosial show'r.   80

    The fierce Curetes circle o'er the ground
In warlike dance, and beat their shields around,

Δικταιαι Μελιαι, σε δε κοιμισεν Αδρηϛεια
Λικνῳ ενι χρυσεῳ. συ δ' εθησαο πιονα μαζον
Αιγος Αμαλθειης, επι δε γλυκυ κηριον εϐρως.
Γεντο γαρ εξαπιναια Πανακριδος εργα μελισσης   50
Ιδαιοις εν ορεσσι, τα τε κλειουσι Πανακρα.
Ουλα δε Κουρητες γε περι πρυλιν ωρχησαντο,

observes, they were the wisest of mankind *. The whole inhabitants of Crete sometimes
received the name Cydonians from a city called Cydon.

    V. 74. And laid thy Godhead in a golden van] I have ventured to translate the
word λικνος literally. It signifies a van for winnowing corn, in which newborn infants
were frequently laid, as we learn from the Greek scholiast. A couch or cradle of this
kind was particularly proper for Jupiter to repose in; especially if we consider him
as representing the air. Cradles of wicker are common in our times, and it is customary
to place a dead-born infant on a sieve, which answers exactly to the Greek λικνος.

                    * Bryant's Mythol. vol. I. p. 246.

V. 85.

That Saturn, for thy cries, might hear alone
The clang of armour on his diſtant throne.

Away thy infant years thus quickly flew,   85
Thy pow'r appearing as thy ſtature grew,

Τευχεα πεπληγοντες, ινα Κρονος ευασιν ηχην
Ασπιδος εισαιοι, κ͵ μη σεο κυριζοντος.
Καλα μεν ηεξευ, καλα δ᾽ ετραφες, υρανιε Ζευ.   55

V. 85. The ſtory of Jupiter's birth] The preceding account of the birth of the
greateſt God of antiquity, though beautifully told by Callimachus, appears at firſt view
wild and extravagant; but upon farther conſideration may be explained partly by
allegory, and partly by hiſtory. We have the authority of Cicero for ſaying that
Chronus or Saturn is the ſame with Χρονος or time, being ſo called, quod ſaturetur annis,
"becauſe he is full of years". It is likewiſe well known that Rhea, Veſta or Cybele,
the wife of Saturn, is only a perſonification of the earth, or rather of the original
Chaos, from which were formed the heavens, the earth, and all the various appearances
of nature *. Jupiter, or the air, comes from the womb of Chaos, in the ſame manner
that Apollo or the ſun is produced by Latona (another name for Chaos) in the fourth
hymn. And the fable of Rhea ſtriking the mountain with her ſceptre, and thus giving
birth to the rivers of Arcadia, ſignifies that air and water exiſted at the ſame inſtant.
I am not ignorant that ſeveral commentators, and among the reſt Spanheim, makes
this paſſage refer to the miracle recorded, Exodus xvi. 6. becauſe Callimachus might
have read the Old Teſtament, being keeper of the Alexandrian Library, at the time
that the ſeptuagint tranſlation is ſuppoſed to have been made. But beſides that the date
of this tranſlation has never been aſcertained, it does not ſeem probable that our Poet
would have borrowed the account of this miracle alone, without introducing other
paſſages from the Old Teſtament in different parts of his works. Thus far the
ſolution is natural and eaſy; but for an explication of the remaining parts of this fable,
we muſt have recourſe to the hiſtory of the Cretan Jupiter.

* Voſſ. de Or. et Progr. Idololatr. Lib. II. cap. 54.

It

And foon thou glow'ft with ev'ry youthful grace,
And foon foft down o'erfpreads thy beauteous face ;
Jove, yet a child, the prize of wifdom bears
From both his brothers in maturer years :   90

Οξυ δ' Ανηβησας, ταχινοι δε τοι ηλθον ικλοι.

Αλλ' ετι παιδνος εων εφρασσαο παντα τελεια·

It is faid that Saturn caufed a very fevere operation to be performed on his father
Uranus, who prayed that his grandfons might ferve Saturn in the fame manner. This
prince, according to the fuperftition of the times, confidered his father's imprecations, as
a prediction, and therefore caufed his children to be fhut up, one by one, immediately
after their birth. His wife Rhea, refenting this ufage, and being delivered of Jupiter
in her hufband's abfence, gave him in charge to three of her maids, Neda, Styx and
Philyrè, who conveyed him into Crete, where he was privately educated by the Curetes
and Corybantes, whom Herodotus calls Phœnician priefts, * and who inhabited mount
Ida. They took great care of the young prince, hid him in a cave, and fed him with
goat's milk, which Lactantius tells us was brought him every day by Amalthea the
daughter of Melittus king of Crete, † and hence the fable of his being fuckled by a
fhe-goat that was afterwards placed among the Stars. The wives of thefe priefts were
called Melifſæ, and thus it was feigned that fwarms of bees fed him with honey ; though
fome fuppofe that they were real bees. Virgil has taken notice of this circumftance :

            Dictæo cœli regem pavêre fub antro. ‡

        The king of heaven in Cretan caves they fed.   DRYDEN.

The Curetes likewife invented a warlike dance called dactylos, in which they clafhed
their fpears againft their bucklers with many contorfions of the body : and hence they
were called Corybants, i. e. people who fhake their heads. By this noife they prevented
the cries of Jupiter from being heard, not by his father Saturn, who was then in a
different country, but by their neighbours unacquainted with the fecret. Such is the
hiftorical account of Jupiter's birth given by the Abbé Banier, who has beftowed much

* Herodot. Lib. I.   † Lactant. de falf. Religion.   ‡ Virg. Georg. IV. v. 152.

time

And both agreed that th' empire of high heav'n,
Tho' theirs by birthright, fhould to Jove be giv'n.

Τῳ τοι και γνωτοι, προτερηγενεες περ εοντες,
Ουρανον ᾶκ εμεγηραν εχειν επιδαισιον οικον.

time and labour upon this fubject *. And one may obferve how exactly the above narration agrees with Callimachus; although Banier feems little acquainted with this poet, and mentions him but twice in his whole book.

V. 92. Tho' theirs by birth-right fhould to Jove be giv'n] Some of the moft ancient poets, and particularly Homer, make Jupiter the eldeft fon. Thus in the fifteenth book of the Iliad, he commands Neptune, by his meffenger Iris, to retire from the field of battle, with this threat in cafe of a refufal.

Μη μ' ᾶδι κρατερος περ ιων, ιπιοντα ταλασση
Μειναι· ιπιι ιο φημι βιη πολυ φιρτερος ιιναι,
Και γινη προτιρος· τᾶδᾶκ ὁβιται φιλον ἡτορ
Ιϳον ιμοι φασθαι, τον τι ϲυγιασι, και ἁλλοι †.

If he refufe, then let him timely weigh
Our elder birth-right and fuperior fway.
How fhall his rafhnefs ftand the dire alarms
If heav'n's omnipotence appear in arms ?
Strives he with me by whom his pow'r was giv'n,
And is there equal to the Lord of Heav'n.   Pope.

But Callimachus, with great judgment, agrees with the prevailing tradition among his countrymen, that Jupiter was the youngeft. And, to promote the caufe of religion, and encreafe their veneration for the fupreme being, affures them, that the two brothers refigned their claims on account of his fuperior power and wifdom. In this refpect he has outdone both Homer and Virgil, who affert, with other ancient poets that Jupiter obtained the empire of heaven by lot ‡.

* Banier's Mythol. Vol. II. p. 205, et feq.   † Hom. Il. XV. v. 164.
‡ Ibid. v. 187. Virg. Æn. I. v. 143.

D   This

Yet ancient poets idle fictions tell
That lots were caſt for heav'n, for earth, and hell,

Δηναιει δ' ἐ παμπαν ἀληθεες ἠσαν ἀοιδοι·   60
Φαντο παλον Κρονιδηϲι δια τριχα δωματα νειμαι·

This diviſion of the world among the three ſons of Saturn has puzzled both hiſtorians and mythologiſts. Some have imagined, with no great probability, that it muſt contain an obſcure hint of the ſacred Trinity *. For as the doctrine of the Trinity was firſt revealed in the New Teſtament, it is not likely that the ancients could know much about it ſeveral hundred years before the New Teſtament was written. Others ſuppoſe that it refers to the diviſion of the world among the three ſons of Noah †. And if we may believe Garcilaſſo de la Vega, this tradition was known even in Peru ‡ But, for my own part, I can ſee no reaſon for ſuppoſing ſuch a diviſion. Shem, Ham, and Japhet were the three principal perſons that came out of the ark ; we are well aſſured that they continued ſome time with their father : and when there were only three or at moſt four families on the whole globe, it is more reaſonable to believe that they would aſſociate together than that one would remain in Aſia, the ſecond travel to Europe, and the third to Africa merely for the ſake of peopling theſe countries. Even allowing the extraordinary longevity of Noahs ſons, and that each of them lived three or four hundred years after the flood, Aſia would be more than ſufficient to contain all their deſcendants. According to ſacred hiſtory, the whole human race journeyed from the *Eaſt*, that is, from the place where the ark reſted, to the building of Babel§, which happened about one hundred years after the flood ; and the diſperſion took place with the confuſion of tongues, when the deſcendants of the three ſons of Noah would be ſo blended together as to make a diſtinction between them impoſſible. If we are to believe the hiſtory of thoſe dark ages, as collected by Banier, Saturn was a great King, and left three ſons who divided his dominions among them. Jupiter poſſeſſed the countries lying towards the riſing Sun; Neptune had Greece, Italy and the adjacent iſles ; and Pluto, Spain, which being ſituated

---

* Notes on Pope's Il. Book XV. v. 210.   † Lactant. de falſ. Relig. lib. I. cap. II.
‡ Hiſtoire des Jncas p. 84.   § Gen. Chap. XI. v. 1.

towards

Our cars thus flatt'ring with amusive tales ;   95
Wit pleases oft'ner than fair truth prevails.
None trust blind chance their fortune to decide,
Unless for equal prizes lots are try'd ;
And who prefers the dark infernal bow'rs
To heav'ns gay courts and bright ætherial tow'rs ?   100
Chance plac'd not Jove in these divine abodes ;
Thy pow'r, thy wisdom, made thee King of Gods !

Τις δε κ' επ' Ὀλυμπῳ τε κ̀ αιδι κληρον ἐρυσσαι,
Ὁς μαλα μη νενιηλος; ἐπ' ἰσαιη γαρ ἐοικε
Πηλασθαι· τα δε τοσσον ὁσον δια πλειςον ἐχυσι.
Ψευδοιμεν ἀιοντρς ἁ κεν πεπιθοιεν ἀκυην.   65
Ου σε θεων ἐσσηνα παλοι θεσαν, ἐργα δε χειρων,

towards the West, was reckoned a gloomy region *. The same author, by a very far-fetched supposition, derives the word Tartarus from Tartessus, a river of Spain, which contradicts his own hypothesis, that the Greek mythology was originally borrowed from Egypt. But, not satisfied with this explication, he deserts his historical system, and follows the opinion of Pausanias, that Jupiter represents the supreme God, who governs Heaven, Earth and Hell under three different names † But if we have recourse to allegory, in which we are supported by the authority of Cicero, the explication is obvious §. Saturn or Time begets three sons, Jupiter or the Air, Pluto or the Earth, and Neptune or the Sea, who naturally enough divide the world among them.

* Banier's Mythol. vol. II. p. 215.   † Ibid.   § Cic. de Nat. Deor. Lib. II. cap. 26.

Then firſt thy bird excell'd th' aërial kind,
Thy mandates waited and reveal'd thy mind ;
Now through the ſkies, at thy command he ſprings,   105
And bears celeſtial aug'ry on his wings.

Ση τε Βιη, το τε Καρτος, ὁ κ̣ πελας εισαο διφρου.
Θηκαο δ' ὀιωνον μεγ' ὑπειροχον αγγελιωτην

V. 103. Then firſt thy bird excelled th' aërial kind] Various reaſons are aſſigned by various authors, why the eagle was thought to be ſacred to Jupiter, to carry his thunderbolts, and to reveal his will to mankind. Pliny tells us that the fiction was founded on truth, becauſe eagles are never deſtroyed by lightning *. This has as much the air of fiction as the ſtory itſelf ; and Spanheim gives two reaſons equally fabulous : firſt, That Jupiter was carried by an eagle into Crete ; and ſecond, That a boy named *Aetos*, the Greek word for an eagle, attended him in the Cretan cave. Others ſay that an eagle appeared to him when he conſulted Augurs in the iſle of Naxos, before he began his wars with the Titans ; and that, this being a bird of good omen, he cauſed a figure of it to be painted on his enſigns † ; which is perhaps the beſt reaſon. Though ſome ſuppoſe that this bird was conſecrated by Jupiter on account of its extraordinary ſtrength and ſwiftneſs ; and others, becauſe in time of a ſtorm, it flies above the higheſt clouds ‡. Horace ſeems to allude to this paſſage of Callimachus in the following lines :

Qualem miniſtrum fulminis alitem,
Cui Rex Deorum regnum in aves vagas
Permiſit,—§
As the majeſtic bird of tow'ring kind,
Who bears the thunder thro' th' etherial ſpace,
To whom the monarch of the Gods aſſign'd
Dominion o'er the vagrant feather'd race.   DUNKIN.

* Plin. Hiſt. Natur. Lib. X. cap. 3.   † Athenæ. Lib. IV.   ‡ Ruæus
in Æn. I. v. 398.   § Hor Lib. IV. Ode 4.

All-gracious-pow'r! protect the friends I love,
And send them fav'ring omens from above.

Lo! rob'd in purple, yonder shining bands
Of chosen youths whom Jove himself commands;   110
Not those who tempt the seas in search of gain,
Or join fierce combat on the dusty plain,
Invent the dance or raise the tuneful song;
These meaner cares t' inferior Gods belong;
But those to whom imperial pow'r is giv'n,   115
Jove's favour'd sons, the delegates of heav'n,

Σων τεραων· ατ᾽ εμοισι φιλοις ενδεξια φαινοις.
Εἱλεο δ᾽ αἰζηων ὁ, τι φερτατον· ὑ συ γε νηων   70
Εμπεραμυς, ὑκ ανδρα σακεσπαλον, ὑ μεν αοιδον.
Αλλα τα μεν μακαρεσσιν ὁλιζοσιν αὐθι παρηκας,
Αλλα μελειν ἑτεροισι. συ δ᾽ ἐξελεο πλολιαρχυς

V. 109. Not those who tempt the seas in search of gain] By the word ιμπεραμυς
I understand merchants who sail the seas, and not simply mariners; and Horace seems
to use the word Nauta or Navita in the same sense.   Vulcanius.

V. 116. Jove's favour'd Sons the delegates of heav'n] Although this sentiment of
the divine right of Kings may not correspond with our ideas of liberty; yet it was
particularly suited to the notions of ancient times, when a limitted monarchy was
unknown, regal government absolute, and every king claimed his descent from Jupiter:
an opinion which runs through the writings of almost every ancient poet; and not to
trouble my readers with long quotations on this subject, I shall only give the following
passage from Hesiod, who deduces poets from Apollo, and kings from Jupiter.

Ἐκ γαρ Μυσαων και ἱκηβολυ Απολλωνος
Ανδρασιδοι ἑασιν ἐπι χθονα, και κιθαρισαι·

Ἐκ

Whom feamen, foldiers, merchants, bards obey,
And wide extended empires own their fway.
  The rough artificer owns Vulcan's pow'r,
And hardy foldiers warlike Mars adore ;   120
The man who fwift purfues the favage brood,
Invokes Diana, huntrefs of the wood,
And he, who ftrikes the Lyre's refounding ftrings
With fkilful hand, from bright Apollo fprings,
But kings from Jove ; except the royal line   125
No rank on earth approaches to divine :

Αυ]ಐς, ὡν ὑπο χειρα γεωμορος, ὡν ἰδρις αἰχμης,
Ων ἐρετης, ὡν ϖαντα· τι δ' ಐ κρατεοντος ὑπ' ἰσχυν;   75
Αυτικα χαλκηας μεν ὑδειομεν Ηφαιςοιο·
Τευχησας δ' Αρηος· ἐπακτηρας δε Χιτωνης
Αρτεμιδος· Φοιϐಐ δε, λυρης εὐ εἰδοτας οἰμಐς.
Εκ δε Διος βασιληες· ἐπει Διος ಐδεν ἀνακτων

    'Εκ δι Διος βασιληες *
    From Jove, great origin, all monarchs fprings
    From mighty Jove, of kings himfelf the King,
    From the Pierian maids, the heav'nly nine,
    And from Apollo, fire of verfe divine
    Far-fhooting deity, whofe beams infpire
    The poets fpring, and all who ftrike the lyre.   COOKE.

And even Plato, though he has written ten books on a republic as the moft perfeft
fyftem of government, deduces a continual feries of kings from Jupiter.*

     * Hef. Theogon. v. 94   † In Alcibiade.

Their ſacred pow'r deſcends from mighty Jove,
And he protects them from high heav'n above.
Beſides from him the pow'r of judges ſprings,
And governors the ſubſtitutes of kings ;   130
He guards the city, o'er the ſtate preſides,
Rewards the governor whom virtue guides ;
But dire diſgrace and ruin keeps in ſtore,
For partial judges that abuſe their pow'r.

Θειοτερον. τω και σφι τεην εκριναο λαξιν·   80
Δωκας δε π7ολιεθρα φυλασσεμεν· ιζεο δ' αυτος
Ακρης εν π7ολιεσσιν, εποψιος οι τε δικησι
Λαον υπο σκολιης, οι τ' εμπαλιν ιθυνεσιν.
Εν δε ρυηφενιην εβαλες σφισιν, εν δ' αλις ολβε·
Πασι μεν, ε μαλα δ' ισον. εοικε δε τεκμηρασθαι   85

V. 134. For partial judges that abuſe their pow'r] The original of this and the
five preceding lines being very laconic, it ſeemed neceſſary to extend the ſentiment a
little, before it could have its full force in Engliſh. Grævius turns this paſſage in the
following manner. " Conſtituiſti qui urbes cuſtodiant : tuque ipſe præſides in arcibus,
inſpector tam eorum qui legibus populum ſub iniquis quam eorum qui aliter gubernant."
Now, for what purpoſe is Jupiter the inſpector of governors and judges, except to
reward the good, and puniſh the partial and unjuſt ? A ſimilar paſſage occurs in Homer :

  Ως δ' υπο λαιλαπι πασακιλαιη, βιβριθι χθων *
  Ηματ' οπωρινω, οτι λαβροτατον χεει υδωρ
  Ζευς, οτι δη ρ' ανδρεσσι κοτεσσαμενος χαλεπηνη,
  Οι βιη ειν αγορη σκολιας κρινωσι θεμιςας,
  Εκ δε δικην ελασωσι, θεων οπιν εκ αλεγοντες.

  * Hom. Il. Lib. XVI. v. 384.

As

Tho' mighty Jove! thy fcepter'd fons obtain   135
Abundant wealth, and means of glory gain,
Yet all receive not, by thy great decree,
An equal fhare of fplendid pomp from thee;
For warlike Philadelphus reigns alone,
And pow'r fupreme fupports his facred throne: 140
Glad evening ftill beholds the vaft defigns
Compleat, to which his morning thought inclines,
Beholds compleat in one revolving fun,
What others, in long ages, but begun.
For Jove, in wrath, makes other kings to mourn   145
Their counfels blafted, and their hopes forlorn.

Ημετερω μεδεοντι· περι προ γαρ ευρυ βεβηκεν.
Εσπεριος κεινος γε τελει τα κεν ηοι νοηση·
Εσπεριος τα μεγιςα, τα μειονα δ' ευτε νοηση·
Οἱ δε τα μεν πλειωνι, τα δ' ἐχ' ἑνι. των δ' απο παμπαν
Αυτος αυτην εκολυσας, ενεκλασας δε μενοινην.   90
Χαιρε μεγα, Κρονιδη πανυπερτατε, δωτορ εαων,

> As when in autumn Jove his fury pours,
> And earth is loaden with inceffant fhow'rs;
> When guilty mortals break th' eternal laws,
> And judges brib'd betray the righteous caufe.   POPE.

V. 139. For warlike Philadelphus reigns alone] This compliment to Ptolemy
Philadelphus is very artfully introduced; and the poet raifes his great patron to a deity,
as much as a mortal can be exalted, by making him the fupreme power on earth, as
Jupiter is in heaven.

V. 156.

Hail! Mighty King; hail! great Saturnian Jove,
Who fends life, health, and fafety from above;
Thy glorious acts tranfcending human tongue,
Nor were, nor fhall by mortal bard be fung!   150
O, from thy bright abodes, let bleffings flow;
Grant wealth, grant virtue to mankind below:
For we with wealth, are not completely bleft,
And virtue fails when wealth is unpoffefs'd;
Then grant us both; for thefe united prove   155
The choiceft bleffing man receives from Jove.

Δωτορ ἀπημονιης. τεα δ᾽ ἐργματα τις κεν ἀειδοι;
Ου γενετ᾽, ἐκ ἐςαι· τις κεν Διος ἐργματ᾽ ἀεισει;
Χαιρε, ττατερ, χαιρ᾽ αὐθι· διδɤ δ᾽ ἀρετην τ᾽ ἀφενος τε.
Ουτ᾽ ἀρετες ἀτερ ὁλϐος ἐπιςαται ἀνδρας ἀεξειν,   95
Ουτ᾽ ἀρετη ἀφενοιο. διδɤ δ᾽ ἀρετην τε κϳ ὁλϐον.

V. 154. The choiceft bleffing man receives from Jove,] It was a favourite fentiment
both with the Greek poets and philofophers, that no man could be happy without
poffeffing riches, a very pleafant and comfortable doctrine, and much more agreeable to
human ears, than the Chriftian precept of felf-denial, which we hear every day inculcated
from the pulpit. And indeed it muft be owned that, in our prefent circumftances,
poverty feems but a negative fort of good, which can be of little fervice to mankind,
except in fo far as it may prevent them from becoming more wicked. He who poffeffes
wealth, and knows how to promote the caufe of virtue by a proper application of it, has
much happinefs in his own power, and, notwithstanding the depravity of mankind,
many fuch characters occur in our times, as well as in the days of Callimachus. Nor
are the fentiments contained in this noble apoftrophe repugnant to facred fcripture, for

E   w

we find the following thoughts in Ecclefiaftes Chap. VII. v. 11. " Wifdom is good with an inheritance, and by it there is profit to them that fee the fun. For Wifdom is a defence, and money is a defence : but the excellency of knowledge is, that wifdom giveth life to them that have it."

END OF THE HYMN TO JUPITER.

THE SECOND HYMN

OF

CALLIMACHUS

TO APOLLO.

W HAT force, what fudden impulfe thus can make
The laurel-branch, and all the temple fhake !

O ION ὁ τω Ἀπολλωνος ἐσεισατο δαφνινος ὁρπηξ,

Hymn to Apollo.] The adoration paid to Apollo or the Sun was the moft ancient, as
well as the moft univerfal fpecies of idolatry, as has been fhewn at full length by the very
learned Mr. Bryant *. It is therefore no wonder that this hymn fhould have been
ranked among the moft celebrated productions of our author. It was held in fuch
eftimation by the ancients, as to be fung for many ages at the feftivals of this deity in the
different countries of Greece, and may be confidered as an exact counterpart to the
foregoing. For the poet, inftead of celebrating the birth of the deity, as in the hymn to
Jupiter, begins by defcribing him in all his glory, enumerates his attributes, traces him
back ftep by ftep to the firft great action of his life, which he is faid to have performed
κυρος ἰων ἐπι γυμος †, " while yet a naked infant," and concludes with juft mentioning his

---

* Bryant's Mythol. Vol. I. paffim.   † Apollon. Lib. II. v. 709.

     birth,

Depart ye fouls profane ; hence, hence! O fly
Far from this holy place ! Apollo's nigh ;

Οἴα δ᾽ ὅλον το μελαθρον, ἑκας, ἑκας, ὅςις ἁλιτρος.

birth, which it was unneceffary to defcribe at full length ; as the whole fourth hymn is
employed in the celebration of that great and important event. The concluding para-
graph has apparently little connexion with what goes before, and feems to have been
artfully introduced for the fake of the poet himfelf, as will be taken notice of in its place.

Voffius derives Apollo from Ἀβελιος, a name given to the Sun by the Cretans *, and
Bryant informs us, that this was a combination of three ancient terms Ab-El-Eon,
Pater fummus Sol, or Pater Deus Sol. Others derive Ἀπολλων from ἀπολλυων, " perdens",
becaufe the Sun was fuppofed to occafion difeafes and peftilence.

V. 2. The laurel branch and all the temple fhake ;

     Depart ye fouls profane !]

The hymn opens with a defcription of the rifing Sun, on the day of the annual
feftival of Apollo in the ifland of Delos ; when the God was faid to appear, becaufe on
that day the Sun firft darted his rays upon the gate of the temple. And the Greek
fcholiaft informs us, that all predictions uttered at that time were true and certainly
fulfilled ; but that thefe proved falfe after the departure of the deity : that is to fay, at
that feafon of the year, when the Sun-beams ceafed to fhine upon the doors of the temple.
The words δαφνιος ἑρπηξ, " the laurel branch" has occafioned difputes among the commentators, fome affirming that a particular laurel-tree is meant, as Mr. Prior tranflated
the phrafe ; but others imagine, with more probability, that it alludes to branches of
laurel, placed over the gates of the temple by young men and maids, who came from
different countries to celebrate this feftival. The priefts likewife ftrewed the innermoft
parts of the temple with laurel, and held laurel branches in their hands during the
celebration of the rites. The ifland of Delos was celebrated not for this tree, but for a
famous palm, which will be mentioned afterwards.

The laurel was facred to Apollo for feveral reafons; becaufe the conical leaf bore
fome refemblance to the rays of the Sun ; becaufe it is an ever-green, and fo may be

       * Voff. de Idolol. Lib. II.

                                                          faid,

He knocks with gentle foot; the Delian palm   5
Submiffive bends, and breathes a fweeter balm :

Και δε που τα Θυρετρα καλω ποδι Φοιβος αρασσει.
Ουχ ορᾳς; επενευσεν ὁ Δηλιος; ἡδυ τι φοινιξ

faid, like him, to enjoy perpetual youth ; and becaufe it was thought to be more eafily
fet on fire than any other fpecies of wood. It was likewife ufual to foretel future events
from the noife of this tree when burning ; a favourable prediction was drawn from its
crackling, but if it burned away in filence the omen was unlucky *. Hence Tibullus fays,

> Laurus ubi bona figna dedit, gaudete coloni.   TIBULLUS, Lib. II.

" Rejoice, O hufbandmen, when the laurel gives you a good omen."

The fcene of this hymn has commonly been laid at Delphos, but I think without
reafon, the temple there being too diftant to give a view of the Delian palm mentioned
V. 4th of the original. And befides, more feftivals were held in honour of Apollo at
Delos than in any other part of the world †. This fuppofition has led all the former
tranflators into a miftake, imagining that the word μιλαθρον muft refer to a cavern, no
doubt becaufe the temple of Delphos was built over a place of this nature. But this
word has a quite contrary import, and fignifies *lacunar*, the main beam that fupports the
roof ; or, as we fay in Scotland, " the roof-tree." I remember only one paffage in
Homer where it occurs, and this Mr. Pope has tranflated with much juftice to the original.

> ————κατα πρηνις βαλιιν Πριαμοιο μιλαθρον
> Αιθαλοιν ‡——

> Be Priam's *Palace* funk in Grecian fires.   POPE.

All the Critics obferve how exactly Virgil has imitated thefe words of our author ἱκας,
ἱκας, ὁτις ἀλιτρος, Procul hinc, procul efte, profani §. And at the folemn Grecian feftivals
when the prieft approached the altar, he always cried out, " Who is here" ? to which
the fpectators anfwered " Many good people." The prieft then faid, " Begone all ye
profane," which the Romans expreffed by the words of Virgil mentioned above.

V. 5. He knocks with gentle foot ; the Delian palm] Apollo knocking with his foot

* Banier's Mythol. Vol. II. p. 416.   † Idem ibid.   ‡ Hom. II. Lib. II.v. 414.
§ Virg. Æn. VI.

alludes

Soft fwans, high hov'ring catch the aufpicious fign,
Wave their white wings, and pour their notes divine.

Ἐξαπινης, ὁ δε κυκνος ἐν ἠερι καλον ἀειδει.   5

alludes to the firſt approach of the Sun-beams to the gates of the temple, as mentioned
before. And the palm was facred to this deity, and an emblem of the Sun, becaufe the
ancients conceived it to be immortal ; or at leaſt, it was thought to recover after death,
and enjoy a fecond life by renewal. And hence the ſtory of the Phœnix is fuppofed to
have been borrowed from this tree, the word Φοινιξ fignifying both a Phœnix and the
Palm-tree *. It was likewife an emblem of victory, probably on account of its tall
growth and ſtately appearance. But the palm mentioned by Callimachus certainly exiſted
in the iſland of Delos, being taken notice of by many ancient authors, although the
origin was undoubtedly fabulous, namely, that when the Goddefs Latona was about to
bring forth Apollo and Diana, the earth that inſtant produced a large palm, againſt which
ſhe reſted in time of her labour, as the reader will find in the fourth hymn. Homer
makes Ulyffes compare the beauty of Naufinaa to this celebrated palm, which he had
obferved from the fea, in his voyage by the iſland of Delos.

> ────────σιζας μ' ἰχιι ἰισοφωντα.
>
> Δηλῳ δη ποτι τοιςι Απολλωιος παρα βωμῳ
>
> Φοινικος νιον ἰρνος ἀνιςχομινον ἰνοησα †.
>
> ────────I gaze and I adore,
>
> Thus feems the palm with ſtately honours crown'd,
>
> By Phœbus' altars ; thus o'erlooks the ground,
>
> The pride of Delos.   Pope.

Cicero tells us that it was ſtill remaining in his time ‡ ; and Pliny that it was coeval with
Apollo. " Necnon Palma Deli ab ejufdem Dei ætate confpicitur §." We are likewife
informed by Plutarch, that Nicias the Athenian prefented a palm-tree of brafs to the

---

* Bryant's Mythol. Vol. I. p. 322.   † Hom. Odyff. Lib. VI. v. 161.

‡ Cicero de Legib. Lib. I.   § Plin. Nat. Hiſt. Edit. Harduin. Lib. XVI. c. 89.

Ye bolts fly back; ye brazen doors expand,
Leap from your hinges, Phœbus is at hand.　　　10
　　Begin, young men, begin the sacred song.
Wake all your lyres, and to the dances throng,

'Αυτοι νυν κατοχχες ανακλινεσθε συλαων,
'Αυται δε κληιδες· ὁ γαρ θεος ὑκετι μακραν.

Delians, which was erected on a piece of confecrated ground bought by him for that purpofe, but was afterwards blown down by the winds *.

V. 7. Soft fwans, high-hov'ring, catch th' aufpicious fign,] The fwan was facred to Apollo, becaufe predictions were known from its motions, and on account of its white colour refembling the beams of the Sun. A farther account of this will be given in the notes on that beautiful paffage of the fourth hymn where the poet defcribes the birth of Apollo.

V. 11. Begin young men, begin the facred fong,] The chief cities of Greece fent choruffes of mufic annually to celebrate the feftival of Apollo in the ifland of Delos, and to fing hymns in honour of this deity. The proceffion was called *Theoria*, and was inftituted by Thefeus, after he overcame the Minotaur, as will be mentioned after- wards. The perfon appointed to conduct this folemnity was always chofen from the chief of the citizens, and it was looked upon as a great honour to be entrufted with that office. But we are informed by Plutarch, that before the time of Nicias this pro- ceffion was generally conducted with much hurry and confufion. For the inhabitants of the ifland ran in crowds to the fhore as foon as the fhip appeared, and without waiting till the Athenians landed, cried out impatiently for them to begin, fo that they were obliged to fing, put on their chaplets (wreaths of laurel) and religious veftments, all at the fame time, which could not be done without much indecency and diforder. Nicias being appointed leader of the proceffion rectified this abufe †.

* Plutarch, in vit. Nic. ad initium.　　　† Potter's Antiquities Vol. I. p. 285.
Plutarch ubi fupra.

V. 22.

Rememb'ring ſtill, the Pow'r is ſeen by none
Except the juſt and innocent alone ;
Prepare your minds, and waſh the ſpots away,　　　　15
That hinder men to view th' all-piercing ray,
Leſt ye provoke his fav'ring beams to bend
On happier climes, and happier ſkies aſcend :
And lo ! the pow'r, juſt op'ning on the ſight,
Diffuſes bliſs, and ſhines with heav'nly light.　　　　20
Nor ſhould the youthful choir with ſilent feet,
Or harps unſtrung, approaching Phœbus meet,
If ſoon they wiſh to mount the nuptial bed,
To deck with ſweet perfumes, the hoary head,

Οἱ δε νεοι μολπην τε ἠ ἐς χορον ἐντύνεσθε.

Ὦ 'πολλων ἐ παντι φαεινεται, ἀλλ' ὁ, τις ἐσθλος.

Ος μιν ἰδη, μεγας ἐτος. ὁς ἐκ ἰδε, λιτος ἐκεινος.　　　　10

Οψομεθ', ὦ Εκαεργε, ἠ ἐσσομεθ' ἐποτε λιτοι.

Μητε σιωπηλην κιθαριν, μητ' ἀψοφον ἰχνος

Τε Φοιβε τες παιδας ἐχειν ἐπιδημησαντος,

Εἰ τελεειν μελλεσι γαμον, πολιην τε κερεισθαι,

V. 22. *Or harps unſtrung, approaching Phœbus meet,*] The word ἐπιδημησαντος alludes to the name of this feſtival, which was called ἐπιδημια Ἀπολλωνος, "The entrance of Apollo among the people," that is, when the Sun beams began to ſhine upon the temple, and in like manner his departure was named ἀπιδημια. Hence it was ſuppoſed that he reſides in ſummer at Delos, and in winter in Lycia.　　　　DACIER.

V. 24. *To deck, with ſweet perfumes, the hoary head,*] The original words πολιην τι κιξιθαι " canos radere" do not ſignify to ſhave the head, but to dye the hair with ſome
fragrant

On old foundations lofty walls to build, 25
Or raife new cities in fome diftant field.

    Ye lift'ning crouds, in awful filence, hear
Apollo's praifes, and the fong revere ;
Even raging feas fubfide, when poets fing
The bow, the harp of the Lycorean king : 30
Nor Thetis, wretched mother, dares deplore
Her lov'd, her loft Achilles, now no more !
But thrill'd with awe, fhe checks her grief and pain
When Io Pæan founds along the main.

Εϛηξειν δε το τειχος επ' αρχαιοισι θεμεθλοις. 15
Ηγασαμην τɤς παιδας, επει χελυς ɤκετ' αεργος.
Ευφημειτ' αιοντες επ' Απολλωνος αοιδη.
Ευφημει κ̑ɉ ποντος, οτε κλειɤσιν αοιδοι
Η κιθαριν, η τοξα, Λυκορεος εντεα Φοιϐɤ.
Ουδε Θετις Αχιληα κινυρεται αιλινα μητηρ, 20
Οππστ' ιη παιηον, ιη παιηον ακουση.

fragrant ointment, a cuftom ufed by perfons of both fexes to conceal their age. SPAN-
HEIM.

    V. 30. The bow, the harp of the Lycorean King] Apollo was called Lycoreus from
a village of that name in the neighbourhood of Delphos.—Grævius.—The very learned
Mr. Bryant tells us that an ancient name for the Sun was El-Uc, which, according to
Macrobius *, the Grecians changed into λυκος, *Lucus*. He was likewife ftyled El-Uc-Or,
and hence the name Lycoreus †.

* Macrob. Saturnal. Lib. I. cap. 17.   † Bryant's Mythol. Vol. I. p. 78.

The weeping rock, once Niobe, fuſpends   35
Its tears a while, and mute attention lends;
No more ſhe ſeems a monument of woe,
Nor female ſighs thro' Phrygian marble flow.

Καὶ μὲν ὁ δακρυοεὶς ἀναβαλλεται ἀλγεα πετρος,
Ος τις ἐνι Φρυγιη διερος λιθος ἐςηρικται,

V. 38. Nor female ſighs thro' Phrygian marble flow] The poet could not have choſen a more proper method to encreaſe the veneration for Apollo, than by making Thetis and Niobe fuſpend their grief and liſten to the hymns in praiſe of the deity; although he had ſlain the only ſon of the one, and the whole family of the other. Thetis, the daughter of the ſea, is very properly joined with that element; and every body knew the ſtory of Niobe, who was ſuppoſed ſtill to exiſt, in form of a rock, on the top of mount Sipylus in Magneſia. Niobe was a Theban princeſs, the daughter of Tantalus and ſiſter of Pelops; according to Homer ſhe had ſix ſons and ſix daughters, but Ovid gives her one more of each. Elated on this account ſhe ran through the ſtreets of Thebes, in order to put a ſtop to the ſacrifices offered to Latona, vainly imagining that ſhe herſelf had a ſuperior claim to divine honours, becauſe of her numerous cffspring. Latona in revenge engaged Apollo and Diana to put all her children to death in the manner related by Homer and Ovid; but the paſſages are two long for inſertion here *. After this the princeſs herſelf was carried away by a whirlwind to mount Sipylus, and there changed into a rock, from which flows a perpetual ſtream of water in commemoration of the tears ſhe ſhed for the loſs of her children. The Abbé Banier ſuppoſes that this fable contains a true but tragical ſtory of a peſtilence which depopulated the city of Thebes, and deſtroyed the children of Niobe, who were here ſuppoſed to periſh by the darts of Apollo and Diana: after which her huſband, unable to bear ſo great a calamity, laid violent hands on himſelf, and ſhe retiring into Lydia ended her days near mount Sipylus ſtupified with grief and aſtoniſhment, and hence ſhe was ſaid to be changed into a

* Hom. Il. **XXIV.** Ovid Metamorph. Lib. **VI.**

rock.

Sound Io! Io! fuch the dreadful end
Of impious mortals, that with Gods contend ;   40
Who dares high heav'ns immortal pow'rs engage,
Againſt our king a rebel war would wage,

Μαρμαρον αντι γυναικος οιζυρον τι χανουσης.
Ιη, ιη φθεγγεσθε· κακον μακαρεσσιν εριζειν.   25
Ος μαχεται μακαρεσσιν, εμῳ βασιληι μαχοιτο.

rock *. This explication is confirmed by Callimachus himſelf, who makes Apollo
denounce vengeance againſt the Thebans, for retaining the fons and daughters of Niobe
in their city, as the reader will find in the hymn to Delos. Others imagine that the
whole ſtory refers to the annual inundation of Egypt. Niobe is the inundation. The
affront offered to Latona denotes the neceſſity ſhe laid the inhabitants under of retreating
to the higher grounds. The fourteen children are the fourteen cubits that marked the
height of the inundation on the Nilometer. Apollo and Diana killing them with their
arrows repreſent either the influence of the Sun and Moon in affuaging the deluge, or
that labour and induſtry overcome all difficulties. The continuance of Niobe was the
preſervation of Egypt. But the word *Selau*, ſignifying ſafety, was by a fmall alteration
changed into *Selaw*, a ſtone. And thus Niobe became a rock. Mr. Bryant, who deduces
all the myſterious rites and fables of antiquity from one event, namely the flood, makes
Niobe the fame with Noah, though by the Greeks repreſented as a woman. His words
are " ſhe is mentioned as one who was given up to grief, having been a witneſs to the
death of all her children. Her tears flowed night and day, till ſhe at laſt ſtiffened with
woe, and was turned into a ſtone †." The reader may choose what ſignification he
pleaſes, and I hope to be excuſed for this long note on one of the moſt celebrated fables
of antiquity.

* Banier's Mythol. Vol. II. p. 409.   † Bryant's Mythol. Vol. II. p. 329.

And who rebels againſt our ſovereigns ſway
Would brave the bright far-ſhooting God of day.
But rich rewards await the grateful choir   45
That ſtill to Phœbus tune the living lyre ;
From him all honour ſprings, and high above
He ſits, in pow'r, at the right hand of Jove.

Ὅς τις ἐμῳ βασίληι, κỳ Ἀπολλωνι μαχοιτο.
Τον χορον ὡ 'πολλων, ὁτι ὁι κατα θυμον ἀειδει,
Τιμησει. δυναται γαρ, ἐπει Διι δεξιος ἡςαι.

V. 44. Would brave the bright far-ſhooting God of day.] The poet, in a manner,
repeats the ſame compliment to Ptolemy which he had before paid to him in the hymn
to Jupiter. And this was agreeable to the ideas of his countrymen, for the Ptolemies
were revered as deities. Therefore Callimachus ſuppoſes that to reſiſt the authority of
the King, and to brave the majeſty of heaven were acts of equal impiety ; and not for
the reaſon aſſigned by the Greek ſcholiaſt, that Ptolemy was φιλολογος, " a patron of
learning and genius." SPANHEIM.

V. 48. He ſits, in pow'r, at the right hand of Jove.] Madam Dacier calls this a
wonderful paſſage, becauſe in ſeveral places of ſacred writ, the ſecond perſon of the
Trinity is ſaid to ſit at the right hand of his father. But the phraſe in Callimachus is
merely metaphorical, in order to expreſs the great power aſcribed to Apollo. Spanheim
obſerves from Ariſtides, that Pindar had ſaid the ſame thing of Minerva long before :
Πινδαρος δ' ἀυ φησι, δεξιαν κατα χειρα τυ πατρος ἀυτην καθιζομενην τας ἱντολας τοις Θεοις ἀπεδιχιοθαι.
" Pindar ſays that ſhe ſits at the right hand of her father to receive his commands, which
ſhe communicates to the other deities." And we find the following paſſage in Horace ;

Proximus illi (i. e. Jovi) tamen occupavit
Pallas honores *.
Yet firſt of all his progeny divine
Immortal honours Pallas claims.   FRANCIS.

* Hor. Lib. I. Ode 12.

The

Beyond the day, beyond the night prolong
The facred theme, to charm the God of fong.   50
Let all refound his praife ; behold how bright
Apollo fhines in robes of golden light ;
Gold are his quiver, harp and Lyctian bow,
And his fair feet with golden fandals glow.
All-bright in gold appears the Pow'r divine,   55
And boundlefs wealth adorns his Delphic fhrine.
Immortal youth and heav'nly beauty crown
His cheeks unfhaded by the fofteft down,
But his fair treffes drop ambrofial dews,
Diftill foft oils, and healing balm diffufe :   6c

Οὐδ᾽ ὁ χορος μετα Φοιϐον ἐφ᾽ ἑν μονον ἡμαρ ἀεισει.   30
Ες-ι γαρ ἐυυμνος· τις ἀν οὐ ρεα Φοιϐον ἀειδοι ;
Χρυσεα τῳ ʼπολλωνι, το, τ᾽ ἐνδυτον, ἡ τ᾽ ἐπιπορπις,
Η τε λυρη, τ϶, τ᾽ ἀεμμα το Λυκτιον, ἡ τε φαρετρη·
Χρυσεα κỳ τα πεδιλα. πολυχρυσος γαρ Απολλων,
Και τε πολυκτεανος. Πυθωνι κε τεκμηραιο.   35
Και κεν ἀει καλος και ἀει νεος· οὐποτε Φοιϐυ
Θηλειαις ὐδ᾽ ὁσσον ἐπι χνοος ἠλθε παρειαις.
Αἱ δε κομαι ϑυεντα πεδῳ λειϐουσιν ἐλαια.
Οὐ λιπος Απολλωνος ἀποςαζυσιν ἐθειραι,

The idea that Callimachus was acquainted with the Septuagint prevails fo much among
the commentators, that every line, bearing the leaft refemblance to a fcripture-phrafe,
is always thought to be borrowed from thence, while fimilar expreffions in other ancient
poets are paffed over unnoticed.

V. 01.

And on what favour'd city thefe fhall fall,
Life, health and fafety guard the facred wall.
To great Apollo various arts belong,
The fkill of archers and the pow'rs of fong ;
By him the fure events of lots are giv'n,   65
By him the prophet fpeaks the will of heav'n,

Ἀλλ' αὐτὴν πανακειαν. ἐν ἀςει δ' ὦ κεν ἐκεῖναι   40
Πρωκες ἐραζε πεσωσιν, ακηρια παντ' εγενοντο.
Τεχνη δ' ἀμφιλαφης ἐ τις τοσον ὁσσον Ἀπολλων.
Κεινος ἀιςευτην ἐλαχ' ανερα, κεινος ἀοιδον.
Φοιβω γαρ κỳ τοξον ἐπιτρεπεται κỳ ἀοιδη.

V. 62. Life, health and fafety guard the facred wall.]   The golden ornaments of
Apollo, his bow, his arrows, his harp and his quiver are all defcriptive of the great
luminary.   And the dews, that fall from his golden locks, fignify the effect of the Sun
in promoting vegetation, purifying the air, and fo diffuſing health on every part of the
globe.   His bow comes from Lyɛtus, a Cretan city, becauſe the Lyɛtians adored Apollo
as their tutelar deity, and likewiſe becauſe they were ſkilful in archery and the art of
bow-making.   The wealth of the famous temple of Delphi is well known, and has been
celebrated by almoſt every ancient poet and hiſtorian.   This edifice ſtood in the country
of Phocis, on the South Weſt extremity of mount Parnaſſus, and encloſed a large hole
or cavern, on the mouth of which was placed a ſtool or tripod, from which the prieſteſs
delivered her oracles.   And it may be obſerved, that many of the ancient temples were
built over caverns.   For when the true religion was loſt, and the minds of men infeɛted
with the gloom of fuperſtition, they always imagined fuch places to be the habitation
of a deity.   Hence, in more civilized ages, the innermoſt part of the temple continued
to receive the appellation of the *cavern* *.

V. 65. By him the fure events of lots are giv'n.]   The lots, as the Greek fcholiaſt

* Bryant's Mythol. Vol. I. p. 218.

remarks,

And wife phyficians, taught by him delay
The ftroke of fate, and turn difeafe away.
   But we to Nomius, heav'nly fhepherd, cry,
Since he, for young Admetus, left the fky ;   70

Κεινυ δε 3ριαι, κ μαντιες. εκ δε νυ Φοιβυ   45
Ιητροι δεδαασιν αναβλησιν 3ανατοιο.
Φοιβον κ Νομιον κικλησκομεν, εξ ετι κεινυ,
Εξοτ επ Αμφρυσω ζευγητιδας ετρεφεν ιππυς,

remarks, were three fmall ftones ufed in divination, and firft difcovered by three Nymphs the daughters of Jupiter, who prefented them to Pallas. But that Goddefs, inftead of accepting the prefent, reproached the Nymphs for offering her what belonged to another deity, namely Apollo, and threw away the ftones in a place called the Thriafian field. Hence lots were called θριαι, *Thriai.* Vulcanius. The learned commentator has not told us whence he copied this fabulous narration ; but it contains an excellent moral, and fhews that thofe perfons who are guided by Pallas or Wifdom, will improve the prefent time, without being too anxious to pry into futurity. And that they will, above all things, avoid the prevalent but pernicious practice of gaming.

   V. 68. ——————————and turn difeafe away.] Apollo is faid to be the patron of archers, becaufe the rays of the Sun dart, like fo many arrows, to the earth. He delights in mufic becaufe being placed in the midft of the feven planets, he makes with them a kind of harmony ; and hence the lyre or harp was faid to have feven ftrings, as the reader will find in the hymn to Delos. He knows all future events, becaufe the beams of the Sun difpel the darknefs of the night ; he is always beardlefs and youthful, becaufe the Sun never grows old nor decays, and he is the patron of the healing art, becaufe his vegetative power makes thofe plants to grow whereof medicines are compofed *.

       * Voff. de Orig. et Progreff. Idololatr.

                  V. 72.

When burning with defire, he deign'd to feed
A mortal's courfers on Amphryfus's mead.
His herds increas'd, and overfpread the ground,
Kids leapt, and fportive lambkins frifk'd around,
Where'er Apollo bent his fav'ring eyes,   75
The flocks with milk abounded, grew in fize,

Ηιθεε ὑπ' ἐρωτι κεκαυμενος Αδμητοιο.

Ρεια κε βεϲοϲιον τελεθοι, πλεον, ὑδε κεν αἰγες   50

Δευοιντο βρεφεων ἐπιμηλαδες, ησιν Απολλων

V. 72. ——————————————he deign'd to feed
     A mortal's courfers on Amphryfus' mead]

    The ftory of Admetus and Apollo is commonly related in this manner. Apollo, to revenge the death of his fon Æfculapius, who had been flain by Jupiter, killed the Cyclops with his arrows, and was, for that reafon, expelled from heaven by his father. Being thus obliged to fhift for his livelihood, he entered into the fervice of Admetus, whence he was called Nomius, or the Shepherd. Callimachus improves this ridiculous fiction, and gives it a more noble turn, by faying that he defcended from heaven voluntarily, and tended the flocks of Admetus out of love to that prince. According to the hiftorical explication of Banier, Apollo was a King of Arcadia, and being dethroned by his fubjects on account of the feverity of his government, retired to the court of King Admetus in Theffaly, who gave him the fovereignty of that part of his dominions, which lay along the banks of the river Amphryfus *. But if we continue the allegory, the meaning muft be, that the fields adjoining to the river Amphryfus were wet and marfhy, and became more fertile in confequence of being dried by the beams of the Sun. Macrobius tells us in confirmation of this, that Apollo was called Nomian, not becaufe he fed the flocks of Admetus, but becaufe the Sun nourifhes every plant that fprings from the earth, " quia Sol pafcit omnia quæ terra progenerat †".

   * Banier's Mythol. Vol. II. p. 415.   † Macrob. p. 239.

And pregnant ewes, that brought one lamb before,
Now dropt a double offspring on the fhore.
Ere towns are built, or new foundations laid,
We ftill invoke the great Apollo's aid, 80
And oracles explore; for with delight
He views new cities rifing on the fight;
And Phœbus felf the deep foundations lays.
The God, but four years old, in former days,

Βοσκομενης οφθαλμον επηγαγεν, ἠδ᾽ αγαλακτοι
Οιες, ἠδ᾽ ακυθοι, πασαι δε κεν ειεν ὑπαρνοι.
Η δε κε μουνοτοκος, διδυματοκος αιψα γενοιτο.
Φοιβω δ᾽ ἑσπομενοι πολιας διεμετρησαντο 55
Ανθρωποι. Φοιβος γαρ αει πολιεσσι φιληδει
Κτιζομεναις, αὑτος δε θεμειλια Φοιβος ὑφαινει.
Τετραετης τα πρωτα θεμειλια Φοιβος επηξε

V. 80. We ftill invoke the great Apollo's aid,] Mr. Bryant obferves that Apollo was called Ὀικιςης and Ἀρχηγετης from being the fuppofed founder of cities, which were generally built in confequence of fome oracle. What colony, fays Cicero, did Greece ever fend into Ætolia, Ionia, Afia, Sicily, or Italy, without having firft confulted about every circumftance relative to it, either at Delphi, or at Dodona, or at the oracle of Ammon *. Spanheim gives the fame account, and we find in Herodotus, that a colony of Spartans made an unfuccefsful voyage to Libya becaufe they had not previoufly confulted the oracle at Delphi †.

* Bryant's Mythol. Vol. I. p. 282.   † Herodot. Lib. V. cap. 42.

First rais'd a structure on th' Ortygian ground   85
Close by the lake that ever circles round ;
When young Diana, skill'd in hunting, laid
Unnumber'd goats, on Cynthus' mountain, dead :
The careful Goddess brought their heads away,
And gave them to the glorious God of day ;   90
He broke the horns, and rais'd with artful toil,
A wond'rous altar from the sylvan spoil,

Καλη εν Ορτυγιη περιηγεος εγγυθι λιμνης.
Αρτεμις αγρωσσασα καρηατα συνεχες αιγων   60
Κυνθιαδων φορεεσκεν, ο δ' επλεκε βωμον Απολλων.
Δειματο μεν κεραεσσιν εδεθλια, πηξε δε βωμον

V. 85. First rais'd a structure on th' Ortygian ground] The island of Delos was called Ortygia from 'Ορτυξ, " a quail," because it was pretended that Latona assumed the shape of that bird, and retired thither in time of her pregnancy, in order to avoid the wrath of Juno. The lake, whose waters are said by Callimachus to have been περιηγες, or circling round, was the source of the river Inopus.

V. 92. A wondrous altar from the Sylvan spoil] This celebrated altar stood in the neighbourhood of the palm-tree mentioned above, and had no doubt been erected by the priests of Apollo, who pretended that it was the work of the deity himself. Goats and bulls were sacrificed to him, and the horns of these animals were emblems both of strength and power, and of the rays of the Sun. Plutarch takes notice of this altar, as will be mentioned towards the close of the hymn to Delos, and says, but without assigning any reason for it, that the horns were all taken from the left side of the head. Eustathius mentions another edifice of the same kind at Ephesus, likewise supposed to have been built by Apollo from the horns of bulls which Diana killed in hunting *.

* Eustath, in Il. VIII.

V. 96.

Plac'd rows on rows, in order ſtill diſpos'd,
Which he with circling walls of horn enclos'd;
And from this model, juſt in ev'ry part,   95
Apollo taught mankind the builders art.

    Beſides Apollo ſhew'd my native place
To Battus, and the fam'd Theræan race,
A crow propitious ſent, that flew before,
And led the wand'rers to the Lybian ſhore.   100

Εκ κεραων, κεραης δε περιξ υπεϐαλλετο τοιχης.
Ωδ' εμαθεν τα πρωτα θεμειλια Φοιϐος εγειρειν.
Φοιϐος κ) βαθυγειον εμην πολιν εφραϲε Βαττω·   65
Και Λιϐιην εϲιοντι κοραξ ηγησατο λαω

V. 96. Apollo taught mankind the builders art.]

Ωδ' ιμαθει ταπρωτα θιμιλιχ Φοιϐος εγιιριιν.

The ſecond aoriſt of the verb μανθανω means either to learn or to teach; and therefore
this verſe is capable of two ſignifications; either that in this manner Apollo learned,
or in this manner Apollo taught others the rudiments of architecture. The laſt is
commonly reckoned the true interpretation; but ſome commentators have rejected the
verſe itſelf as ſpurious.

V. 99. A crow propitious ſent, that flew before,] A ſimilar ſtory is told of Alexander,
when he went to conſult the oracle of Jupiter Ammon, the Apollo of Egypt. " Jam
haud procul oraculi ſede aberant, cum complures corvi agmini occurrunt, modico volatu
prima ſigna antecedentes, et modo humi reſidebant, cum lentius agmen incederet, modo
ſe pennis levabant, antecedentium iterque monſtrantium ritu *. " They were now not
far from the ſeat of the oracle, when a great flock of ravens came towards them, and
flew gently before their van, and ſometimes pitched to give them time to come up; and

* Quint. Curt. Lib. IV. c. 7.

G 2   then

Apollo, marking from unclouded ſkies,
Beheld Cyrenè's lofty tow'rs ariſe,
And faithful ſwore, that Ægypt's king ſhould gain
The new-built city and the fertile plain.

　　To tuneful Phœbus, ſacred God of ſong,　　　　　　105
In various nations, various names belong';
Some Boëdromius, Clarius ſome implore,
But nam'd Carneüs on my native ſhore.

Δεξιος οικιϛηρ· χJ ωμοσε τειχεα δωσειν
Ημετεροις βασιλευσιν· αει δ᾽ ευορκος Απολλων.
Ω 'πολλον, πολλοι σε Βοηδρομιον καλευσι,
Πολλοι δε Κλαριον· (παντη δε τοι ουνομα πουλυ)　　　70

then taking wing again preceded them, ſhewing them the way, and as it were diſcharging the office of a guide." DIGBY.

　　Mr. Bryant ſuppoſes that theſe were the prieſts that came to meet Alexander, and who were denominated crows or ravens from their black complexion *. Probably the crow, mentioned by our author, may be explained in the ſame manner.

　　V. 103. And faithful ſwore, that Egypt's king ſhould gain
　　　　　　The new built city]
Mr. Pitt, Mr. Prior, and Dr. Dodd have all tranſlated this paſſage in reference to the Cyrenian monarchs, the deſcendants of Battus. But the Greek ſcholiaſt explains it of Ptolemy, and this agrees with ancient hiſtory. For the territory of Cyrene was added to the dominions of Egypt by the firſt Ptolemy the father of Philadelphus. And it is much more probable that Callimachus would make Apollo promiſe this country to the preſent poſſeſſor, with whom the poet was in high favour, than to a race of Kings extinct long before the time of writing the hymn.

　　V. 108. But nam'd Carneüs on my native ſhore.] The poet ſeems to have mentioned

　　　　　　* Bryant's Mythol. Vol. II. p. 289.

the

Thee, great Carneüs! Sparta firſt poſſeſs'd,
Next Thera's iſle was with thy preſence bleſs'd;   110
You croſs'd the ſwelling main from Thera's bow'rs,
And then reſided in Cyrenè's tow'rs.

Αὐταρ ἐγω Καρνειον· εμοι ϖατρωιον ἠτω.

Σπαρτη τοι, Καρνειε, τοδε ϖρωτιςον ἐδεθλον,

Δευτερον αὐ Θηρη, τριτατον γε μεν αϛυ Κυρηνη.

the altar of horns, in order to introduce the building of his native city, where Apollo was worſhipped under the name of Carneüs, which Mr. Bryant derives from the word Keren, a horn. He obſerves "that the Greeks often changed the *Nu* final into *Sigma:* hence from Keren they formed κιρας, κιρατος. and thence they deduced other words all relating to ſtrength and eminence. Gerenius, Γιρηνος, applied to Neſtor by Homer ſignifies a princely and venerable perſonage. The Egyptian Crane, for its great ſervices, was held in high honour, being ſacred to the God of light, Abis, or as the Greeks expreſſed it Ibis; from whence the name was given. It was alſo called Keren, and Kerenus, by the Greeks Γιρηνος, the noble bird being moſt honoured of any. It was a title of the Sun himſelf: for Apollo was named Craneüs, and Carneüs; which was no other than Cereneüs, the ſupreme deity, the Lord of light: and his feſtival ſtyled Carnea, Καρνια, was an abbreviation of Cerenea, Κιρηνια *." Clarius was a term of the ſame import; and the Greek ſcholiaſt informs us that the Athenians having conſulted the oracle of Apollo about the iſſue of a war, in which they were engaged, the deity adviſed them to ruſh upon their enemies with loud ſhouts and violent clamours. They obtained the victory, and hence gave the name Boëdromius (from βοη clamor, and δριμω curro) both to the God, and to the month of Auguſt in which the battle was fought; inſtituting at the ſame time an annual feſtival, in commemoration of this event, called alſo Boë-dromian.

* Bryant's Mythol. Vol. I. p. 46.

V. 116.

The fixth from Oedipus convey'd the God
From Lacedæmon o'er the wat'ry road
To Thera's ifle ; but brought from Thera's ftrand   115
By blamelefs Battus to Afbyftis' land.
He rais'd a temple to record thy praife,
Appointed annual feafts, on folemn days,
In fair Cyrenè ; facred hymns refound,
And flaughter'd bulls lie bleeding on the ground.   120

Εκ μεν σε Σπαρτης εκτον γενος Οιδιποδαο
Ηγαγε Θηραιην ες αποκτισιν· εκ δε σε Θηρης   75
Ουλος Αριςοτελης Ασβυςιδι παρθετο γαιη.
Δειμε δε τοι μαλα καλον ανακτορον· εν δε πολη
Θηκε τελεσφοριην επετησιον, η ενι πολλοι
Υςατιον πιπτυσιν επ᾽ ισχιον, ω ανα, ταυροι.

V. 116. By blamelefs Battus to Afbyftis' land.] The Afbyftæ or Afbytæ inhabited the
region of Afbyftis, fo near to the territory of Cyrenè, that Callimachus makes them the
fame. Vide Salmafü exercitationes Plinianas ad cap. 28. Solini. GRÆVIUS.

V. 118. Appointed annual feafts, on folemn days,] The poet means the annual
feftival to Apollo Carneüs, which was called Καρμα, and was firft inftituted at Sparta in
the XXVI. Olympiad, as we learn from Athenæus. The rites began upon the feventh
day of the month Carneüs, about the beginning of winter. MEURSIUS.

V. 120. The ftory of Battus and the building of Cyrenè.] The poet, by a very
artful and beautiful tranfition, introduces the building of his native city, and dwells with
pleafure on every circumftance, relating to the famous expedition of Battus, whom he
regarded not only as the founder of Cyrenè, and the firft who eftablifhed the worfhip of
Apollo in Libya, but as his own anceftor. He tells us, that Theras, the fixth from
Oedipus, led a colony of Spartans to the ifland Callifta, afterwards called from his name

Thera,

Iö ! Carneän Phœbus ! all muſt pay
Their vows to thee, and on thine altars lay
Green herbs and painted flow'rs, when genial ſpring
Diffuſes ſweetneſs from Favonius' wing ;

Ιη ἰη, Καρνειε πολλυλιτε, σειο δε βωμοι   80
Ανθεα μεν φορευσιν ἐν εἰαρι, τοσσα περ ὡραι
Ποικιλ' ἀγινευσι ζεφυρȣ πνειοντος; ἑερσην,

Thera, whence they were conducted by Battus the ſon of Polymneſtus to Cyrnus or
Cyrenè, and carried a ſtatue of Apollo along with them. According to Herodotus,
Theras was ordered by the oracle of Apollo to build a city in Libya ; but he anſwered,
" I am old and unfit for ſuch an enterpriſe ; therefore rather command one of theſe
young men to undertake this expedition," and at the ſame time pointed to Battus. The
reſponſe of the oracle being thus ſlighted, Apollo puniſhed the Theræans with a drought
that laſted for ſeven years, in conſequence of which Battus undertook the voyage. He
was born with an impediment in his ſpeech, and having conſulted the oracle in what
manner it might be removed, was ordered not to mind his ſtammering, but to go and
build a city in Libya *. To this the Greek ſcholiaſt adds, that Africa was at that time
much infeſted with Lions : and that Battus, being frightened at the appearance of a
monſtrous lion ſoon after his arrival, cried out with ſuch vehemence as to break the
ligament or membrane which confined his tongue, and ſo obtained the uſe of his ſpeech.
After this he built the city of Cyrenè. His attendants Δωριες, Dorians, were ſuppoſed to
be deſcended from Hercules. Herodotus imagines that the prieſteſs gave him the title of
Battus, which in the Libyan language ſignifies a king, and that he had another name
before *. This, according to Callimachus, was Ἀριϛοτελης, Ariſtotle.

V. 123. Green herbs and painted flow'rs,——] In the firſt ages of idolatry, and
before the refinements of ſuperſtition had introduced the cruel rites afterwards put in
practice, offerings to the deities were for the moſt part very ſimple. The perpetual fire
on the altars was fed with herbs and flowers, and the offerings to Apollo conſiſted chiefly

* Herodot. Lib. IV. cap. 151.   † Ibid. ubi ſupra.

But when ſtern winter his dark pow'r diſplays   125
With yellow crocus feed the riſing blaze :
So flames unceaſing deck thy hallow'd ſhrine,
And breathe ſweet odours to thy pow'r divine.
With tranſport Phœbus views the warlike dance
When fierce Bellona's ſons in arms advance, ·   130
And, with brown Lybian virgins, tread the ground,
When annual the Carnean feaſt comes round.
Nor yet Alcides ſons had Cyrne feen,
Her cryſtal fountain and extended green,

Χειματι δε κροκον η̃δυν. αει δε τοι αεναον πυρ,
Ουδε ποτε χθιζον περιβοσκεται ανθρακα τεφρη.
Η ῥ εχαρη μεγα Φοιβος, οτε ζωςηρες Ενυ̃ς   85
Ανερες ωρχεσαντο μετα ξανθησι Λιβυσσης,
Τεθμιαι ευτε σφιν Καρνειαδες ηλυθον ωραι.
Οι δ' υπω πηγης Κυρης εδυναντο πελασσαι

of meal and conſecrated bread which were purchaſed at the gates of the temples *. It
may be obſerved that our poet always deſcribes the moſt innocent part of theſe ceremonies,
and particularly avoids mentioning the horrible practice of offering human ſacrifices,
then cuſtomary among the moſt civilized nations on the globe.

V. 129. With tranſport Phœbus views the warlike dance] Pyrrhus the ſon of
Achilles was the ſuppoſed inventor of this dance, called from his name Pyrrhic. In
ſome places it was eſteemed a martial exerciſe, and exhibited by perſons in armour, who
gave it the name of Betarnius. They uſed to dance round a large fire in honour of the
Sun, whoſe orbit they affected to deſcribe †.

* Bryant's Mythol. Vol. I. p. 296.   † Idem ibid. p. 286.

But thro' Azilis' woods the wand'rers ftray'd,   135
And hid their heads within the dufky fhade,
When Phœbus ftanding on the horned hill
Beheld the foreft and the murm'ring rill,
And fhew'd the warriors to his lovely bride,
Cyrenè fair attending at his fide,   ➤   140
Who kill'd the lion on Myrtufa's rocks,
That tore the good Eurypylus's flocks.
Apollo faw not from the realms above,
A city more deferving of his love ;

Δϲριεϛ, ϖυκινην δε ναπαιϛ Αζιλιν εναιον.
Τϲυϛ μεν αναξ ιδεν αυτοϛ, εη δ' επεδειξατο νυμφη   90
Σταϛ επι Μυϛτϐϲηϛ κερατωδεωϛ· ηχι λεοντα
Υψηϛ κατεπεφνε, βϖον ϲινιν Ευϛυπυλοιο.
Ου κεινϐ χοϛον ειδε θεοτεϛον αλλον Απολλων.

V. 143. That tore the good Eurypulus's flocks] Λιοντα——γϙιν Ευϛυπϲλϙιϛ. Σινιϛ, Sinis was a famous robber celebrated both for inhuman cruelty in putting to death every traveller that fell in his power, and for enormous ftrength, which was fo great, that he ufed to bend pine-trees to the earth, and tie the limbs of his captives to branches of different trees, which upon being let loofe returned to their natural pofition with fuch vi lence, as to tear the poor wretches afunder. Plutarch relates that he was killed by Thefeus, and Ovid mentions both his death and his cruelty in thefe words.

        Occidit ille Sinis, magnis male viribus ufus,
        Qui poterat curvare trabes, et agebat ab alto
        Ad terram late fparfuras corpora pinus *.

        * Ovid. Metamorph. Lib. VII. v. 440.

No rifing town, no mighty ftate obtain'd   145
Such gifts from Phœbus as Cyrenè gain'd,
In dear remembrance of the ravifh'd dame,
That crown'd his love, and gave the city's name.

Ουδε πολει τοσ' ενειμεν οφελσιμα τοσσα Κυρηνη,

Μνωομενος προτερης αρπακτυος. ηδε μεν αυτοι   95

          By him the tort'rer Sinis was deftroyed,
          Of ftrength (but ftrength to barb'rous ufe employ'd)
          That tops of talleft pines to earth could bend,
          And thus in pieces wretched captives end.   TATE.
Afterwards the name Sinis came to be ufed as an adjective, expreffive of wickednefs.
Thus Ariftotle calls the robber Sciron Σιν; ανηρ, a wicked or mifchievous perfon.
MEURSIUS.

Eurypulus, faid to be the fon of Neptune, was king of the territory of Cyrenè before
the arrival of Battus. The foreft of Azilis ftood in the neighbourhood of Myrtufa a
mountain in Libya, called κερατωδης, or horned, on account of its two lofty promontories,
and the city was built over the fountain Cyrne or Cyre facred to Apollo. DACIER.

V. 148. 'That crown'd his love, and gave the city's name.] Apollo having fallen in
love with Cyrenè, the daughter of Hypfeus King of Theffaly, conveyed her from Pelion
to the mountain of Myrtufa in Africa, where fhe killed a monftrous lion that defolated
the country, much about the time that Battus and the Spartans under his command
arrived on the coaft. And Apollo, ftanding on the top of the mountain, fhewed them
to his bride, before they had reached the place deftined for their future habitation, and
while they wandered in the woods of Azilis, where they concealed themfelves after their
landing, being at firft afraid to venture up the country. If there is any truth in the
ftory of Battus, Cyrenè had probably accompanied him in his voyage, and fhe being
either his wife or his miftrefs, he called the new city by her name. And fhe might be
faid to kill a Lion, becaufe the fcouting parties would have frequent rencounters with
thefe terrible animals, and no doubt deftroy numbers of them. But I muft not forget
to mention that Mr. Bryant treats this whole narrative as a fable. He tells us from

          4   Palæphatus,

Nor were her fons ungrateful, but beſtow'd
Superior honours on their guardian God.   150
    Now Iö! Iö Pæan! rings around
As firſt from Delphi roſe the ſacred ſound,
When Phœbus ſwift deſcending deign'd to ſhew
His heav'nly ſkill to draw the golden bow.
For when no mortal weapons could repel   155
Enormous Python horrible and fell,

Βαττιαδαι Φοιβοιο πλεον θεον αλλον ετισαν.

Ιη ιη παιηον, ακουομεν, ουνεκα τυτο

Δελφος τοι πρωτιϛον εφυμνιον ευρετο λαος,

Ημος εκεβολιην χρυσεων επεδεικνυσο τοξων.

Πυθω τοι κατιοντι συνεντετο δαιμονιος θηρ,   100

Αινος οφις. τον μεν συ κατεναρες, αλλον επ' αλλω

Palæphatus, that the Cyrenians were a colony of Cuthites or Ethiopians, and he ſuppoſes that this nation carried traditions of the deluge wherever they went. According to him, Battus is the fame with Boutus, a city of Egypt, where was a floating temple, in comme-moration of the fame event; and the name Boutus ſignified an ark or float. He derives Cyrenè from Cur, a very ancient epithet of the Sun, takes the name of her father 'Υψευ;, Hypſeus, in the literal ſenſe, and hence interprets her own name 'Υψη;, Hypſeis, the daughter of the Moſt High; that is, the Sun or Apollo *. If we adopt this explica-tion (which is both plauſible and ingenious) the voyage of the Spartans, and the crow that led them to the deſtined ſhore, contain obſcure traditions of the deluge; and Cyrenè killing the Lion ſignifies the effect of the Sun in aſſuaging the waters, drying the ground, and rendering the world once more habitable.

    * Bryant's Mythol. Vol. II. p. 326. Vol. I. p. 40, 82.

From his bright bow inceſſant arrows flew,
And, as he roſe, the hiſſing ſerpent flew.
Whilſt Iö! Iö Pæan! numbers cry,
Haſte launch thy darts, for ſurely from the ſky,   160
Thou cam'ſt the great preſerver of mankind,
As thy fair mother at thy birth deſign'd.

Ηαλλων ωκυν ὁ·ςον· επηυτησε δε λαος,
Ιη ιη παιηον, ιει βελος. ευθυ σε μητηρ
Γεινατ' αοσσητηρα· το δ' εξ ετι κειθεν αειδη.

V. 159. Whilſt Iö! Iö Pæan! numbers cry,] This famous exclamation, ſo frequently
repeated by the votaries of Apollo during the performance of the ſacred rites, is derived
by ſome παρα το παυιν τας ανας, a ſedendo moleſtias, and by others παρα το παιιν, a
feriendo *, agreeable to the explication of Callimachus ἱι βλος, mitte ſagittam. And the
poet informs us, that this triumphant ſhout or acclamation was firſt raiſed by the inhabitants of Delphi, in the time of the dreadful combat between Apollo, and the monſter
Python. From that time the hymns in honour of Apollo were called Pæans, and the
ſame acclamation was repeated in every ſong of triumph. Hence Ovid has uſed it to
commemorate a victory of a ſofter kind ;

> Dicite Iö Pæan : et Iö bis dicite Pæan :
> Decidit in caſſes præda petita meos †.
> Now Iö Pæan ſing ! now wreaths prepare !
> And with repeated Iös fill the air :
> The prey is fall'n in my ſucceſsful toils ;
> My artful nets encloſe the lovely ſpoils. DRYDEN.

But Spanheim quotes two verſes of Apollonius, to ſhew that Iö Pæan had another origin,
having been firſt introduced by certain Nymphs of Parnaſſus called Corycian. See
Apollonius Lib. II. v. 714.

---

* Rami Panth, Mythic. p. 29.   † Ovid. Art. Amator. Lib. II. v. 1.

An equal foe, pale envy, late drew near,
And thus fuggefted in Apollo's ear;
I hate the bard, who pours not forth his fong, 165
In fwelling numbers, loud, fublime, and ftrong;
No lofty lay fhould in low murmurs glide,
But wild as waves, and founding as the tide.

Ὁ φθονος Απολλονος ἐπ' ἑατα λατριος εἰπεν, 105
Οὐκ ἀγαμαι τον ἀοιδον, ὁς ἐδ', ὁσα ϖοντος, αειδει.

V. 162. The ftory of Python.] The death of Python was the firft memorable action
afcribed to Apollo. It is mentioned by almoft every ancient poet and hiftorian. Hence
Apollo had the name Pythius; the Pythian games were inftituted in memory of the
combat, the prieftefs at Delphi was called Pythia; and the deity himfelf was worfhipped
under the form of a ferpent, with rays around his head to denote the beams of the Sun.
According to the poets, the goddefs Juno, in order to be revenged of her rival Latona,
the mother of Apollo, defcended from heaven, and caufed noxious vapours to arife from
the earth. Of thefe fhe formed a hideous ferpent, who engaged in combat with Apollo,
almoft as foon as he was born *. Both the Abbé Banier and Mr. Bryant agree, that the
Greek Python was the fame with the Egyptian Typhon. The former fuppofes that this
monfter was an allegorical reprefentation of the noxious vapours arifing from the
Nile, after the annual inundation begins to fubfide; and that the victory of Apollo
fignified the effects of the Sun-beams in difperfing the clouds, improving the air, and
thus removing difeafes occafioned by the Steams iffuing from the ftagnant waters †. This
agrees pretty well both with the narrative in the text, and with what was faid before of
the healing dews falling from the locks of Apollo. Mr. Bryant makes Typhon the
univerfal deluge ‡. And either of thefe opinions is more probable than the explication
of Voffius, who fuppofes this tremendous monfter to have been the fame with Og, King
of Bafhan, of whom fo many wonders are related by the Jewifh Rabbins §.

* Banier's Mythol. Vol. I. p. 504.   † Banier's Mythol. Vol. I. p. 512.
‡ Bryant's Mythol. Vol. II. p. 226. § Voff. de Idololat. Lib. I. cap. 26.

V. 170

Fierce with his foot, indignant Phœbus spurn'd
Th' invidious monster, and in wrath return'd ;   170
Wide rolls Euphrates' wave, but soil'd with mud,
And dust and slime pollute the swelling flood :
For Ceres still the fair Melissæ bring
The purest water from the smallest spring,
That softly murm'ring creeps along the plain,   175
And falls, with gentle cadence, to the main.
     Propitious Phœbus ! thus thy pow'r extend,
And soon shall envy to the shades descend.

Τον φθονον ω 'πολλων ποδι τ' ηλασεν, ωδε τ' εειπεν·
Ασσυριη ποταμοιο μεγας ροος, αλλα τα πολλα
Λυματα γης κ) πολλον εφ' υδατι συρφετον ελκει.
Δηοι δ' εκ απο παντος υδωρ φορεεσι Μελισσαι,   120
Αλλ' ητις καθαρη τε κ) αχρααντος ανερπει
Πιδακος εξ ιερης ολιγη λιβας, ακρον αωτον.
Χαιρε αναξ. ο δε Μωμος, ιν' ο φθορος, ενθα νεοιτο.   —

V. 178. The story of envy.]   This beautiful hymn ends with the victory of Apollo
over Python, but Callimachus has, with much art, added a Satire on a cotemporary poet,
whom all the commentators agree to have been Apollonius Rhodius, author of the
Argonautics.   According to them Apollonius had privately endeavoured to prejudice their
common patron Ptolemy against our author, on account of the brevity of his poems, which
Callimachus considered as a particular excellence ; And we learn from Athenæus that he was
the author of that quaint saying " A great book is a great evil."   Καλλιμαχος ο γραμματικος
το μεγα βιβλιον ισον ελεγεν ειναι μεγαλῳ κακῳ*.   In the present passage he both ridicules his

* Athenæ. Lib. III. cap. 1.

adverfary, and celebrates his patron by comparing the former to Python and the latter to Apollo. And by the fate of Μωμος or envy we are informed, that the invidious attempts of his enemy proved unfuccefsful. Callimachus wrote another Satire againft Apollonius entitled Ἰϛις *, which is now loft. But Ovid confeffes that he has copied the greateft part of this performance in his book againft Hyginus which is ftill extant under the fame title.

> Nunc quo Battiades inimicum devovet Ibin,
>
> Hoc ego devoveo teque tuofque modo.
>
> Utque ille, hiftoriis involvam carmina cæcis:
>
> Non foleam quamvis hoc genus ipfe fequi.
>
> Illius ambages imitatus in Ibide dicar,
>
> Oblitus moris judiciique mei †.

The Meliffæ were the prieftelles of Ceres or Rhea, as has been already mentioned. And as pure water from a fmall fpring was a more acceptable offering to that Goddefs than the muddy waves of a great river, the poet infinuates, that his illuftrious fovereign received more pleafure from his fhort performances than from the verbofe but heavy productions of his jealous rival.

Before concluding the notes on this hymn I fhall juft obferve that Apollo was the chief of the eight great Gods of Egypt, frequently mentioned by Herodotus, though he has not favoured us with their names. Mr. Bryant fuppofes thefe to have been the eight perfons preferved in the Ark, who were deified by their pofterity, and that all the myfterious rites of Egyptian worfhip were fymbolical reprefentations of the deluge ‡. The Greeks and Romans increafed their number to twelve, as will be mentioned in the notes on the following Hymn.

* Suid in Callim. † Ovid. Ibis. v. 53. ‡ Bryant's Mythol.
Vol. II. p. 231, & feq.

END OF THE HYMN TO APOLLO.

THE THIRD HYMN

OF

CALLIMACHUS.

TO DIANA.

T H O' great Apollo claim the poet's lyre,
Yet cold neglect may tempt Diana's ire,

ΑΡΤΕΜΙΝ (ἐ γαρ ἐλαφρον ἀειδοντεσσι λαθεσθαι)

Hymn to Diana.] This hymn to Diana, or the Moon, has justly been reckoned one of the finest poems of antiquity, and superior to either of the foregoing. The poet has exerted all his powers in celebrating this famous divinity, who was supposed to be a female; and therefore he represents her both as the Moon, and as a beautiful lady possessed of many amiable qualifications. She enjoys perpetual virginity by her own choice; she delights in hunting, an exercise in great repute among the young women of antiquity; she ranges the woods and mountains attended by a train of virgins as virtuous as herself, and she never visits the habitations of mankind, except with an intention of doing good. At the same time she is represented as a strict lover of justice; she punishes vice with severity, and rewards virtue with generosity. The poet has artfully omitted those terrible attributes which the ancients ascribed unto her under the name of Hecate; and the Diana of Callimachus is perhaps one of the most agreeable characters that the reader has yet been made acquainted with.

Artemis,

Come, virgin-goddefs, and infpire my fong,
To you the chace, the fylvan dance belong,

Υμνεομεν, τη τοξα Λαγοβολιαι τε μελονται,

Artemis, the Greek name for Diana, is derived by Plato δια το αρτεμις * from integrity,
or according to Macrobius παρα τε τον αερα τεμνειν †, becaufe the light of the Moon difpels
the darknefs of the night. Mr. Bryant fuppofes it to be the fame with Ar-temis, the
city of ‡ Themis or Thamis ; the Thamuz of Sidon and Egypt.

V. 1. Tho' great Apollo claims the poet's lyre,] Apollo is not named in the original,
but it feemed neceffary to mention him in the tranflation, partly to preferve a connexion
betwixt this and the preceding hymn, Diana being the fifter of Apollo, but chiefly on
account of that jealoufy for her brother's fuperior power, which fhe expreffes a few lines
afterwards. This is a diftinguifhed mark of her character, and runs through the whole
poem. A literal tranflation of the firft verfe would be as follows : " Let us now fing a
hymn in praife of Diana, left her wrath fhould fall heavy on the bard who forgets her ;"
i. e. the bard who praifes Apollo and neglects Diana. For we cannot fuppofe the
meaning of Callimachus to be that every poet fhould celebrate Diana in every fong ;
but only that thofe poets incur the difpleafure of the goddefs, who praife her brother and
neglect herfelf. Spanheim feems to be of the fame opinion by his obfervation on this
paffage. " Quod Phæbi foror eofdemque juxta eum cultores nacta." And Callimachus,
contrary to the practice of Homer, Hefiod, and the more ancient Greek poets, expreffes
himfelf with fo much brevity, that one is fometimes obliged to tranflate him by his idea,
as much as by his words. At the fame time his ftyle is pleafant and well adapted to his
fubject, except now and then that he degenerates into *pun* and *burlefque*, of both which
there are inftances in the prefent hymn.

V. 4. To you the chace, the fylvan dance belong.] The word λαγοβολιαι, which is
tranflated *chafe*, properly fignifies *hare-hunting* ; but Spanheim obferves that this term was
ufed for the chafe in general, as well as θαραθολιαι. Grævius renders this word *retia*,
nets, but furely not according to the original. And Erneftus, who has made many

* Plato in Cratylo.   † Macrob. Lib. VIII. fub fin.   ‡ Bryant's Mythol.
Vol. I. p. 107.

valuable

And mountain sports ; since first with accents mild,   5
Whilst on his knee the Thund'rer held his child,
O grant me, Father, thus the Goddefs said,
To reign a virgin, an unspotted maid.
To me let temples rise, and altars smoke,
And men by many names my aid invoke ;   10

Και χορος αμφιλαφης, κ) εν ερεσιν εψιαασθαι.
Αρχομεν ως οτε πατρος εφεζομενη γονατεσσι
Παις ετι κυριζυσα, ταδε προσσεειπε γονηα,   5
Δος μοι παρθενιην αιωνιον, αππα, φυλασσειν,
Και πολυωνυμιην· ινα μη μοι Φοιβος εριζη.

valuable emendations on the Latin verfion gives the true meaning of the original in this
paffage.   The commentators are much divided in their opinions concerning the dance to
which the poet alludes.   From the word αμφιλαφης, amplus, copiofus, Vulcanius imagines
that the Nymphs of Diana were fuppofed to dance in fmall parties, and Stephens that
they formed a large circle holding one another by the hand, to which Spanheim agrees.
And he obferves from Ælian, that it was ufual in this kind of dance, to move the hands
and head as well as the feet, and to fhake the body with great agility.

V. 8. To reign a virgin, an unfpotted maid.]   Ovid has imitated this verfe in the
ftory of Daphne :

Da mihi perpetua, genitor chariffime, dixit,
Virginitate frui : dedit hoc pater ante Dianæ *.
Give me, my Lord, fhe faid, to live and die
A fpotlefs maid, without the marriage tie,
'Tis but a fmall requeft : I beg no more
Than what Diana's father gave before.   DRYDEN.

V. 10. And men by many names my aid invoke ;]   Here the Goddefs begins to fhew

* Ovid's Metamorph. Lib. I. v. 486.

that

Proud Phœbus elfe might with thy daughter vie,
And look on Dian with difdainful eye.
To bend the bow and aim the dart be mine,
I afk no thunder nor thy bolts divine ;

Δος δ᾽ ἰκς κỳ τοξα. ἰα πατερ᾽ κ̔ σε φαρετρην,
Οὐδ᾽ αἰτεω μεγα τοξον (ἐμοι Κυκλωπες δἰςκς

that jealoufly of her brother already taken notice of.   She wifhes to have as many names
as he, who was characterized as πολυωνυμος.   And indeed her requeft feems to have been
fully granted; for none of the ancient deities were invoked by a greater number of titles
than Diana.   Many of thefe appellations are mentioned in this hymn, and many more
are enumerated by Spanheim, which, as they would be too tedious to tranfcribe, probably
there would be no pleafure in reading.   Nor was this cuftom confined to the Grecians
alone ; for Stephens obferves from Selden, that all the oriental nations, and particularly
the Arabians, implored the affiftance of their deities by an almoft infinite number of
names.   And in the Greek Anthologia there are two addreffes, one to Bacchus, and one
to Apollo, confifting entirely of epithet, contained in as many lines as there are letters
in the Greek alphabet, and digefted in the fame order.   Mr. Bryant fuppofes the reafon
of thefe numerous appellations to have been, that the Grecians often miftook the place of
worfhip for the deity worfhipped ; fo that the different names of the Gods were only the
names of as many temples *.

   V. 13. I afk no thunder, nor thy bolts divine ;]   κ̔ σε Φαρἰτρην, κδ᾽ αἰτιν μεγα τκξκ.   As
the tranflation of this paffage may be thought a deviation from the original, I fhall
fubjoin the reafon for rendering it in this manner, after premifing, that all the commentators, Spanheim excepted, have paffed it over in filence ; and his explication I take to
be foreign to the purpofe.   He produces a paffage from Æfchylus to fhew that the
Scythians ufed long bows, which were afterwards introduced into Greece ; and that
Diana does not afk from her father a Scythian or Grecian bow, but one of a fmaller fize.
Now it is not likely that a Goddefs jealous of her honour would fupplicate her father

* Bryant's Mythol. Vol. I. p. 107.

Jupiter

At your defire the Cyclops will beftow   15
My pointed fhafts and ftring my little bow.
Let filver light my virgin fteps attend,
When to the chace with flying feet I bend,
Above the knee be my white garments roll'd
In plaited folds, and fring'd around with gold.   20
Let Ocean give me fixty little maids
To join the dance amid furrounding fhades;

Αὐτίκα τεχνησονται, ἐμοι δ᾽ ἐυκαμπες ἀεμμα.)   10
Αλλα φαεσφορinν τε, κ᾽ ἐς γονυ μεχρι χιτωνα
Ζαννυσθαι λεγνωτον, ἱν᾽ ἀγρια θηρια καινω.
Δος δε μοι ἑξηκοντα χορητιδας Ωκεανινας,
Πασας εινετεας, πασας ἐτι παιδας ἀμιτρυς.

Jupiter to give her a high rank among the gods, and to degrade her below a mortal at
the fame inftant. Befide, we learn from Homer that Teucer and Merion the two beft
arches in the Grecian army came from Crete and Salamis, two iflands remote from the
Scythians, with whom they could have but little intercourfe in a rude age, and while
the art of navigation was yet in its infancy. I am therefore of opinion that this difficult
paffage may be better explained in this manner, and agreeable to the common ideas of
ancient Mythology. Chronus, Saturn or time devours his children, but Jupiter or the
air efcapes. Latona brings him two children at a birth, namely Apollo and Diana, or
the Sun and the Moon. The arms of Jupiter are the thunder-clouds, which the poet
allegorically calls a great bow, and certainly with as much propriety as the two great
luminaries are denominated bows from their fhape. The goddefs addreffes her father
with much feeming diffidence, but with a good deal of art. She infinuates that his power
will be no ways injured by granting her requeft, at the fame time that fhe begs permiffion
to have her arms made by the fame workmen that forge his thunderbolts.

V. 23.

Let twenty more from fair Amnisius come,
All nine years old, and yet in infant-bloom,
To bear my buskins, and my dogs to feed,   25
When fawns in safety frisk along the mead,
Nor yet the spotted lynx is doom'd to bleed.
Be mine the mountains and each rural bow'r,
And give one city for thy daughter's dow'r;
On mountain-tops shall my bright arrows shine,   30
And with the mortal race I'll only join,
When matrons torn by agonizing throws
Invoke Lucina to relieve their woes;

Δος δε μοι αμφιπολυς Αμνισιδας εικοσι νυμφας,   15
Αι τε μοι ενδρομιδας τε, κ̀, οπποτε μηκετι λυγκας;
Μητ᾽ ελαφυς βαλλοιμι, θους κυνας ευ κομεοιεν.
Δος δε μοι ἐρεα παντα. πολιν δε μοι ἠντινα νειμον,
Ηντινα λης· σπαρνον γαρ ὁτ᾽ Αρτεμις ἀςυ κατεισιν.
Ουρεσιν οικησω· πολεσιν δ᾽ επιμιξομαι ανδρων   20
Μυνον ὁτ᾽ οξειαισιν ὑπ᾽ ωδινεσσι γυναικες
Τειρομεναι καλευσι βοηθοον· ἡσι με μοιραι
Γεινομενην τοπρωτον επεκληρωσαν αρηγειν·

V. 23. Let twenty more from fair Amnisius come,] Amnisius was a river, or according to Stephens, a city of Crete, from which the Cretan virgins were called Amnisiades. And Strabo tells us that there was a temple in this city sacred to Diana Lucina. Pausanias mentions that the Cretans, in the neighbourhood of Gnossus, imagined this deity to have been born at Amnisius, and that she was the daughter of Juno. Frischlinus.

V. 37.

For at my birth the attendant Fates affign'd
This tafk to me, in mercy to mankind,   35
Since fair Latona gave me to thy love,
And felt no pangs when bleft by fav'ring Jove.

Οττι με κỳ τικτυσα κỳ ἐκ ἤλγησε φερυσα
Μητηρ, ἀλλ' ἀμογητι φιλων ἀπεθηκατο κολπων.   25

V. 37. The fpeech of Diana.] As this fpeech explains the principal attributes of
Diana, whether we confider her as the Moon, or as the goddefs of hunting; I have here
collected the comments of Spanheim and Frifchlinus on the fubject.

The goddefs afks of her father fame, honour and perpetual virginity; the habit and
arms of a huntrefs, a number of attendants, and the dominion of the mountains and
woods: all which may be underftood of the Moon. She retains the vigour of youth, and
never grows old, becaufe the heavenly bodies are not fubject to change or decay. She
has many attendants, becaufe the Moon is furrounded by a multitude of ftars. She is
faid to hunt wild beafts, and to kill them with her arrows, becaufe thefe animals fly at
the approach of light, particularly in the night time. She is patient of labour and
indefatigable in the chace, becaufe the Moon is unwearied in her courfe and performs it
in a fhort time. She is faid to inhabit the mountains and woods, becaufe from them fhe
feems to arife, and there fhe feems to defcend. Hence Horace juftly celebrates her, as being

> Montium cuftos, nemorumque virgo *.
> Of groves and mountains guardian maid.

Her nymphs, like herfelf, enjoy perpetual virginity; fhe choofes them when they are
only nine years old, and ἐτι παιδας ἀμιτρυς, i. e. not yet marriageable. For the young
women of ancient Greece conftantly wore a μιτρα or Zone after nine years old, but laid
it afide when they were married.

Thus far the commentators; to which it may be added that the goddefs is barren and
a virgin, becaufe fhe has no light of her own, fhines brighteft in Autumn or Winter, and
is not endowed with the fame power of promoting vegetation as the Sun. The circular

* Hor. Lib. III. Ode 22.

dance

She fpoke, and ftretch'd her hands with infant-art,
To ftroak his beard, and gain her father's heart;
But oft fhe rais'd her little arms in vain,   40
At length with fmiles he thus reliev'd her pain.

Fair daughter, lov'd beyond th' immortal race,
If fuch as you fpring from a ftol'n embrace,
Let furious Juno burn with jealous ire,
Be mine the care to grant your full defire,   45

Ὡς ἡ παις εἰπ8σα, γενειαδος ἠθελε πατρος
Αψασθαι, πολλας δε ματην ετανυσσατο χειρας,
Μεχρις ἱνα ψαυσειε. πατηρ δ' επενευσε γελασσας·
Φη δε καταρρεζων, Οτε μοι τοιαυτα Θεαιναι
Τικτοιεν, τυτθον κεν εγω ζηλημονος; Ηρης   30
Χωομενης αλεγοιμι. φερευ τεκος ὁσσ' εθελημος

dance of her nymphs evidently alludes to the motion of the ftars; and they come from
rivers and the fea, becaufe, like the Sun and Moon, they feem to fet in the ocean *.
Hefiod reckons three thoufand of thefe nymphs; but why only eighty, or, as fome fay
a hundred accompanied Diana it is difficult to determine. Perhaps this opinion may
have proceeded from fome ancient aftronomical obfervation concerning the motion of
the ftars. The city fhe demands is no doubt Ephefus, where this goddefs was adored as
the fupreme deity, and where the poet takes leave of her at the conclufion of the hymn.
She prefides over women in child-bed, becaufe the term of pregnancy confifts of nine
lunar refolutions; her hunting habit, quiver and bufkins were ufed by the huntreffes of
old. Virgil gives the fame to the young women of Carthage:

> Virginibus Tyriis mos eft geftare pharetram,
> Purpureoque alte furas vincire cothurno ‡.

† Hef. Theogon. v. 364.   ‡ Virg. Æneid. I. v. 340.

And greater gifts beside: from this bleft hour
Shall thirty towns invoke Diana's pow'r,
Full thirty towns (for fuch high Jove's decree)
Ungirt by walls, fhall pay their vows to thee:
O'er public ways Diana fhall prefide   50
And ev'ry port, where fhips in fafety ride.
Nor fhall thefe towns alone your pow'r obey,
But you with other Gods divide the fway
Of diftant ifles amid the wat'ry main,
And cities on the continental plain,   55
Where mighty nations fhall adore your name,
And groves and altars your protection claim.

Αἰτίζεις, κỳ δ' ἄλλα πατηρ ἔτι μείζονα δώσει·
Τρις δέκα τοι πτολιεθρα κỳ ἔχ ἕνα πυργον ὀπασσω.
Τρις δέκα τοι πτολιεθρα, τα μη Θεὸν ἄλλον ἀέξειν
Εἴσεται, ἀλλα μονην σε, κỳ Αρτεμιδος καλεεσθαι.   35
Πολλας δὲ ξυνῃ πολιας διαμετρησασθαι,
Μεσσογεως, νησους τε· κỳ εἰν ἁπασησιν ἔσονται
Αρτεμιδος βωμοι τε κỳ ἄλσεα. κỳ μεν αγυιαις;

V. 57. The fpeech of Jupiter.] Whether the oratory of Diana, or her fucceeding
blandifhments were the moft prevailing arguments with her father, the poet has not
informed us; but fhe feems to have gained his affections entirely. He informs his
beloved daughter, that fhe has a powerful enemy, whom yet fhe has no occafion to fear,
as he is refolved to protect her. He makes no mention of Apollo, in order to fhew
that her fufpicions concerning him are ill-founded; he grants all her petitions, with
many diftinguifhed privileges which fhe did not expect, and inftead of one town he gives
her

The Thund'rer fpoke, and gave th' almighty nod,
That feals his will, and binds th' immortal God.
Meantime the joyful Goddefs wings her flight   60
To Creta's ifle with fnowy mountains bright ;

Εσση κ λιμενεσσιν επισκοπος.   Ως ο μεν ειπων
Μυθον επεκρηηνε καρηατι. βαινε δε κυρη   43
Λευκον επι Κρηταιον ορος κεκομμηενον ὑλη·

her thirty. By this we are informed that Diana was the tutelar deity of thirty cities, the
chief of which according to Frifchlinus were Perga in Pamphylia, Tauri in Scythia,
Pitane in Æolia, Aulis in Bœotia; Miletus, Ephefus, Chefius in Ionia; Pelle and Petra
in Achaia ; and Caftabala in Cilicia.   The reft are enumerated by Strabo and Paufanias.
This was one caufe of the many names given to Diana ; for her adorers never failed to
implore her affiftance by the name of their native city.   In the fame manner, as goddefs
of ftreets and highways fhe received from the Romans the appellation of *Trivia*, and
from the Greeks that of Τριοδιτις, as Madam Dacier informs us from Varro *.   That fhe
was the guardian of iflands and harbours is eafily underftood from the Moon being the
caufe of the flux and reflux of the ocean.   But all the commentators have left us in the
dark, why the cities over which fhe prefides are faid to be unfortified.   And this would
have been a very neceffary piece of information ; as we are well affured that Ephefus,
Perga, Miletus, and indeed all the capital cities of antiquity were furrounded by lofty
walls and ftrong fortifications.   Perhaps the meaning may be, that Jupiter intends to
compliment Diana, by telling her that fhe is to be the guardian goddefs of thirty citie. ;
becaufe while fhe continues her protection they have no need of any other defence.

V. 61. To Creta's ifle with fnowy mountains bright ;
       Thence from Dictynna's hills and bending wood]

Βαινε δε κυρη

Λευκον επι, Κρηταιον ορος, κεκομμηνον ὑλη.

There are various opinions with regard to the meaning of the word ᴋᴏᴘᴋ, fome con-

---

* Varro Lib. VIII. de L. L.

K

Thence from Dictynna's hills, and bending wood,
She feeks the caverns of the rolling flood,
And at her call th' attendant virgins come,
All nine years old, and yet in infant bloom.   65
With joy Cæratus views the fmiling choir,
And hoary Tethys feels reviving fire,
When her bright offspring o'er th' enamel'd green,
Trip with light footfteps and furround their queen.

Ενθεν επ' Ωκεανον· πολεας δ' επελεξατο νυμφας,
Πασας εινετεας, πασας ετι παιδας αμιτρυς.
Χαιρε δε Καιρατος ποταμος μεγα, χαιρε δε Τηθυς,
Ουνεκα θυγατερας Λητωιδι πεμπεν αμοργυς.   45

tending that it is the name of a mountain, and others only an epithet; but Spanheim
removes the difficulty, by the following quotation from Theophraftus: ιν Κρητη γυν φασιν
εντοις Ιδαιοις οριςι, και εν τοις ΛΕΥΚΟΙΣ καλυμενοις επι των ακρων υπερ υδιποτε επιλιιπιν χιων κυπαριττον
υναι *. Cyprefs is faid to grow in Crete on the mountains of Ida, and on thofe called
white, whofe tops are always covered with fnow. The chief of thefe cliffs was the promontory of Dictynna fituated on the weft part of the ifland, ftretching far into the
ocean, and fo lofty, that mariners frequently miftook the fnowy fummits of this immenfe precipice for white clouds rifing in the air †.

V. 66. With joy Cæratus views the fmiling choir.] The river Cæratus wafhed the
walls of the city Gnoffus, the capital of the kingdom of the famous Minos; and hence
the city was fometimes called by the name of the river ‡. The joy of Cæratus and
Tethys reprefents the reflection of the beams of the Moon and ftars from the waves of
the fea and the ftreams of the river.

V. 69. The opinion that the ftars or the nymphs of Diana were the daughters of

* Theophraft. Hift. Plant. Lib. IV. cap. 1.   † Solinus cap. XI.
‡ Univerf. Hift. Vol. VI.

But thence to Melegunis' ifle in hafte   7●
(Now Lipara) the fylvan Goddefs pafs'd,
Her nymphs attending, and with wond'ring eyes
Saw the brown Cyclops of enormous fize,

Αὐθι δε Κυκλωπας μετεκιαθε. τȣς μεν ἐτετμε
Νεσῳ ἐνι Λιπαρῃ (Λιπαρῃ νεον, ἀλλα τοτ᾽ ἐσκεν
Οὐνομα οἱ Μελιγουνις) ἐπ᾽ ἀκμοσιν Ηφαιϛοιο

the ocean, and that their dancing fignifies either the various motions of the heavenly bodies; or the reflection of their beams from woods, rivers and mountains may have occafioned thefe lines of Milton :

> Now the bright morning-ftar, day's harbinger,
> Comes dancing from the Eaft.

And again

> So finks the day-ftar in the ocean's bed,
> And yet anon repairs his drooping head,
> And tricks his beams, and with new-fpangled ore,
> Flames in the forehead of the morning fky.

V. 70. But thence to Meligunis' ifle in hafte

Now Lipara]

This vulcanic ifland, fituated to the weft of Sicily, was firft called Meligunis, from the fertility of the foil, and the great plenty of honey found there; and afterwards Lipara, from Liparus the fucceffor of Æolus, who was fuppofed to have reigned in this ifland. The modern name Strombolo is derived from the Greek ϛρογγυλη; it was fo called on account of its circular appearance * ; and was faid to be the habitation of the winds, becaufe fmoke arifing from thence produced a fea ftorm in three days after †. For a particular account of Strombolo fee Brydone's Tour, Vol. I. Letter 2.

† Plin. Hift. Natural. Lib. III. cap. 9. Edit. Harduin.   ‡ Ruœus in Æn. Lib. I. v. 56.

K 2   Deep

Deep in their darkſome dwelling under ground,
On Vulcan's mighty anvil turning round   75
A maſs of metal hiſſing from the flaine :
The Sea-god urges, and for him they frame
A wond'rous vaſe, the liquor to contain
That fills his courſers on the ſtormy main.

With horror chill'd, the tim'rous virgins eye   80
Stupendous giants rear their heads on high,
Like cloud-capt Oſſa riſing o'er the field ;
One eye, that blaz'd like ſome refulgent ſhield,
From each ſtern forehead glar'd pernicious fire.
Aghaſt they gaze, when now the monſters dire   85
With ſtubborn ſtrokes ſhake the refounding ſhore,
And the huge bellows thro' the caverns roar.
But when from fiercer flames the metal glows,
And the fix'd anvil rings with heavier blows,
When pond'rous hammers break the tortur'd maſs,   90
Alternate thund'ring on the burning braſs,

Εςαοτας ϖερι μυδρον. επειγετο γαρ μεγα εργον.
Ιππειην τετυκοντο Ποσειδαωνι ϖοτιςρην.   50
Αἱ νυμφαι δ' εδδεισαν ὁπως ἰδον αινα ϖελωρα,
Πρηοσιν Οσσειοισιν ἐοικοτα· (ϖασι δ' ὑπ' οφρυν
Φαεα μουνογληνα, σακει ἰσα τετραβοειω,
Λεινον ὑπογλαυσοντα,) κϳ ὁππoτε δκπον ακεσαν
Ακμονος ἠχησαντος ἐπει μεγα ϖκλυ τ' αημα   55

V. 96.

The nymphs no more endure the dreadful fight,
Their ears grow deaf, their dim eyes lose the light;
A deeper groan through lab'ring Ætna runs,
Appals the hearts of old Sicania's fons,   95
Redoubles from Hefperia's coaft around,
And diftant Cyrnus thunders back the found.

Φυσκων, αὐτων τε βαιυν ςονον. αὐε γαρ Λιτνη,
Αὐε δε Τρινακοιη, Σικανων ἑδος, αὐε δς γειτων
Ιταλιη· μεγαλην δε βοην ἐπι Κυρνος αὐτει.
Εὐθ' οἱγε ῥαιςτηρας ἀειραμενοι ὑπερ ὡμων,
Η χαλκον ζειοντα καμινοθεν, ἠς σιδηρον,   60
Αμϐολαδις τετυποντες. (ἐπει μεγα μοχθησειαν,)
Τῳ σφεας ἐκ εταλασσαν ἀκηδεες Ωκεανιναι
Οὐτ' αὐτην ἰδεειν, ὐτε κτυπον ἐᾰτι δεχθαι.

V. 96, The ftory of the Cyclops] The vifit of Diana and her nymphs to the caves of the Cyclops, with all the attendant circumftances, is one of the fineft remains of ancient poetry. But the original lines feem to have been mifplaced by the error of fome tranfcriber; and the Commentators are much divided both with regard to the proper pofition of the verfes and the right conftruction of the words. According to the Greek Scholiafts (whofe opinion is followed in the tranflation) verfe 56, 57, and 58, fhould be placed immediately after verfe 63, and, by this tranfpofition, the defcription will confift of three parts, each rifing above another by natural, though terrible gradations. I. Though Diana herfelf continues undaunted, the Nymphs are very much frightened at their firft entrance into the cave, when they behold terrible monfters, with one eye in their foreheads, ftanding round a huge mafs of metal juft taken from the fire. II. Their fears increafe, when they hear the groans of the bellows, and the noife of the hammers which the huge workmen lifts with one hand. III. They fall into fainting fits when thefe enormous giants ftrike the metal alternately with heavier hammers raifed over

No wonder that Diana's tender maids   ... ̇ ̈
Should fink with terror in thefe gloomy fhades;

Οὐ νεμεσις· κεινυς δε ᾖ αἱ μαλα μηκετι τυτθαι
Οὐδεποτ᾽ ἀφρικτι μακαρων ὁροωσι θυγατρες.   65

their fhoulders, and lifted with both hands. Nor are the effects of this dreadful noife confined to the caverns alone; Mount Ætna fhakes to the foundation, and fends forth terrible groans that refound along the coaft of Italy, and return from the diftant ifle of Cyrnus or Corfica. And it muft be owned that the Goddefs feems rather inattentive to her new attendants amidft this terrible commotion. For we have no account how they recovered their fenfes, or made their efcape from the dungeon; nor are they mentioned again, till the Poet defcribes them unloofing the hinds from the chariot of their miftrefs. She probably imagined that, as their fears were groundlefs, they might be left to recover at leifure.

Virgil has not failed to imitate this beautiful paffage in various parts of his works; but though his defcriptions are longer, they have not in general that ftrength and fublimity which we find in this of our author. The moft fuccefsful imitation is in the following fimile.

> Ac veluti lentis Cyclopes fulmina maffis
> Cum properant: alii taurinis follibus auras
> Accipiunt, redduntque: alii ftridentia tingunt
> Æra lacu: gemit impofitis incudibus Ætna:
> Illi inter fe magna vi brachia tollunt
> In numerum, verfantque tenaci forcipe ferrum *.
> As when the Cyclops at that mighty nod,
> Now thunder haften for their angry God:
> Subdued in fire the ftubborn metal lies,
> One brawny Smith the puffing bellows plies,
> And draws and blows reciprocating air;
> Others to quench the hiffing mafs prepare.

* Virg. Georg. IV. V. 170.

With

For when the daughters of th' immortal Gods,   100
With infant-clamours fill the bleſt abodes,
Arges or Steropes the mother calls
(Two Cyclops grim) from their infernal halls

Αλλ' ότε κυραων τις απειθεα μητερι τευχοι,

Μητηρ μεν Κυκλωπας έη επι παιδι καλιςρει,

Αργην, ή Στεροπην· ό δε δωματος εκ μυχατοιο

> With lifted arms they order ev'ry blow,
> And chime their ſounding hammers in a row
> With labour'd anvils Ætna groans below.
>
> Strongly they ſtrike; huge flakes of flames expire;
> With tongs they turn the ſteel, and vex it in the fire. **DRYDEN.**

But this deſcription, however beautiful, is inferior to that of Callimachus; becauſe the noiſe of the hammers is confined within the cavern, and only ſhakes the bottom of the mountain below. Claudian's account of Pluto ſtriking the rocks of Sicily with his ſceptre makes a kind of counterpart to our author, but much inferior. For inſtead of thoſe dreadful echoes, which alarm Sicily, Italy, and Corſica, and may be conceived to ſhake the very centre of the earth, the ſound of Pluto's ſceptre contracts inſtead of expanding, and at laſt ends in a ſingle point.

> Saxa ferit ſceptro, Siculæ tonuere cavernæ;
>
> Turbatur Lipare; ſtupuit fornace relicta
>
> Mulciber, et trepidus dejecit fulmina Cycclops †.

In order to explain this paſſage as an allegory we have only to remember that Diana repreſents the Moon, and her virgins the Stars. She viſits the manſions of the Cyclops without fear, but her attendants loſe their ſenſes, becauſe the light of the moon, penetrates deeper into theſe caverns than the twinkling of the ſtars. And ſhe recieves her arms from thence, becauſe the appearance of the moon often foretells tempeſtuous weather.

† Claudian de Rapt. Proſerp. Lib II. v. 173.

V. 109.

To feize the froward child; no Cyclops come,
But, loudly threat'ning, from fome inner room   105
Obfequious Hermes fwift before her ftands,
With blacken'd face, and with extended hands :
The frighted infant, thus compos'd to reft,
Forgets its cries, and finks upon her breaft.

Ερχεται Ερμειης σποδιη κεχρημενος αιθη.
Αυτικα την κκρην μορμυσσεται. η δε τεκκσης   70
Δυνει εσω κολπκς, θεμενη επι φαεσι χειρας.

V. 109. Forgets its cries and finks upon her breaft.] I am afraid our author finks below himfelf in this paffage, by making fo quick a tranfition from the fublime to the burlefque. And by his laying the fcene among the Gods, one would almoft imagine he had
intended to ridicule the very deities he had been celebrating. All that can be faid for him
is, that he has preferved the memory of an ancient cuftom, which according to Spanheim, is not taken notice of by any other author. The fame conmentator gives a long
difcourfe on the preceeding verfes, and quotes a curious paffage from St. Chryfoftom, by
which we are informed, that the opinion of this venerable father, all good fathers and
mothers ought to caufe their fervants to perfonate Hobgoblins, in order to terrify froward children into a fenfe of their duty. Madam Dacier likewife mentions, that the
nurfes of ancient Greece ufed to frighten crying infants with a terrible female Spectre
called Μορμω, of whom fhe gives no account. Callimachus, in the word μορμισσεται, alludes to this imaginary being, who is alfo mentioned by Theocritus;

——— ηκ αξω τυ, τεκνον, μ'ρμω δακνει ιππος *.

You muft not go, dear chuck, my dear delight;
For there are bugbears, and the horfes bite. CREECH.

It is not probable, that modern parents will incline to adopt this cuftom, though fanctioned
by the poets, nurfes and divines of antiquity

* Theocrit Idyll. XV. v. 40.

V. 113.

But fair Diana, fcarce three fummers old,   110
Could with her mother thefe dread realms behold,
When Vulcan, won by her enchanting mien,
With welcome gifts receiv'd the fylvan queen:
Stern Bronte's knee the little Goddefs preft,
And pluck'd the briftles from his brawny breaft,   115
As if dire Alopecia's pow'r had torn
The hairs that fhall no more his cheft adorn.

Κκρα, συ δε προτερω περ, ετι τριετηρος εκσα,
Ευτ' εμκλεν Λητω σε μετ' αγκαλιδεσσι φερκσα,
Ηφαιςκ καλεκντος οπως οπτηρια δοιη,
Βροντεω σε ςιβαροισιν εφεσσωμενκ γονατεσσι,   75
Στηθεος εκ μεγαλκ λασιης εδραξαο χαιτης,
Ωλοψας δε βιηφι· το δ' ατριχον εισετι κ νυν
Μεσσατιον ςερνοιο μενει μερος, ως οτε κορςην
Φωτος ενιδρυνθεισα κομην επενειματ' αλωπηξ.

V. 113. With welcome gifts received the fylvan Queen] Prefents were ufually made
to the young children of Ancient Greece, on their vifit at the houfe of a relation or fometimes of a ftranger; and fuch gifts were called οπτηρια. Diana made a prefent of this kind
to her brother Apollo:

    φοιβη διδωσιν δ' η γενεθλιον δοσιν
    φοιβω *.

Phœbe hæc autem dedit natale donum
Phœbo.

Prefents called οπτηρια were likewife given by the bridegroom to the bride on the nuptial

* Æfchyl. Eumen. v. 7.

L   day;

Now undifmay'd, as then, the Goddefs cry'd,
Ye mighty Cyclops, fet your tafks afide,
And for Jove's daughter forge immortal arms,   120
To fright the favage race with wild alarms ;
Sharp arrows to purfue the flying foe,
A founding quiver, and a dreadful bow,
Such as Cydonians ufe ; for know that I
Defcend, like Phœbus, from the realms on high,   125

Τῷ μαλα Θαρσαλεη σφε ταδε προσελεξαο τημος,   80
Κυκλωπες, η μοι τι Κυδωνιον ει δ' αγε τοξον,
Ηδ' ιυς, κοιλην τε κατακληιδα βελεμνων
Τευξατε· κ̃ γαρ εγω Λητωιας, ωσπερ Απολλων.

day ; and another fort named ἀνακαλυπτηρια on the third day after marriage, when the bride
was unveiled, and made her firft appearance in public.   Spanheim.

V. 116. As if dire Alopecia's pow'r had torn] The Alopecia was a cutaneous diforder well known to the ancients, and is mentioned by Hippocrates, who makes it a fpecies
of leprofy, called by the Greeks Elephantiafis*.   According to the more particular defcription given by Celfus, a fcaly whitenefs extends in a circle from the back part of the
head, round the ears and over the forehead, but he obferves that it is oftener cured by
nature than by art†.   The name alopecia is derived from αλωπηξ vulpes; either becaufe
foxes are liable to baldnefs, or becaufe the urine of thefe creatures makes the hair fall
off, and the ground barren. Sauvage gives the following definition of the alopecia. Ca-
pillorum lapfus, cum cuticulœ defquamatione.   The beft cure for this and every other
fpecies of baldnefs is thought to be a decoction of Boxwood.

* Hippocrat. πηρι παθων.   † Celf. de Medicina, Lib. VI.

V. 129.

And, when fome tufky boar refigns his life,
Beneath my darts amid the fylvan ftrife,
Th' unwieldy victim fhall reward your toil,
And hungry Cyclops gorge the grateful fpoil.

She fpoke; the tawny workmen fwift obey'd,   130
And in one inftant arm'd th' immortal maid.

But now the Goddefs fought, nor fought in vain,
Pan the protector of th' Arcadian plain;

Αἰ δε κ' εγω τοξοις μονιον δακος ἠ τι πελωρον
Θηριον αγρευσω, το δε κεν Κυκλωπες εδοιεν.   85
Εννεπες· οἱ δ' ετελεσσαν. αφαρ δ' ὡπλισσαο δαιμον.
Αιψα δ' επι σκυλακας παλιν ἠιες· ἱκεο δ' αυλιν

V. 129. The fpeech of Diana.] This fpeech is entirely agreeable to the character of the Goddefs, who never forgets Apollo, but take care to inform the Cyclops that they are obliged to obey her commands, becaufe like him fhe is the offspring of Jupiter. And the poet has fhewn great judgment by making them almoft prevent her wifhes. For it was not to be fuppofed, that a powerful Goddefs would wait a whole night for new armour like the mortal heroes of the Iliad and Æneid. She receives her arms as quick as thought, and departs immediately, which is likewife defcriptive of the moon, always changing and never fhining long on the fame place. It may be obferved that Callimachus takes every opportunity of praifing the Cretan archery. In the fecond hymn the bow of Apollo, comes from Lyctus (a city of Crete) and here Diana demands to be armed like the Cydonians, who inhabited the weftern parts of that Ifland lying towards the promontory of Dictynna.

V. 133. Pan, the protector of th' Arcadian plains] The Commentators not having affigned any reafon for this vifit to the Arcadian deity; and as the ftory is not mentioned by any other ancient Poet, all attempts to give a rational account of it may now be in vain. At the fame time, if we fuppofe the univerfe to be reprefented by Pan, as his name implies, this fiction of our Poet may mean no more than that the moon darts her

She found the God dividing 'mongſt his hounds
The fleſh of Lynxes from Mænalea's grounds.   135
Six beauteous dogs, when firſt ſhe came in view,
Swift from the pack the bearded ſhepherd drew.

Αρκαδικην επι Πανος. ο δε κρεα λυγκος εταμνε
Μαιναλις, ινα οι τοκαδες κυνες ειδαρ εδοιεν.

rays all over the world. And this opinion ſeems the more probable, when we conſider
that Pan was one of the great Gods of Egypt, from whence the Grecians received their
accounts of him: that he was painted with horns on his head to repreſent the rays of the
Sun, as the ruddineſs of his complexion denotes the luſtre of the heavens. That the Star
on his breaſt was a ſymbol of the firmament, and that his feet and legs overgrown with
hair, ſignified the lower parts of the creation, covered with plants and trees *.

Nor could the Poet have found a more proper employment for the rural deity than what
is here deſcribed; ſince, according to Virgil, who doubtleſs had this paſſage in his eye,
he was the guardian of ſhepherds, preſerved their flocks from wild beaſts, and for that
reaſon muſt always be provided with a number of ſtrong and ſwift hounds, who become
more fierce by devouring the fleſh of ſavage animals; as the bravery of Achilles is ſaid
to have encreaſed from his being fed with the marrow of lions.

     Pan, ovium cuſtos, tua ſi tibi Mœnala curæ

     Adſis, O Tegæe favens * :

     And thou, the ſhepherds tutelary God,

     Leave for a while, O Pan, thy lov'd abode;

     And if Arcadian fleeces be thy care,

     From fields and mountains to my ſong repair.   DRYDEN.

Mænalus was a mountain, and Tegæa a city of Arcadia both ſacred to this deity. He
obeys the Goddeſs Diana with the ſame alacrity that the Cyclops had done before; and
hence we may learn of what importance the ancients conceived the Moon to be, and that
her influence was thought capable of producing the greateſt revolutions in the affairs of
mankind, as will be further ſhewn in the progreſs of the preſent hymn.

* Banier's Mythol. Vol I. p. 540.   † Virg. Georg. I. v. 16.

One filver fpangles round his body bears,
Two ftreak'd with white, and three with fpotted ears,
All fierce in blood; the weaker prey they flew,   140
And living lions to their kennel drew.

Τιν δ' ὁ γενειητης δυο μεν κυνας, ἡμισυ πηγους,   90
Τρεις δε παρσατιας, ἑνα δ' αιολον· ὁι ῥα λεοντας
Αὐτες αυ ἑρυοντες, ὁτε ἐραξαιντο δεραων,

V. 141.   And living lions to their kennel drew.]   Upon the fuppofition that the God
Pan reprefents the univerfe, the dogs which he prefents to Diana muft be, like her
nymphs, an emblem of the ftars; and this is confirmed by what the Poet fays of their being
covered with fpots and party-coloured.   But, though we confider them as real hounds,
the account of their carrying home lions alive does not feem any ways exaggerated.
Quintus Curtius has informed us, that Sophites, an Indian king, kept a pack of hounds
for hunting lions only.   The paffage (towards the end of the ninth book) is too curious
to be omitted, but being fomewhat long, I fhall only give Mr. Digby's tranflation,
which conveys the exact meaning of the original.

"This country affords very fine dogs for hunting; they are faid to refrain their cry,
after they have once feen their game, which is the Lion particularly.   That he (viz.
Sophites) might therefore fhew Alexander the ftrength and nature of thefe dogs, he
caufed a very large lion to be brought forth, and only four of them to be let loofe upon
him.   The dogs prefently faftened upon the beaft; then one of thofe, whofe proper
bufinefs it was, took hold of the leg of one of them, and pulled it with all his ftrength,
but the dog not yielding thereunto, he began to cut it off; notwithftanding which, the
dog kept his hold, fo that the keeper cut him in another place, and finding him to ad-
here ftill tenacioufly to the beaft, he by degrees cut him in pieces, the dog keeping his
teeth ftill fixed in the Lion till he died; fo great is the eagernefs nature has implanted
in thefe creatures for their game, as it is tranfmitted to us by our predeceffors."

Curtius concludes this relation by faying that he is doubtful of the fact.   However a

* Plin. Hiftor. Natural. Lib VIII. cap. 40.

ftory

Seven more he gave of Sparta's hardy race,
Fleet as the winds, and active in the chace
Of fauns, that climb the mountains lofty steep,
And hares that never shut their eyes in sleep ;   145

Εἴλκον ἔτι ζώοντας ἐπ' αὔλιον· ἑπτὰ δ' ἔδωκε
Θάσσονας αὔραων κυνοσκρίδας, αἱ ῥα διῶξαι
Ὤκισαι νεβρούς τε κᾳ ὺ μύοντα λαγωον,   95

story of the same kind is told by Pliny*, and Oppian mentions dogs that were not afraid
to encounter the Lion.

 Ὅσσοι μη.δι λέοντας ἰης τριικσιν ἀιακτας *.

In the passage before us, there is some difficulty about the meaning of the word
παρωτιος. Vulcanius contends that it should be rendered *auripetas*, long or trailing ears ; but
Madam Dacier, with much more probability, thinks that it signifies spotted ears, as in the
translation. For very long ears would have given their dreadful adversary too great an
advantage, as a game-cock would soon be defeated, if his comb were uncut. The Spar-
tan dogs, mentioned a few lines afterwards, and called κυνοσκριδας, from Cynosuris a district
of Laconia, said were to be a breed betwixt the dog and the fox. Madam Dacier, maintains that these were the worst species of such animals; but this must probably be a mis-
take : for doubtless Callimachus had better opportunities of knowing the nature of La-
cedæmonian dogs than any modern however learned can pretend to. Xenophon has
left us some marks to distinguish the good or bad disposition of a hound from his colour,
though some commentators imagine that the following words relate as much to the nature as to the swiftness of the animal. Τα δὲ χρωματα ὺ χρη ἰναι των κυιων, ὺτι πυρρα, ὺτι με
λαια, ὺτι λευκα παιτιλως. ἰσι γαρ ὺ γειαιον τουτο, ἀλλ' ἀπλων και Σημωδς. "Dogs should be neither
red, black, nor entirely white; for these colours are a sign, not of a generous but of a
savage disposition". The worthy sportsmen of this island will not be displeased to
see so many learned quotations on the present subject, and to find in what high esti-

* Oppian Cyneget. Lib. I. v. 416.

z   mation

Skill'd thro' the porcupine's dark haunts to go,
And trace the footsteps of the bounding roe.
   The nymph accepting leads her hounds with speed
To verdant hills above the Arcadian mead,
And on the mountains airy summit finds   150
(Sight wond'rous to behold) five beauteous hinds,
That on Anaurus' flow'ry margin fed
(Where mossy pebbles fill'd his ample bed)

Καὶ κοιτην ἐλαφοιο, κ᾽ ὑςριχος ἐνθα καλιαι
Σημηναι, κ᾽ ζορκος ἐπ᾽ ἰχνιον ἡγησασθαι.
Ενθεν ἀπερχομενη (μετα κ᾽ κυνες ἐσσευοντο)
Εὑρες ἐπι προμολης ὀρεος τε Παρρασιοιο
Σκαιρυσας ἐλαφυς, μεγα τι χρεος. αἱ μεν ἐπ᾽ ὀχθης   100
Αἰεν ἐβυκολεοντο μελαμψηφιδος Αναυρυ,

mation their favourite quadrupeds were held by Xenophon, Alexander, and other
great men of antiquity.

   V. 146. And hares that never shut their eyes in sleep] ἃ μυοντα λαγωον, "the hare
that never winks". Oppian has a verse to the same purpose.

ἐπποτι γαρ δη
Ὑπνον ἐπιβλιφαροισιν ἀποβριξαντες ἱλαντο *.

   " Hares may be drowsy, but they never close their eye-lids in sleep." Xenophon observes, that they constantly move their eye-lids even when awake. But this does not
seem to be founded on fact. For the eyes of hares appear open, fixed, and as it were
immoveable. Hence the proverb *Lepus dormiens*, or the sleeping hare, which Erasmus
applies to those who seem busy about one thing, while they are employed in another.

   V. 152. That on Anaurus's flow'ry margin fed] Anaurus, according to Frischi-

* Oppian. Cyneget. Lib. III. v. 154.

In fize like bulls, and on their heads divine
High horns of beaming gold refplendent fhine.   155
Soon as the vifion opened on her eyes,
Thefe, thefe, fhe faid, fhall be Diana's prize,
Then, o'er the rocks, purfu'd the mountain-winds,
Outftripp'd the dogs, and feiz'd the flying hinds;
One unobferv'd efcap'd, but four remain   160
To draw her chariot thro' th' ætherial plain.

Μασσονες η ταυροι· κερκων δ' απελαμπετο χρυσος.
Εξαπινες δ' εταφις τε κ̣ ον ποτι θυμον εειπες,
Τυτο κεν Αρτεμιδος πρωταγριον αξιον ειη.
Πεντ' εσαν αι πασαι· πισυρας δ' ελες ωκα θευσα,   105
Νοσφι κυνοδρομιης, ινα τοι θοον αρμα φερωσι.

linus, was a Theffalian river, that flowed from the famous mount Pelion. It is a-
gain mentioned in the hymn to Delos, and likewife by Lucan,

　　　Nec tenues ventos fufpirat Anaurus *.

Celadon was a branch of the river Alpheus, and Cerynæus a fummit of mount Mænalus, as we learn from the Greek Anthologia.   Spanheim.   ᵕ

　　V. 155.   High horns of beaming gold refplendent fhine]   Bochart and Swartius
are of opinion with Ariftotle, that hinds never have horns; and that there muft be an
error in the text.   But the experience of our own age fhews this obfervation to be
groundlefs; for not many years ago the king of Denmark had a doe in his poffeffion
furnifhed with very large horns, an account of which was publifhed by the learned
Morhooft. Vulcanius.

　　　　　* Lucan. Pharfai: Lib. VI. v. 307.

　　　　　　　　　　　　　　V. 165.

The fifth by Juno's wiles, took fwift her way
Thro' Celadon's dark flood ; the glorious prey
To Cerynæus' diftant mountains run ;
A future prize for great Alcmena's fon.   165

Τὴν δε μιαν, Κελαδοντος ὑπερ ποταμοιο φυγεσαν,
Ἡρης αἰνεσιησιν, ἀεθλιον Ηρακλῃι
Υςατον ὀφρα γενοιτο, παγος Κερυνειος ἐδεκτο.

V. 165. The ftory of the hinds] The Goddefs being now furnifhed with her hunting equipage, immediately takes leave of the fields of Arcadia, agreeable to her changeful difpofition, and repairs to her favourite mountains; where fhe is as fuccefsful in the
chace, as her fondeft hopes could fuggeft. To the horns of gold mentioned by our
author, Virgil has added hoofs of brafs, an emblem of fwiftnefs, though he gives only
a very fhort account of the fifth hind, which was killed by Hercules after a whole
year's purfuit.

> Nec vero Alcides tantum telluris obivit;
> Fixerit æripedem cervam licet *.
>
> Nor Hercules more lands or labours knew;
> Not tho' the brazen-footed hind he flew.   DRYDEN.

Both the prepofition ὑπερ, and the adjective ὑςατον are tranflated according to the opinion of Spanheim.   The prepofition fignifies *per* as well as *fuper*, and it is the nature of
deer to fwim thro' the neareft river when clofely purfued. The adjective is often rendered *poftra*, and the chace of this hind was not the laft, but the fourth labour of Hercules, as we learn from the Anthologia.

> Χρυσοκερον δ' ἐλαφον μετα ταυτ' ἠγρευει τιταρτον †
> Auricornam cervam pofthac venatus eft quarto.

The fame Commentator informs us, that hinds were facred to Diana, on account of
their fwiftnefs and longevity; the former being an emblem of time, and the latter of
eternity.   Her chariot was likewife faid to be drawn by mules and oxen, fymbols of

---

* Virg. Æneid. Lib VI. v. 801.   † Anthol. Græc. Lib. IV. cap. 8.

Hail, fair Parthenia, beauteous queen of night,
Who hurl'd fierce Tityus from the realms of light;
I fee the nymph in golden arms appear,
Mount the fwift car, and join th' immortal deer:
A golden zone around her waift fhe binds,   170
And reins of gold confine the bounding hinds.

Αρτεμι παρθενιη, τιτυοκτονε, χρυσεα μεν τοι   115
Εντεα κ̓ ζωνη, χρυσεον δ̓ εζευξαο διφρον,
Εν δ̓ εβαλευ χρυσεια, θεα, κεμαδεσσι χαλινα.

virginity and barrennefs; and fometimes by a black and white horfe to exprefs the various changes of the moon. The poet has related this fable with all that elegance and
concifenefs, for which his writings have been fo juftly admired; and in order to comprehend his meaning, we have only to confider Diana in her true charaƈter; namely, as
reprefenting the moon. Aftronomy teaches us that a lunar revolution, or from one change
to another is divided into eight parts commonly called oƈtants, two of which make a
quarter. Callimachus has not told us the colour of the hinds, but according to other
authors they were white, whitenefs being an emblem of virginity. The Goddefs finds
them by a river fide on the top of a hill, becaufe the moon feems to arife from rivers and
mountains. They are four in number to reprefent the four phafes or quarters of the
moon, the horns of gold fignify the eight Oƈtants; the hind that efcapes denotes the ftars
which are not fubjeƈt to the lunar influence; and her catching four out of five denotes the
fuperior proportion of her luftre to theirs. Juno, as well as Jupiter, fometimes reprefented the heavens or æther; fhe affifts the fifth in her flight, becaufe the ftars, like the
moon, appear in the firmament. Thus, from every fable of Callimachus, we are at
once entertained with beautiful fiƈtion, and made acquainted with ufeful truth.

The ftory of Hercules killing the fifth hind feems only a different account of Endy-
mion's amour with Diana, which will be more particularly mentioned afterwards. En-
dymion was much addiƈted to the ftudy of aftronomy; and in like manner, we may fuppofe that Hercules, or whoever is meant, fpent a twelvemonth in obferving the motions of the Stars.   V. 176.

But whether firft, O facred virgin, fay,
Did your bright chariot whirl its airy way?
To Hæmus' hills, whence Boreas fiercely blows
On wretched mortals froft and winter fnows.   175
But whence the pine, and whence the kindling flame?
The pine from Myfia's lofty mountain came;
Jove's thunder roar'd; red lightning ftream'd on high
To light the torch that blazes through the fky.
Say next, how oft the filver bow you drew,   180
And where, bright queen, your vengeful arrows flew.
An elm receiv'd the firft, an oak the next;
The third a mountain favage deep transfix'd;

Πᴜ δε σε τοπρωτον κερσεις οχος ηρξατ' αειρειν;
Αιμω επι Θρηικι, τοθεν βορεαο καταιξ
Ερχεται αχλαινοισι δυσαεα κρυμον αγᴜσα.   115
Πᴜ δ' ιταμες ᴣευκην; απο δε φλογος ηψαο ᴣοιης
Μυσω εν Ουλυμπω; φαεος δ' εννηκας αυτμην
Ασβεςᴜ, το ρα ᴣατρος αποςαζᴜσι κεραυνοι.
Ποσσακι δ' αργυρεοιο Θεη ᴣειρισαο τοξᴜ;
Πρωτον επι ᴣτελεην, το δε δευτερον ηκας επι δρυν,   120

V. 176. But whence the pine, and whence the kindling flame] The wrong pointing
of the original has occafioned fome obfcurity in this place, which is now corrected according to the emendation of Vulcanius. He obferves very juftly that the fecond interro-
gation ends with the word ᴣοιης; as the phrafe Μυσω εν Ουλυμπω is an anfwer to the firft.
Myfian Olympus was that famous mountain in leffer Afia, fo much celebrated by Homer
for the defcent of the Gods during the Trojan war. There were feveral other mountains
of that name; the moft famous in Theffaly.

More fwift the fourth, like rattling thunder fprings,
And hurls deftruction from its dreadful wings   185
On realms accurft, where juftice ne'er was fhewn
To fons of foreign ftates, or of their own,
Deep funk in crimes!—How miferable they
'Gainft whom thy vengeance wings its diftant way!
Difeafe devours the flocks, dire hail and rain   190
Deftroy the harveft, and lay wafte the plain.
The hoary fire, for guilty deeds undone,
Shaves his grey locks, and mourns his dying fon.
In agonizing pangs, her babe unborn,
The matron dies, or from her country torn   195
To fome inhofpitable clime muft fly,
And fee th' abortive birth untimely die.

Το τριτον αυτ᾽ επι Θηρα. το τετρατον ἐκετ᾽ επι δρυν,
Αλλα μιν εις αδικων ἑβαλες πολιν, οἰτε περι σφεας
Οἰτε περι ξεινυς αλιτημονα πολλ᾽ ετελεσκον.
Σχετλιοι, οἱς τυνη χαλεπην ἐμμαξεαι οργην.
Κτηνεα φιν λοιμος καταβοσκεται, εργα δε παχνη.   125
Κειρονται δε γερcντες εφ᾽ υιασιν. αἱ δε γυναικες,
Η βληται Θνησκυσι λεχοιδες, ἠε φυγυσαι
Τικτυσιν᾽ των δ᾽ υδεν επι σφυρον ορθον ανεςη.

V. 197. And fee th' abortive birth untimely die] The preceeding lines in which
the poet may be fuppofed to fpeak by the immediate infpiration of the Goddefs, are
perhaps more beautiful than any other part of his writings. Here fhe appears as
Diana Lucifera, in which character fhe was reprefented bearing fometimes one, and

Thrice happy nations, where with look benign
Your afpect bends ; beneath your fmiles divine

Ους δε κεν ευμειδης τε κ] ιλαος αυγασσηαι,

fometimes two torches, whence fhe had the name of Δαδυχος, or torch bearer. In reading this admirable paffage we have a view of Diana feated in her chariot, with a flaming
pine-tree in her hand; while the poet appears below looking upwards. firft in filent adoration, and then putting queftions, with the proper anfwers to which he is immediately infpired. At firft fight indeed, we would imagine that our Author was miftaken in fuppofing that the pine, the torch of Diana, or in other words the Moon was firft
kindled by lightning, inftead of borrowing her luftre from the beams of the Sun. This
cannot be imputed to ignorance; as it is well known that the Egyptians were much
given to the ftudy of aftronomy, and had brought it to great perfection long before the
days of Callimachus. But, on a clofer examination, we fhall find this feeming miftake a
proof of his genius, and entirely agreeable to the character of Diana. Her jealoufy continues; and even when fhe is fo tranfported with the praifes of her poet, as to infpire him
with anfwers to his queftions, fhe infinuates that fhe is under no obligation to Apollo, but
that fhe receives her fplendour from the lightning of Jupiter. Thus while the poet
beftows on his favouring patronefs all the perfection of a Goddefs, he never lofes fight
of her character as a woman. In the twenty fecond Ode of the fecond Book of Horace
the poet dedicates a pine to Diana,

> Imminens villæ tua pinus efto,
>
> To you I confecrate the pine,
>
> That nodding waves my villa round.   FRANCIS.

On which Mr. Francis has the following note

" The Commentators are much perplexed in their learning to know why Horace con-
fecrates a pine to Diana; whether it was an emblem of perpetual virginity, quod femel
excifæ nunquam repullulafcit ; or becaufe Ifis and Cybele, to whom this tree was facred,
were only other names for Diana. But perhaps the Poet did not intend to perplex his
gueffing commentators, and only defigned to make a prefent of his favourite tree to the
Goddefs."

Now it is plain that if Mr. Francis himfelf, or any of thefe commentators had read

I   the

The fields are with increafing harvefts crown'd,   200
The flocks grow faft, and plenty reigns around,

Κεινοις ευ μεν αρβρα φερει ςαχυν, ευ δε γενεθλη   130
Τετραποδων, ευ δ' ολβος αεξεται, εδ' επι σημα

the third hymn of Callimachus, they would have been able to give a more fatisfactory
explication. For we are here informed that the pine was facred to Diana, becaufe the
torch which fhe held in her hand, in the character of Lucifera, was fuppofed to be a
pine-tree, that abounds with turpentine, fparkles as it burns, and was therefore moft
proper to reprefent the rays of the moon.

Spanheim obferves that the epithet κεραις, or horne.l, given to the chariot of the Goddefs
alludes to the horns of the hinds, which is a farther proof that thefe horns were intended
by the Poet to reprefent the various appearances of the moon, as mentioned in a former
note. And he probably intended to fubftitute them in place of the crefcent, with which
Diana is fo often defcribed by other authors, but never by Callimachus.

Nor will this fine paffage be found deficient in beauty if we confider it as an allegory, according to the method which has been hitherto followed. The Goddefs flies firft
to mount Hæmus, whence the north wind blows, becaufe high winds, that feem to come
from the mountains, are occafioned by the influence of the moon. The darts of Diana
are emblems of a violent ftorm, which fhatters the trees on the hills, kills wild beafts,
deftroys the harveft, and brings infectious vapours along with it, that occafion misfortunes
yet more fevere, namely malignant and peftilential difeafes. The bow of the Goddefs
is filver, for the fame reafon that her hinds are white; and fhe darts four arrows to denote her four principal appearances. In ancient times, when the moon was adored as a
principal divinity, thefe terrible effects were attributed to her difpleafure; as a favourable feafon was thought to proceed from her fmiles, which are defcribed in the next para-
graph. The anger of this Goddefs was thought to be the caufe of fudden deaths, and
hence fhe was worfhipped in every country under different reprefentations. Nay, fome
moderns have fuppofed this planet to poffefs almoft the fame power afcribed to her by
the ancients; for which the curious reader may confult the late learned Dr. Mead's ingenious treatife De imperio Solis et Lunæ.

The

Nor fire, nor infant-fon black death fhall crave,
Till ripe with age they drop into the grave ;
Nor fell fufpicion, nor relentlefs care,
Nor peace-deftroying difcord enter there,   205
But friends and brothers, wives and fifters join
The feaft in concord and in love divine.

O ! grant your bard, and the diftinguifh'd few,
His chofen friends, thefe happy climes to view,
So fhall Apollo's love, Diana's praife,   210
And fair Latona's nuptial's grace my lays ;

Ερχονται, πλην εὐτε πολυχρονιον τι φερωσιν.
Οὐδε διχοςασιη τρωγει γενος, ἡ τε κ᾽ εὐ περ
Οἰκἀς ἑςηωτας ἑσινατο. ται δε θυωρον
Εἰνατερες γαλοῳ τε μιαν περι διφρα τιθενται.   135
Ποτνια, των εἰη μεν ἐμοι φιλος ὁς τις ἀληθης,
Εἰην δ᾽ αὐτος, ἀνασσα· μελοι δε μοι αἰεν ἀοιδη,
Τη ἐνι μεν Λητους γαμος ἐσσεται, ἐν δε συ πολλη,
Εν δε κ᾽ Απολλων, ἐν δ᾽ οἱ σεο παντες ἀεθλοι.

The ancient cuftom of fhaving the head on the death of a fon, or other near relation is well known. But it may be obferved, that the Grecians fhaved the eye brows, as well as the head, on mournful occafions. And Madam Dacier informs us that the fame cuftom prevails in fome parts of Turkey to this day. The phrafe ἐπισφυρ᾽ ὀξθον ἀνιςη has been copied by Horace recto talo ftare *. It is here tranflated according to the interpretation of Vulcanius, minime vitale, which coincides with the dreadful effects of the arrows of Diana.

V. 211. And fair Latona's nuptials grace my lays]   From thefe words Spanheim

* Horat Epift. ad Auguft. v. 176.

imagines

And when my foul infpiring tranfport feels,
Your arms, your labours, and the fervid wheels
Of your fwift car, that flames along the fky
To yonder courts of thund'ring Jove on high.　　　215
Your coming Acacefian Hermes waits,
And great Apollo ftands before the gates,
To lift from off the car the fylvan prey,
While Hermes joyful bears your arms away.
Nor Phœbus e'er his helping hand denies ;　　　220
But when Alcides fcal'd the lofty fkies,

Εν δε κυνες, κỳ τοξα, κỳ αντυγες, αἱ τε σε ρεια　　　140
Θνητην φορεωσιν, ὁτ' ἐς Διος οικον ἐλαυνεις.
Ενθα τοι αντιοωντες ἐνι προμολησι δεχονται,
Οπλα μεν Ερμειης ἀκακησιος, αὐταρ Απολλων,
Θηριον ὁ, τῇι φερησθα, παροιθε δε, πριν περ ἱκεσθαι

imagines that Callimachus had written other poems (now loft) in praife of Apollo, Diana,
and Latona's marriage, or rather amour with Jupiter.

V. 216. Your coming Acacefian Hermes waits] Mercury was the tutelar deity of
Acacecus a city of Arcadia, fo called from Acacus the fon of Lycaon an Arcadian King.
A ftatue of the God was placed on a neighbouring mountain. Vulcanius
The fame title is given to Mercury by Homer, viz. 'Ακακητης*, the fame with Ακακος,
and fignifies a preferver from evil.—Two reafons may be affigned why Mercury and
Apollo are faid to wait for Diana at the gates of heaven. The firft is becaufe ftatues
were erected to thefe deities before the doors of houfes: but the laft and beft is from
aftronomy. The Sun and Moon frequently appear in the firmament at the fame time,

* Hom. Odyf. XXIV. v. 10.

This taſk to him was by the Gods decreed,
So from his ancient labours ſcarcely freed,
Before th' eternal doors the hero ſtands,
Expects the prey, and waits your dread commands.   225
In laughing crowds the joyous Gods appear,
But chief th' imperious ſtep-dame's voice you hear
Loud o'er the reſt, to ſee Tirynthius pull
Th' unwieldy weight of ſome enormous bull.

Καρτερον Αλκειδην· νυν δ' ἐκ ἐτι τετον ἀεθλον   145
Φοιϐος ἐχει. τοιος γαρ ἀει Τιρυνθιος ἀκμων
Εϛηκε προ πυλεων, ποτιδεγμενος εἰ τι φερѫσα
Νειαι πιον ἐδεσμα. Θεοι δ' ἐπι παντες ἐκεινω
Αλληκτον γελοωσι, μαλιϛα δε πενθερη αὑτη,
Ταυρον ὁτ' ἐκ διφροιο μαλα μεγαν, ἡ ὁτε χλευην   150

and Mercury has the ſame phaſes with the moon, appearing ſometimes horned, ſometimes gibbous, and ſometimes ſhining with a round face. And from this reſemblance the poet could not have found a more proper attendant on Diana.

V. 228. To ſee Tirynthius pull] Hercules had the Name Tirynthius from Tiryn-thia a city of Peloponneſus, where he was ſaid to have paſſed his infancy. Juno be-came his mother in law, becauſe, after his deification he married her daughter Hebe, or in other words attained the enjoyment of immortal youth. But Juno, who was alſo his ſtep-mother ſeems ſtill to retain part of her ancient malice, when the ſight of her ſon-in-law in an awkward ſituation gives her ſo much pleaſure. She adopted Her-cules after he was ranked among the Gods, and the ceremony of his adoption is thus related. Juno laid herſelf on a bed, as if in labour, and placed Hercules in ſuch a man-ner, that he fell to the ground as from under her petticoats *. His marriage with Hebe

* Diodor. Sicul. Lib. IV cap. 40.

N   ſignifies

That with his hinder foot impatient fpurns   230
The lab'ring God, as from the car he turns.
The brawny hero, tho' with toil oppreſt,
Approach'd the nymph, and quaintly thus addreſt.

Καπρον επισθιδιοιο φεροι ποδος ασπαιροντα.
Κερδαλεω μυθω σε, θεη, μαλα τωδε πινυσκει,

ſignifiesthat ſtrength and youth always go hand in hand. And befides Hebe or youth being
the daughter of Juno or the air, implies that nothing contributes fo much to the prefer-
vation of health and ſtrenth as open air and plenty of exercife. Hercules making ſport
to the other deities is doubtlefs an imitation of that paffage of Homer, where Vulcan appears as Cup-bearer at the celeſtial feaſt.

Αυταρ ο τοις αλλοισι θεοις ενδεξια πασιν
Ωιοχοει, γλυκυ νεκταρ απο κρητηρος αφυσσων,
Ασβιρος δὲ ενωρτο γελως μακαρεσσι θεοισιν,
Ως ιδον Ηφαιρον δια δωματα ποιπνυοντα*.

Then to the reſt he filled; and in his turn,
Each to his lips apply'd the nectar'd urn,
Vulcan, with awkward grace, his office plies,
And unextinguiſh'd laughter ſhakes the ſkies.   POPE.

But it is plain to an impartial obferver that in this inſtance Callimachus excells Homer;
for Vulcan attends the Gods, but they run to the gates of heaven to·enjoy the buffoon-
ery of Hercules, whom other authors mention to have poffeffed no ſmall ſhare of humour,
as well as generofity. Thus, when Jupiter offered him a place among the twelve fuperior
deities, after his marriage with Hebe, the hero declined the honour, alleging that there
was no vacancy and that it would be unreafonable to degrade any other God to make
room for him †. But being endowed with a moſt excellent appetite, whence he had the
furname of Βυφαγος, or Beef-eater, it is moſt probable that, like Sancho, he chofe to devour
his victuals ‚in private where no fpectator could animadvert on the quantity ſwallowed.

* Hom Il. I. v. 596.   † Diodor. ubi fupra.

And

Strike sure the savage beast, and man to thee
Will give the name before bestow'd on me,   235
The great Deliv'rer; let the timid hare,
And bearded goat to native hills repair,
And there securely range. What ills proceed
From hares or goats that on the mountains feed?
Wild boars, and trampling bulls oft render vain   240
The peasant's toil, and waste the rip'ning grain;
Aim there your darts, and let the monsters feel
The mortal wound, and the sharp-pointed steel.

Βαλλε κακυς ἐπι Θηρας, ἱνα Θνητοισα βοηθον,
Ὡς ἐμε, κικλησκωσιν. ἐα προκας ἡδε λαγωυς
Οὐρεα βοσκεσθαι· τι δε κεν προκες ἡδε λαγωοι   155
Ρεξειαν; συες ἐργα, συες φυτα λυμαινουται.
Και βοες ἀνθρωποισι κακον μεγα. βαλλ' ἐπι κ̔ τυς.

And hence it appears, that our author had an intention of ridiculing this hero, from the strange employment allotted to him in heaven. For the ancients were of opinion, that departed spirits possessed the same faculties, appetites, passions, and indeed the same imperfections as before the separation of the soul from the body. Thus the giant Orion is armed with a huge mace of brass, and hunts wild beasts in the infernal shades; the ghosts of Achilles and Patroclus are inseparable companions, and Sisyphus sweats as he rolls the stone up the mountain *.

V. 243. The speech of Hercules] These words are admirably adapted to the character of the speaker. He begins with all the bluntness of an ancient hero, and without the least mark of respect for the Goddess, Βαλλι κακυς ἱπιτρας, Kill destructive animals. The

* Hom. Odyss. Lib. XI.

will

He fpoke, renew'd his toil, and heav'd away
With fecret gladnefs the reluctant prey.   245
Beneath the Phrygian oak his bones were burn'd,
And his immortal part to heav'n return'd,

Ὡς ἐνεπεν, ταχινος δε μεγαν περι θηρα πονειτο.
Οὐ γαρ ὁγε Φρυγιη περ ὑπο δρυι γυια θεωθεις

wit or quaintnefs of the fpeech, as the word κιρλαλω fignifies, plainly confifts in this : he
defires, indeed commands Diana to fpare fmall and harmlefs animals, and to employ her
arrows on wild-boars, and bulls, that often hinder population, and lay wafte whole provinces. But the true reafon is, that he may have an opportunity of fatiating his gluttony,
a quality for which many modern Heroes have been equally remarkable. Thus, with
all his feeming roughnefs, he contrives both to fatisfy his own appetite, and to flatter
Diana's vanity, of which with all her good qualities, fhe feems to have poffeffed no inconfiderable fhare; as appears by the many names fhe wifhes to be invoked, by the number of her attendants, and the eagernefs with which fhe purfues the white hinds. If the
poet intends any ridicule on Hercules, it muft be contained in this fpeech. For one would
imagine that all the great actions of this hero proceeded from one fource, namely, an in-
fatiable defire of eating. And I may be allowed to remark that he was eminent for a
fifter-property of almoft equal importance, namely drinking, in which he is faid to have
arrived at a degree of perfection unknown either before or fince; for he never travelled
without a Cup of fuch immenfe magnitude, that it ferved him at once for a boat and a
drinking glafs *.

V. 246. Beneath the Phrygian oak his bones were burned] Spanheim and Frifchilinus
obferve, that the kingdom of Phrygia is not meant here, but one of the fummits of mount
Oeta, called Phrygia, where an oak tree grew; by the fide of which Hercules raifed a
funeral pile, and threw himfelf into it, yet alive. For the particulars of this ftory fee
Ovid. Metamorph. Lib. IX.

* Macrob. Lib V.

V. 249.

Yet ſtill tormented with fierce hunger's rage,
As when Theiodamas he durſt engage.
Amniſian virgins from the car unbind   250
The ſacred deer, and dreſs each panting hind ;
Ambroſial herbage by their hands is giv'n
From meadows ſacred to the queen of heav'n,
Where Jove's immortal courſer's feed.   They bring
Refreſhing water from a heav'nly ſpring   255
In golden ciſterns of ætherial mold,
The draught more grateful from a vaſe of gold.

Παυσατ' ἀδηφαγιης ἐτι οἱ παρα νηδυς ἐκεινη   160
Τη ποτ' ἀροτριχοντι συνηντετο Θειοδαμαντι.
Σοι δ' Αμνισιαδες μεν ὑπο ζευγληφι λυθεισας,
Ψηχεσιν κεμαδας, παρα δε σφισι πελυ νεμεσθαι
Ηρης ἐκ λειμωνος ἀμησαμεναι φορεεσιν
Ωκυθοον τριπετηλον ὁ κϳ Διος ἱπποι ἐδεσι,   165
Εν κϳ χρυσειας ὑποληνιδας ἐπλεσαντο
Ὑδατος, ὁφρ' ἐλαφοισι ποτον θυμαρμενον ειη.

V. 247. As when Theiodamas he durſt engage] Theiodamas or Theodamantus according to Banier, was a king of Myſia, whom Hercules in the courſe of his travels met
one day plowing a field with oxen. The hero being, according to cuſtom, ready to
faint with hunger, demanded ſome victuals, which the king refuſing, Hercules immediately killed him, and ſnatching up one of the Oxen, devoured it without ceremony,
ſkin, bones and all. And from this it was uſual among the ancients, to ſwear by Hercules the Beef-eater: Μα τοι βαθωαι Ἡρακλεα*. However, to make ſome amends, he took
the king's ſon Hylas along with him, who afterwards became his friend.

* Antholog. cap. VIII. Epigr. 40.

V. 263.

But you, fair nymph, call'd by the pow'rs above,
Afcend the manfions of imperial Jove;
The Gods rofe graceful, when the virgin queen,   260
With beauteous afpect, and with look ferene
By Phœbus' fide affum'd her filver throne,
Next him in power, and next in glory fhone.
    But when, with fportive limbs, the nymphs are feen
To dance in mazy circles round their queen,   265
Near the cool fountains whence Inopus rofe,
Broad as the Nile, and like the Nile o'erflows;

Αὐτη δ' ἐς πατρος δομον ἐρχεαι· οἱ δε σ' ἐφ' ἑδρην
Παντες ὁμως καλευσι. συ δ' Απολλωνι παριζεις;.
Ηνικα δ' αἱ νυμφαι σε χορῳ ἐνι κυκλωσονται   170
Αγχοθι πεγαων Αιγυπτιϑ Ινωποιο,

V. 263. Next him in pow'r and next in glory fhown] Claudian has imitated the
paffage where Callimachus defcribes the nymphs unbinding the hinds from the chariot.
         Cervi currum fubière jugales
         Quos decus effe Deœ primi fub limine cœli
         Rofcida fæcundis concepit Luna cavernis†.
And thefe hinds (who muft likewife be fuppofed Goddeffes) feem to have imbibed part
of their miftrefs's tafte for magnificence, by refufing to drink, unlefs they are ferved from
veffels of gold. The Gods inviting Diana to the fkies, and fhe taking her feat by the fide
of Apollo plainly intimate that the moon is next to the fun the brighteft Luminary in the
heavens.
    V. 266. Near the cool fountains whence Inopus rofe] A river of Delos that over-
flows and decreafes annually like the Nile, and hence was named the Egyptian river.

                 * Claud. fec Conf. Stilich. v. 268.

Or when to Pitane or Limnæ's meads,
Or Alæ's flow'ry field, the Goddefs leads
The choir, from Taurus black with human blood, 270
And turns difguftful from the Scythian brood.
That day my heifers to the ftall retire,
Nor turn the green fward for another's hire ;

Η Πιτανης, (κỳ γαϱ Πιτανη σεθεν) ἡ ἐνι Λιμναις,
Η ἱνα, δαιμον, Λλας Αϱαϕηνιδας οἰκησɛσα
Ηλθες ἀπο Σκυθιης, ἀπο δ' εἰπαο τεθμια Ταυϱων,
Μη νειον τημɛτος ἐμαι βοες· εἰνεκα μισθɛ   175
Τετϱαγυον τεμνοιεν ὑπ' ἀλλοτϱιῳ ἀϱοτηϱι.
Η γαϱ κεν γυιας τε κỳ αὐχενα κεκμηκυιαι

The Delians imagined that there was a fubterraneous communication betwixt the fountains of Inopus and the Nile. It will be feen in the next hymn that this was likewife the
opinion of Callimachus. Dacier.

V. 268--271. Two Grecian cities were called Pitane, one in Laconia near the Eurotas, and the other in Æolia, near the mouth of the river Alpheus. The former is fuppofed to be meant here. Limnæ was a diftrict fituated on the borders of Laconia, and
poffeffed in common, by the Dorians, Spartans and Meffenians. Here ftood a temple facred to Diana Limnas. Alæ was part of Attica. Spanheim and Frifchlinus.

Taurus was a diftrict of that part of Scythia, now called leffer Tartary fituated on the
North of the ancient Cherfonefus Taurica, now Crimea. In this country human facrifices were offered to Diana Taurica *; and the Poet expreffes his deteftation of this horrid
practice, by telling us that Diana turns with difguft from thefe inhofpitable climes.

* Heredot. Lib. IV.

Tho'

Tho' nine years old, and in Tymphæa born,
Their limbs tho' sturdy, and tho' strong of horn　　　275
To drag the plough, and cleave the mellow soil ;
Yet would their necks, o'erlabour'd bend with toil,
When Sol himself leans downward from the sky,
Beholds the virgins with enraptur'd eye,
Detains his chariot, whence new glories pour,　　　280
Prolongs the day, and stops the flying hour.

　What city, mountain, or what sacred isle,
What harbour boasts your most auspicious smile ?
And of th' attendant nymphs, that sportful rove
Along the hills, who most enjoys your love,　　　285
O Goddess tell : If you inspire their praise,
Admiring nations will attend my lays.

　Your favour Perga, green Doliche boasts,
Taygettus' mountains, and Euripus' coasts ;

Κοπρον επι προγενοιντο, κ̀ ει Τυμφανδες ειεν,
Εἰναετιζομεναι, κεραελκεες, αἱ μεγ' αρισαι
Τεμνειν ωλκα βαθειαν. επει θεος ἑποτ' εκεινον　　　180
Ηλθε παρ' Ηελιος καλον χορον· αλλα θεηται
Διφρον επιςησας, τα δε φαεα μηκυνονται.
Τις δε νυ τοι νησων, ποιον δ' ορος εὑαδε πλειςον ;
Τις δε λιμην ; ποιη δε πολις ; τινα δ' εξοχα νυμφεων
Φιλαο, κ̀ ποιας ἡρωιδας εσχες εταιρας ;　　　185
Ειπε θεα, συ μεν ἀμμιν, εγω δ' ετεροισιν αεισω.
Νησων μεν Δολιχη, πολιων δε τοι εὑαδε Περγη,

2

And

And Britomartis, from Gertynas' grove,   290
Of all the nymphs enjoys diftinguifh'd love :
Fair Britomartis (fkill'd to wing the dart,
And pierce with certain wound the diftant hart)
Imperial Minos chac'd with wild defire,
O'er Cretan hills, and made the nymph retire   295
To fome far diftant oak's extended fhade,
Or fheltring grove, or marfh's wat'ry bed.
Nine months the king purfued, with furious hafte,
O'er rocks abrupt, and precipices vaft,
Nor once gave back, but when the blooming maid   300
Was juft within his pow'r, and none gave aid,
His grafp eluding, from the impending fteep
Headlong fhe plung'd amid the fwelling deep.
But friendly fifhers on the main difplay'd
Their nets wide-ftretching to receive the maid,   305

Τηϋγετον δ' ορεων, λιμενες γε μεν Ευριποιο.
Εξοχα δ' αλλαων Γορτυνιδα φιλαο νυμφην,
Ελλοφονον, Βριτομαρτιν, εϋσκοπον· ἧς ποτε Μινως   190
Ποιηθεις ὑπ' ερωτι κατεδραμεν ὑρεα Κρητης.
Η δ' οτε μεν λασιησιν ὑπο ὁρυσι κρυπτετο νυμφη,
Αλλοτε δ' ειαμενησιν. ὁ δ' εννεα μηνας ἐροιτα
Παιπαλα τε κρημνες τε· κ̀ ὑκ ανεπαυσε διωκτυν,
Μεσφ' οτε μαρπτομενη κ̀ δη σχεδον ἡλατο ποντον   195
Πρηονος ἐξ ὑπατοιο· κ̀ ἐνθορεν εἰς ἁλιηων

                    O   And

And thus preferv'd her from a wat'ry death,
Worn out with toil, and panting still for breath.
And in succeeding times Cydonians hence
Dictynna * call'd the nymph; the mountain, whence
She leapt into the sea, bear Dictè's name,   310
Where annual rites record the virgin's fame.
On that blest day, fair nymph, is wove for thee
A Garland from the pine or mastich tree;
The myrtle-branch untouch'd, that durst assail
The flying maid and rent her snowy vèil,   315
And hence the man must bear the virgins frown,
Who shall her altars with fresh myrtles crown.
    The name Dictynna too the Cretans gave
(From her who fearless plung'd beneath the wave)

Δικτυα, τα σφ᾽ ἐσαωσεν. ὁθεν μετεπειτα Κυδωνες
Νυμφαν μεν, Δικτυναν, ὁρος δ᾽ ὁθεν ἡλατο νυμφη,
Δικταιον καλευσιν. ανεστησαντο δε βωμυς,
ἱερα τε ρεζυσι. το δε ςεφος ἡματι κεινω,   200
Ἡ πιτυς, ἡ σχινος· μυρτοιο δε χειρες ἀθικτοι.
Δη τοτε γαρ πεπλοισιν ενεσχετο μυρτινος οζος
Τῃς κυρης, ὁτ᾽ εφευγεν· ὁθεν μεγα χωσατο μυρτω.

---

* The Greek word δικτυον signifies a net; in the plural δικτυα; hence the name of the
nymph, in memory of the means by which she was saved from drowning, and of the admirable chastity, which exposed her to that danger. Virgil in his Ciris mentions this
story, and says that the Moon, or Diana, was called Dictynna from the name of the nymph.
Dictynnam dixere tuo de nomine lunam.

To you fair Upis, * from whofe facred brows   320
Refplendent glory with mild luftre flows;
But in your breaft the nymph Cyrene fhares
An equal place, and equal favour bears,
To whom in days of old your hands convey'd
Two beauteous hounds, with which the warlike maid
Acquired renown before th' Jolcian tomb.
All-bright with locks of gold fee Procris come,
Majeftic matron, Cephalus's fpoufe,
Whom, tho' no virgin, you great Goddefs choofe
Companion of the chace, but o'er the reft   330
Mild Anticlea your regard poffeft:
Fair as the light, and dearer than your eyes,
She claims protection by fuperior ties.

Οὔπι ἄνασσ' εὐῶπι, φαεσφόρε κỳ δε σε κεινης
Κρηταεες καλευσιν ἐπωνυμιην ἀπο νυμφης.   205
Και μην Κυρηνην ἐτα·ισσαο, τη ποτ' ἐδωκας;
Αυτη Θηρητηρε δυω κυνε, τοις ἐνι κυρη
Υψηις παρα τυμ-ον Ιωλκιον ἐμμορ' αεθλυ.
Και Κεφαλυ ξανθην ἀλοχον Δηιονιδαο
Ποτνια σην ὁμοθρον ἐθηκαο· κỳ δε σε φασι   210
Καλην Αντικλειαν ἰσον φαεεσσι φιληται.

---

* Upis is an appellation of Diana either, απο τυ επιζισθαι τας τικτυσας, from her attending
women in child-bed, or from υπις, (ab. υπτομαι) denoting the difpenfer of light.

Thefe

Thefe firft bore quivers, thefe you taught to wing
The founding arrow from the trembling ftring,   335
With their right fhoulders, and white bofoms bare,
They lead the chace, and join the fylvan war.
Your praifes too fwift Atalanta charm,
Jafius' daughter, whofe refiftlefs arm
O'erthrew the boar; you fhew'd the nymph with art   304
T' incite the hounds, and aim the unerring dart.
But Calydonian hunters now no more
Difpute the prize, fince the fair virgin bore
The glorious trophy to th' Arcadian plain,
Where his white teeth record the monfter flain.   345
Nor now fhall Rhœcus, nor Hylæus young,
With luft inflam'd, or with fell envy ftung,

Αἱ πρῶται θοα τόξα κỳ ἀμφ' ὤμοισι φαρετρας
Ιοδοκυς ἐφορησαν· ἀσυλωτοι δε φιν ὠμοι
Δεξιτεροι, κỳ γυμνος ἀει παρεφαινετο μαζος.
Ἡνησας δ' ἐτι παγχυ ποδορρωην Αταλαντην   215
Κυρην Ιασιοιο συοκτονον Αρκασιδαο,
Και ἑ κυνηλασιην τε και εὐστοχιην ἐδιδαξας.
Οὐ μιν ἐπικλητοι Καλυδωνιυ ἀγρευτηρες
Μεμφονται καπροιο. τα γαρ σημηια νικης
Αρκαδιην εἰσηλθεν, ἐχει δ' ἐτι θηρος ὀδοντας.   220
Οὐδε μεν Ὑλαιον τε κỳ ἀφρενα Ροικον ἐολπα,
Οὐδε περ ἐχθαιροντας, ἐν ἀιδι μωμησεσθαι

                                        ε   Lay

Lay hands unhallow'd on the beauteous maid,
Or once approach her in th' Elyfian fhade;
Since their torn entrails on Mænalia tell　　　　350
How by her arm th' inceftuous monfters fell *.

Hail! Bright Chitone, hail! Aufpicious queen,
With robes of gold, and with Majeftic mien!
In many temples, many climes adore
Your name, fair guardian of Miletus' fhore.　　　355
The name Imbrafia, Chefias too is giv'n
To you high thron'd among the pow'rs of heav'n,
Since happy Nelus and th' Athenian hoft
By your protection reach'd the fertile coaft.

Τοξοτιν· ἐ γαρ σφιν λαγονες συνεπιψευσονται,
Ταων Μαιναλιη ναεν φονω ακρωρεια.
Ποτνια, πᾳλυμελαθρε, πολυπτολι, χαιρε Χιτωνη,　　225
Μιλητω επιδημε. σε γαρ ποιησατο Νηλευς
Ηγεμονην, ὁτε νηυσιν ανηγετο Κεκροπιηθεν,
Χησιας, Ιμβρασιη, πρωτοθρονε· σοι δ' Αγαμεμνων

* The fcoliaft fays, Hylacus and Rhæcus were Centaurs in Arcadia, flain by Atalanta
for attempting to violate her chaftity. They were transfixed by her arrows; and as the
ancients believed that the wounds of which any perfon died, were ftill vifible in his fhade,
thefe wounds, the poet fays, which attefted their difgrace, would reprefs their infolence.
In the 6th Eneids, 495, the fhade of Deiphobus appears covered with wounds.

　　Atque hic Priamidem laniatum corpore toto,
　　Deiphobum videt, et lacerum crudeliter ora;
　　Ora manufque ambas.

Great

Great Agamemnon's hand a rudder bore,   360
To grace your temple on Bœotia's fhore,
And gain your love, while adverfe winds detain
The impatient Grecians from the roaring main;
Wild with delay, on rugged rocks they mourn
Rhamnufian * Helen from her country torn.   365
　　When fudden frenzy fiez'd the madd'ning brains
Of Prætus' † daughters on the' Achaian plains;
While o'er th' inhofpitable hills they roam,
You fought the maids, and fafe conducted home:
Of this two facred fanes preferve the fame,   370
One to Corefia from the virgin's name;

Πηδαλιον νηος σφετερης εγκατθετο νηω,
Μειλιον απλοιης, οτε οι κατεδησας αητας,   230
Τευκρων ηνικα νηες Αχαιιδες αςτα κηδειν
Επλεον, αμφ' Ελενη Ραμνησιδι θυμωθεισαι.
Η μεν τοι Προιτος γε δυω εκαθισσατο νηους·
Αλλον μεν Κοριης, οτι οι συνελεξαο κηρας

* Helen was called Rhamnufian from Rhamnus, a town of Attica; where, according to
the fcholiaft, Jupiter lay with Nemefis, the protecting Divinity of the place.   Nemefis in
order to fhun the embraces of Jupiter metamorphofed herfelf into a fwan, and the effects
of his compreffing her in that fhape, was the famous egg, which produced Helen and her
brothers Caftor and Pollux.

† The ftory of Prætus daughters who fancied themfelves heifers is well known.   See
Ovid. Metamorph. l. 15. v. 327 who afcribes their cure to Melampus, who employed for
this purpofe black hellebore, fince called from his name Melampodion.

To

To Hemeresia one in Lousa's shades,
Mild Hemeresia cur'd the furious maids.
Fierce Amazonian dames to battle bred,
Along th' Ephesian plains by Hippo led,   375
With pious 'hands a golden statue bore
Of you, bright Upis, to the sacred shore
Plac'd where a beech-tree's ample shade invites
The warlike band to join the holy rites.
Around the tree they clash their maiden shields,   380
With sounding strokes that echo thro' the fields;
Swift, o'er the shores, in wider circles spring,
Join hand in hand to form a mazy ring,
And beat, with measur'd steps, the trembling ground
Responsive to the shrill pipe's piercing sound;   385

Ουρεα πλαζομενας αζεινια· τον δ᾽ ενι Λυσσοις   235
Ημερη. ουνεκα θυμον απ᾽ αγριον ειλεο παιδων.
Σοι κ᾽ Αμαζονιδες πολεμυ επιθυμητειραι
Εν κοτε παρραλιη Εφετυ βρετας ιδρυσαντο,
Φηγω υπο πρεμνω. τελεσεν δε τοι ιερον Ιππω.
Αυται δ᾽. Ουπι ανασσα, περι πρυλιν ωρχησαντο,   240
Πρωτα μεν εν σακεεσσιν ενοπλιον, αυθι δε κυκλω
Στησαμεναι χορον ευρυν. υπηεισαν δε λιγειαι
Λεπταλεον συριγγες, ινα πλησσωσιν ομαρτη.
Ου γαρ πω νεβρεια δι᾽ οςεα τετρηνοντο,

                                                          The

The bones of deer yet uninfpir'd and mute,
From which Minerva form'd a fofter flute.
Difcordant notes to lofty Sardis fly,
And Berecynthus' diftant hills reply;
Hoarfe-rattling quivers o'er their fhoulders rung   390
While from the ground, with bounding feet they fprung.
And after ages faw, with glad furprize,
A wond'rous,* fabric round the ftatue rife,
More rich, more beautiful, than Phœbus boafts,
With all his glory on the Delphic coafts :   395
Nor yet Aurora's morning beams have fhone
On fuch a temple, or fo fair a throne.

Εργον Αθηναιης ελαφω κακον. εδραμε δ' ηχω   245
Σαρδιας, ες τε νομον Βερεκυνθιον. αξ δε ποδεσσιν
Ουλα κατεκροταλιζον, επεψοφεον δε φαρετραι.
Κεινο δε τοι μετεπειτα περι βρετας ευρυ θεμεθλον
Δωμηθη. τυ δ' υτι θεωτερον οψεται ηως,
Ουδ' αφνειοτερον· ρεα κεν Πυθωνα παρελθοι.   250

* The temple of Ephefian Diana, which rofe with encreafing fplendour from feven repeated misfortunes, and was finally burnt by the Goths in their third naval invafion.   It
was fupported by an hundred and twenty-feven marble columns of the Ionic order, each
fixty feet high; and the length of the temple was four hundred and twenty-five feet, about
two thirds the meafure of the length of St. Peters at Rome.   See Gibbon's Hiftory of
the Decline and Fall, &c. Vol. 1. p. 325.   This temple was early enriched by
the dedication of devout monarchs, and adorned by the arts of Greece, which rendered it
truly worthy of Callimachus's panegyric.

But

But foon fierce Lygdamis * defcending down,
With impious threats to burn th' Ephefian town,
In numbers like the fand an hoft prepares   400
Of ftrong Cimmerians, fed with milk of mares :
The bands unbleft their fudden march began
From frozen plains, where lowing Io ran.
Ah ! wretched Monarch, fated now no more
To lead your legions to the northern fhore ;   405
Who drove their chariots o'er Cayefter's mead
Shall ne'er in Scythian climes their courfers feed:
For bright Diana guards the facred towers,
And on th' approaching foe deftruction pours.

Τῳ ῥα κỵ ἠλαινων αλαπαζεμεν ἠπειλησε
Λυγδαμις ὑϐρισης· ἐπι δε ϛρατον ἱππημολγων
Ηγαγε Κιμμεριων, ψαμαθῳ ἰσον, οἱ ῥα παρ' αὐτον
Κεκλιμενοι ναιᾰσι βοος πορον Ιναχιωνης.
Α δειλος βασιλεων, ὁσον ἠλιτεν. ᾽ὖ γαρ ἐμελλεν   255
Οὐτ' αὐτος Σκυθιηνδε παλιμπετες, ᾽ὖ τε τις ἀλλος
Οσσων ἐν λειμωνι Καῦϛριῳ ἐ᾽ϛαν ἁμαξαι,
Νοϛησειν· Εφεσᾰ γαρ ἀει τεχ τοξα προκειται.

* The Cimmerian invafion is mentioned by Heredotus as a predatory incurfion. Strabo, l. i. p. 12, and l. iii. p. 222, fays, that it happened in the time of Homer or a little be-fore the age of that Poet. The Cimmerians, who inhabited the Taurica Cherfonefus, were as unfortunate in their attempt to plunder the temple of Ephefus, as the Gauls, many centuries afterwards, were in attempting to plunder Delphi. Paufanias Phocic. And the memorable defeats of both thofe warlike northern nations tended to confirm the popular fuperftition of Greece.

P   Hail.

Hail ! great Munychia; for th' Athenian bay   410
And Pheræ's fertile fhores confefs your fway;
Hail ! bright Pheræa ; and let none prefume
T' offend Diana, left th' avenging doom
Fall heavy on their heads, which Oeneus * mourn'd,
When unfuccefsful, from the field he turn'd   415
For vows unpaid.   Like her let none pretend
To dart the javelin or the bow to bend ;
For when Atrides † durft her grove profane,
No vulgar death remov'd the fatal ftain.
Let none, with eyes of love, the nymph behold;   420
Left, like fond Otus and Orion ‡ bold,

Ποτνια Μουνυχιη, λιμενοσκοπε χαιρε, Φεραιη.
Μη τις ατιμηση την Αρτεμιν· ᴕδε γαρ Οινει   260
Βωμον ατιμασαντι καλοι ᴨτολιν ηλθον αγωνες.
Μηδ' ελαφηϲολιην, μηδ' ευϛοχιην εριδαινειν.
Ουδε γαρ Ατρειδης ολιγω επεκομπασε μισθω.
Μηδε τινα μνασθαι την παρθενον· ᴕδε γαρ Ωτος,

* Oeneus' offence, we are told by Lucian in Sympos, confifted in facrificing to the
other Gods, and neglecting Diana.   The Goddefs punifhed him by fending the Calydonian boar to ravage his territories.   Saphocles & Euripides.

  † Agamemnon's offence confifted in hunting a goat in Diana's grove.   The price,
or mulct, was his daughter Iphigenia.

          ‡ Et integræ
          Tentator Orion Dianæ
          Virginea domitus fagitta. HORACE.

                                                    They

They fink beneath her darts ; let none decline
The folemn dance, or flight the pow'r divine :
Ev'n favour'd Hippo feels her vengeful ire,
If, from th' unfinifh'd rites, fhe dares retire.   425
  Hail ! Virgin queen, accept my humble praife ;
And fmile propitious on your poet's lays.

Οὐδε μεν Ωαριων ἀγαθον γαμον ἐμνηςευσαν.   265
Μηδε χορον φευγειν ἐνιαυσιον· ὁδε γαρ Ιππω
Ακλαυτει περι βωμον ἀπειπατο κυκλωσασθαι.
Χαιρε μεγα κρειυσα, κỳ ἐυαντησον ἀοιδη.

END OF THE HYMN TO DIANA.

P 2

THE FOURT HYMN

O F

CALLIMACHUS.

TO DELOS.

O WHEN, my foul, wilt thou refound the praife
Of Delos, nurfe to Phœbus' infant-days,
Or of the Cyclades †. Moft facred thefe
Of ifles, that rife amid furrounding feas;

ΤΗΝ ἱερην, ὦ θυμε, τινα χρονον ἡ ποτ' αεισεις
Δηλον, Απολλωνος κυροτροφον ; ἡ μεν απασαι
Κυκλαδες, αἱ νησων ἱερωταται εἰν ἁλι κεινται,

---

* Hymn to Delos.] This is one of the innumerable hymns compofed to celebrate the
birth of Apollo and Diana, and to ennoble, by the charms of poetry, the Delian feftival
which returned in the fpring, at the beginning of every fifth year.

† The Cyclades fo called from forming a circle around Delos, are a clufter of feventeen
fmall iflands, rifing above the Ægean fea nearly oppofite to the territories of Argos and
Attica. During the liberty of Greece thefe iflands were rich and profperous; and their
vallies, fertilized by labour, formed a ftriking contraft with the favage rudenefs of their
rocky

And fame and hymns divine to them belong: 5
But Delos chief demands the Mufe's fong.
For there the God, who leads the vocal train,
Was fwath'd around ; and on the Delian plain
His infant-limbs were wafh'd : the facred lay
Triumphant rofe to hail the God of day.   10
As who forgets, Pimplea the divine,
Is foon forfaken by the tuneful Nine ;
Thus on the bard, neglecting Cynthus' * fhores,
Avenging Phœbus all his fury pours :
To Delos then let votive lays belong,   15
And Cynthian Phœbus will approve my fong.

Εὔιμνοι' Δηλος δ' ἐθελει τα πρωτα φερεσθαι.
Εκ Μϑϭεων, ὁτι Φοιϭον ἀοιδαων μεδεοντα   5
Λϑϭε τε ἰὐ σπειρωσε, κἰ ὡς ϑεον ἠνϭε πρωτῃ.
Ὡς Μϑϭϰι τον ἀοιδον, ὁ μη Πιμπλειαν ἀειϭει,
Εχθϭϭιν, τως Φοιϭος ἰτις Δηλοιο λαθηται.
Δηλῳ νυν οιμης ἀποδαϭϭομαι, ὡς ἀν Απολλων

recky mountains. Paros was celebrated for its marbles; Andros and Naxos for their vines
equaling nectar; Siphnos for its mines of gold and filver; Melos for its alum, fulphur, and
other minerals; Amorgos for its manufactures of cloth, and its fkill in dying fcarlet
with a fpecies of lichen abounding in that ifland. Ceos was the birth place of Simonides, the poet; Syros, of the hiftorian Pherecydes; Ios contained the tomb of Homer ;
each ifland had its peculiar excellence, but Delos far ecclipfed the reft, for the reafons
affigned in the text.

   * Cynthus a mountain overhanging the Delian temple.

Tho'

Tho' beat by billows, and tho' vex'd with ftorms,
The facred ifle its deep foundations forms *
Unfhook by winds, uninjur'd by the deep.
High o'er the waves appears the Cynthian fteep;   20
And from the flood the fea-mew bends his courfe
O'er cliffs impervious to the fwifteft horfe † :
Around the rocks th' Icarian furges roar,
Collect new foam, and whiten all the fhore
Beneath the lonely caves, and breezy plain   25
Where fifhers dwelt of old above the main.
No wonder Delos, firft in rank, is plac'd
Amid the fifter ifles on ocean's breaft;

Κυνθιος αινησῃ με φιλης αλεγοντα τιθηνης.   10
Κεινη δ' ηνεμοεσσα κ̀ ατροπο:, οια θ' αλιπληξ,
Αιθυιῃς κ̀ μαλλον επιδρομος ἠεπερ ιπποις,
Ποντῳ ενεςηρικται. ὁ δ' αμφι ἑ ϖηλυς ἑλισσων,
Ικαρι8 ϖολλην απομασσεται ὑδατος αχνην,
Τῳ σφε κ̀ ιχθυβολῃες αλιπλοοι ενναςαντο.   15
Αλλα οἱ 8 νεμεσητον ενι ϖρωτῃσι λεγεσθαι,
Οππετ' ες Ωκεανον τε κ̀ ες Τιτηνιδα Τηθυν
Νησοι αολλιζονται· αει δ' εξαρχος; οδευει.

For

For when the fea-Gods o'er the liquid plains,
Seek thefe dark cells where hoary Tethys reigns,   30
Majeftic Delos leads* beneath the deeps
The wat'ry train ; clofe foll'wing Cyrnus keeps .
Her fteady courfe ; Eubæa floats along,
And fair Sardinia † glides amid the throng.
Laft, o'er the main, fee flow'ry Cyprus move,   35
That from the waves receiv'd the queen of love ;
And in return the Nymph, with fav'ring fmile,
Bleft the bright fhores, and guards the facred ifle.

Η δ' όπιθεν Φοινισσα μετ' ιχνια Κυρνος οπηδει.
Ουκ ονοτη· κ̀ Μακρις Αβαντιας Ελλοπιηων,   20
Σαρδω ϑ' ιμεροεσσα, κ̀ ην επενηξατο Κυπρις
Εξ υδατος ταπρωτα· σαοι δε μιν αντ' επιβαθρων.
Κειναι μεν πυργοισι περισκεπεεσιν ερυμναι,

* Scholiafts and commentators do not explain, how this is confiftent with the immobility of Delos, juft mentioned. The motion here afcribed to Delos is common to it with
other iflands, and merely poetical. The iflands being perfonified, it was natural to tranf-
fer to them the attributes fuiting their refpective ranks; and Delos, as the nobleft, is defcribed as the Choryphaeus, or leader of the dance]

† Sardinia was the Botany Bay of the Romans; and neither that ifland nor Cyrnus,
or Corfica, above mentioned feem from their prefent ftate entitled to the rank, which
Callimachus affigns them. But in ancient times, both Corfica and Sardinia were adorned
by Phœnician and Grecian Colonies; and are celebrated for the fertility of their foil, the
excellence of their fruits, the tallnefs and beauty of their trees, and other circumftances
of panegyric, by Herodotus, Theophraftus, Polybius, and Diodorus Siculus.

Tho'

Tho' tow'rs in thefe and lofty bulwarks ftand,
Apollo ftill defends the Delian land,   40
A ftronger fortrefs, and a furer truft:
Strymonian * Boreas levels with the durft
The work of human hands; but Delos' God
Stands unremov'd, and guards his lov'd abode.
Hail! favour'd ifle, where walls nor tow'rs arife,   45
A ftronger pow'r defends you from the fkies.
  O facred Cynthus, much in fong renown'd,
What theme delights.   What fhall the mufe refound
To thee moft pleafing.   Wilt thou bend thine ear
The mighty fea-God's glorious acts to hear.   50
With thofe dread weapons, which the Telchins † form,
He fhook the mountains, like a burfting ftorm,

Δηλος δ᾽ Απολλωνι. τι δε ςιβαρωτερον ἑρκος;
Τειχεα μεν κ̄ λαες ὑπαι ῥιπης κε πεσοιεν   25
Στρυμονιυ βορεαο· θεος δ᾽ αει ἀς-υφελικτος.
Δηλε φιλη, τοιος σε βοηθοος ἀμφιβεβηκεν.
Εἰ δε λιην πολεες σε περιτροχοωσιν ἀοιδαι,
Ποιη ἐν᾽πλεξω σε ; τι τοι θυμηρες ἀκυσαι ;
Η ὡς ταπρωτιςα μεγας θεος ὑρεα θεινων   30
Ἀορι τριγλωχινι, το οἱ Τελχινες ἐτευξαν,

  * Strymon.   The name of a river and city in Thrace, a northern country in refpect
of the Cyclades.
  † Crete was called Telchinia; and its natives Telchins.   They were famous for work-
ing metals, and their fkill incurred the reproach of juggling and impofture; a reproach
                                                                                    from

In times of old ; from their foundations hurl'd
Rocks, hills and vales amid the wat'ry world :
In rush the seas, and from the land divide   55
The num'rous isles now rising from the tide,
And fix'd for ever in the boundless main.
But Delos isle along the liquid plain
Still floated uncontroll'd ; her sacred name
Asteria then ; to her immortal fame,   60
She shot from heav'n like a descending star,
Amid the roaring deeps and wat'ry war,
To shun th' embrace of Jove *.   Asteria fair
She still was call'd ; till, bright with golden hair,
Distress'd Latona sought the shady shore,   65
Hence Delos nam'd, Asteria now no more.

Νησυς ειναλιας ειργαζετο ; νε θε δε πασας
Εκ νεατων ωχλισσε κỳ εισεκυλισσε θαλασση ;
Και τας μεν κατα βενθος, ιν' ηπειροιο λαθωνται,
Πρυμνο⁚εν ερριζωσε· σε δ' εκ εθλιψεν αναγκη,   35
Αλλ' αφετος πελαγεσσιν επεπλεες· ενομα δ' ην σοι
Αςεριη το παλαιον, επει βαθυν ηλαο ταφρον
Ουρανοθεν φευγεσα Διος γαμον, αςερι ιση.
Τοφρα μεν επω σοι χρυσεη επεμισγετο Λητω,
Τοφρα δ' ετ' Αςεριη συ κỳ εδε πω εκλεο Δηλος.   40

from which Eustachius in his notes on Dionysius the Geographer, takes pains to rescue
them. They made Saturn's hook, and Neptune's trident. Vulcanius.

  * The poet makes fine use of this circumstance as will be seen in the sequel.

         Oft

Oft failors wand'ring o'er the briny main
From Lycian Xanthus, or Trœzene's plain
Stood for the Ephyrian coaft, and there defcry'd
Afteria floating on Saronia's tide :   70
But when returning to their native fhore,
Wide o'er the main the rolling ifle no more
Appear'd in view ; but held its rapid courfe,
Driv'n by th' impetuous flood's refiftlefs force,
Where black Euripus' gulphs tempeftuous roar,   75
And dafh the whit'ning waves on Chalcis fhore *,
Then mounting o'er the furging billows, bounds
From Sunium's † rocks to Chios' flow'ry grounds,
Or foftly feeks Parthenia's ‡ fruitful foil,
Not Samos yet ; and from the virgin ifle   80

Πολλακις ἐκ Τροιζηνος ἀπο Ξανθοιο πολιχνης
Ερχομενοι Εφυρηνδε, Σαρωνικα ἐνδοθι κολπω
Ναυται ἐπεσκεψαντο· κ᾽ ἐξ Εφυρης ἀνιοντες,
Οἱ μεν ἐτ᾽ ἐκ ιδον αὐθι· συ δε ϛεινοιο παρ᾽ ὀξυν
Εδραμες Εὐριποιο πορον καναχηδα ῥεοντος.   45
Χαλκιδικης δ᾽ αὐτημαρ ἀνηναμενη ἁλος ὑδωρ,
Μεσφ᾽ ἐς Αθηναιων προσενηξαο Σουνιον ἀκρον,
Η Χιον, ἠ νησοιο διαϐροχον ὑδατι μαϛον
Παρθενιης, (ἐπω γαρ ἐην Σαμος) ἠχι σε νυμφαι

* Chalcis, a city of Eubœa.
† A promontory of Attica.
‡ Parthenia, the deftined mother of Samos, not yet born.

The

The Mycalefian nymphs rejoicing pour,
And hail thee to the hofpitable fhore
Of kind Ancæus *.　But thy facred earth
Supplied a place for great Apollo's birth,
Hence thy new name the grateful failor's gave　　85
And Delos † call'd along the tracklefs wave
An undiftinguifhed courfe no more you keep,
But fix'd and rooted in the Ægean deep.

　Nor didft thou dread imperial Juno's ire,
That burft impetuous, like the force of fire,　　90
On ev'ry goddefs, from whofe fecret love
A rifing offspring crown'd th' embrace of Jove,
But chief purfu'd Latona; well fhe knew
That from Latona's bed would rife to view

Γειτονος Αγκαιε Μυκαλησιδες εξεινισαν.　　50
Ηνικα δ' Απολλωνι γενεθλιον εδας επεσχες,
Τετο τοι αντιμοιβον αλιπλοοι ενομ' εθεντο,
Ουνεκεν εκετ' αδηλος επεπλεες, αλλ' ενι ποντε
Κυμασιν Αιγαιοιο ποδων ενεθηκαο ριζας.
Ουδ' Ηρην κοτεεσαν υπετρεσας· η μεν απασαις　　55
Δεινον επεβρωματο λεχωισιν, αι Διϊ παιδας
Εξεφερον· Λητοι δε διακριδον, ενεκα μουνη

* Ancæus, the Scholiaft fays, was the king of Parthenia or Samos.

† The Greek word fignifies plain, manifeft; formerly the ifland was often looked for in vain, and not to be feen by the mariners.

Q 2　　The

The brighteſt pow'r in heav'n, and dearer far   95
To thund'ring Jove than the ſtern God of war *.
Amid the ſkies th' obſerving Goddeſs ſat,
And brooded dire revenge, and furious hate
Unutterable ; watch'd the painful hour
Of labour, and detain'd the ſtruggling pow'r :   100
Then ſent two faithful meſſengers on earth
To guard the ſhores and wait th' approaching birth.
Bright in immortal arms ſtern Mars appears
On Hæmus' hills ; o'er their proud ſummits rears
His tow'ring head, and from the mountain's height   105
Wide o'er the continent directs his ſight :

Ζηνι τεκειν ἠμελλε φιλαιτεϱον Αϱεος ὑια.
Τῳ ϱα κ̓ αὑτη μεν σκοπιην ἐχεν αἰθεϱος εἰσω,
Σπεϱχομενη μεγα δη τι κ̓ ὐ φατον· εἰϱγε δε Λητω   60
Τειϱομενην ὡδισι. δυω δε οἱ εἰατο φϱυϱοι
Γαιαν ὑποπτευοντες. ὁ μεν ϖεδον ἠπειϱοιο
Ἡμενος ὑψηλης κοϱυφης ἐπι Θϱηικος Αἱμυ

---

* The jealouſy of Juno is, on this occaſion, envenomed by envy; and her conduct be-
trays the combined influence of thoſe baſe and deteſtable paſſions. The fruit of Latona's
amour with Jupiter is to become the ſource of her ſufferings, which are induſtrouſly pro-
longed by her unrelenting adverſary. The meanneſs of the cauſe is, however, ennobled
by the grandeur of the effect. Mars ſtationed on mount Hæmus; Iris centinel on
mount Mimas, threatening the earth, the iſlands, the rivers and the ſea—theſe are
ſublime images, which throw an undeſerved luſtre on the ignoble paſſions of Juno. Mimas is a high mountain in the iſle of Chios.

    Th'

Th' immortal fteeds meanwhile ftood far behind
In fev'n receffes of the northern wind.
Next Iris fierce defcends on Mima's brows,
And o'er the fcatter'd ifles obferving throws   110
Her careful eyes ; with inaufpicious threats
Denounces vengeance on the pitying ftates,
Where bright Latona turns diftrefs'd with grief;
She bars accefs, and ftill denies relief.

Before the dreadful voice Arcadia fled,   115
And high Parthenius * bow'd his rocky head
(Fair Auge's facred hill) Phenæus † bends
His aged fteps, and clofe behind attends ;
And all the climes of Pelop's ifle, that lie
Along the northern ifthmus, fwiftly fly,   120

Θηρος Αρης εφυλασσε συν εντεσι. τω δε οι ιππω
Επταμυχον βορεαο παρα σπεος ᵃχυλιζοντο.   65
Η δ᾽ επι νησαων ετερη σκοπος ευρειαων
Ηςο κορη Θαυμαντος, επαιξασα Μιμαντι.
Ενθ᾽ οι μεν πολιεσσιν οσαις επεβαλλετο Λητω,
Μιμνον απειλητηρες, απετρωπων δε δεχεσθαι.
Φευγε μεν Αρκαδιη, φευγεν δ᾽ ορος ιερον Αυγης   70
Παρθενιον· φευγεν δ᾽ ο γερων μετοπισθε Φεναιος.

* Parthenius is a mountain of Arcadia, where Hercules ravifhed Auges, the daughter
of Aleus, and the prie'efs of Minerva   The fcholiaft.
† Phenæus, an ancient city of Arcadia.

Save

Save Argos and Ægiale * : but there
All entrance is deny'd by Juno's care,
To whom the realms of Inachus belong.
Aonia † frighted holds her courfe along
The felf-fame path ; and Dirce fwift fucceeds,   125
And Strophie ‡ wat'ring green Bœotia's meads,
Upon whofe hands their fire Ifmenus hung,
As black with mofly ftones he roll'd along.
And fore difabled by the lightnings blaft §,
Slow moves Afopus, with inactive hafte ;   130

Φευγε δ᾽ ὅλη Πελοπηΐς ὅση παρακεκλιται Ισθμώ,
Εμπλην Αιγιαλε τε κ᾽ Αργεος. ε γαρ εκεινας
Ατραπιτες επατησεν, επει λαχεν Ιναχου Ηρη.   75
Φευγε κ᾽ Αονιη τον ενα δρομον. αἱ δ᾽ εφεποντο
Διρκη τε, Στροφιη τη, μελαμψηφιδος εχεσαι
Ισμηνε χερα πατρος. ὁ δ᾽ ηιπετο πολλον οπισθεν
Ασωποι βαρυγευνος, επει πεπαλακτο κεραυνω.
Ηδ᾽ υποδινηθεισα χορε απεπαυσατο νυμφη

* Cities or the river Inachus, facred to Juno,
          Plurimus in Junonis honorem
          Aptum dicit equis Argos.   HORACE.
† Aonian, ancient name of Bœotian Thebes.
‡ Dirce and Strophiæ, fountains in Bœotia.
§ Afopus the father of Ægina who was ravifhed by Jupiter. The unfortunate Sify-
phus told to Afopus the difgrace of his daughter; and Afopus, in his fury, purfuing the
God was ftruck with thunder. The Scholiaft.

                                                      But

But native Dryads *, pale with facred awe
Swift from the dance their trembling feet withdraw,
And fhriek and figh, when oaks coeval bend
Their green heads, and from Helicon defcend.
Ye fav'ring Pow'rs, immortal Mufes fay,   135
Do nymphs with oaks exift, with oaks decay?
The nymphs rejoice, when oaks refrefh'd with dew
Put forth their leaves, and fpread their arms anew,
The nymphs lament, when winter black with ftorms,
Sweeps off the leaves, and the green boughs deforms. 140
 Apollo heard, and from his mother's womb
Furious denounc'd th' unalterable doom
On Thebæ's guilty realms, unhappy ftate !
Why thus provoke thy fwift-approaching fate ?

Αὐτοχθων Μελιη, κὴ ὑπόχλοον ἐσχε παρειην,   80
Ηλικος ἀσθμαινεσα περι δρυος ὡς ἰδε χαιτην
Σειομενην Ελικωνος. ἐμαι θεαι εἰπατε Μεσαι,
Η ῥ' ἐτεον ἐγενοντο τοτε δρυες, ἡνικα νυμφαι.
Νυμφαι μεν χαιρεσιν ὁτε δρυας ὁμβρος ἀεξει,
Νυμφαι δ' αὐ κλαιεσιν ὁτε δρυσιν εκ ετι φυλλα. 85
Ταις μεν ἐτ' Απελλων ὑποκολπιος αινα χολωθη,
Φθεγξατο δ' εκ ἀτελεςον ἀπειλησας επι Θηβη·

---

 * The Dryads, called alfo Hamadryads, from the circumftance of their growing, flou-
rifhing, and decaying, along with the oaks which they inhabit. Callimachus ftarts a queftion refpecting the truth of this circumftance, and decides it obliquely.

               Why

Why tempt the God unwilling, to declare   145
The woes ungrateful Thebes is doom'd to bear?
For tho' no prieſteſs on the tripod feels
Inſpiring pow'r, nor thence our will reveals;
Nor yet, by darts divine, has Python bled
Slow moving on from Pliſtus' oozy bed,   150
Hideous and huge he rears his ſhaggy cheſt,
Black with infernal hairs (tremendous peſt!)
Aſcends Parnaſſus' hill, and dreadful throws
Nine ſable volumes round his hoary brows *.

Θηβη, τιπτε ταλαινα τον αυτικα ποτμον ελεγχεις;
Μηπω μη μ' αεκοντα βιαζεο μαντευεσθαι.
Ουπω μοι Πυθωνι μελει τριποδηϊος εδρη,   90
Ουδε τι πω τεθνηκεν οφις μεγας, αλλ' ετι κεινο
Θηριον αινογηνειον απο Πλεισοιο καθερπον
Παρνησον νιφοεντα περιστεφει εννεα κυκλοις.

* The killing of this dreadful and deſtructive ſerpent was one of the earlieſt exploits of
Apollo, by which he got poſſeſſion of Pytho or Delphi. The ſolemn terrors of the place
were well fitted to engender in the fancy, this ſerpent and ſuch like hideous monſters. "That
branch of the celebrated mount Parnaſſus, dividing Phocis and Locris, contained towards
its ſouthern extremity a profound cavern, emitting ſulpherous vapour, deemed capable
of inſpiring thoſe who breathed it with religious frenzy and prophetic enthuſiaſm. Around
the principal mouth of the chaſm, the city of Delphi aroſe in the form of a theatre,
upon the winding declivity of Parnaſſus; whoſe fantaſtic tops over ſhadowed it like a ca-
nopy on the north, which two immenſe rocks rendered it in acceſſible on the eaſt and weſt,
and the rugged and ſhapeleſs mount Cirphris defended it on the ſouth. The foot of the
laſt-named mountain is waſhed by the rapid Pliſtus, which diſcharges itſelf foaming
into

Yet hear thy doom; more awful the decree   ·155
Than e'er the laurel shall pronounce by me:
Fly hence; but Fate pursues: my burning darts
Shall soon be quench'd in blood of Theban hearts.
Since thou retain'st the guilty race that sprung
From that vile woman * with blasphemous tongue;   16○
Apollo's hallow'd birth shall never crown
Cithæron's hill, nor Thebæ's impious town.
The God is good, and only will bestow
Distinguish'd blessings on good men below.

So spake the pow'r unseen: Latona mourn'd,   165
And to th' Achaian states again return'd.

Αλλ' εμπης ερεω τι τομωτερον η απο δαφνης,
Φευγε προσω· ταχινος σε κιχησομαι, αιματι λυσων   95
Τοξον εμον. συ δε τεκνα κακογλωσσοιο γυναικος
Ελλαχες. ε συ γ' εμειο φιλη τροφος, εδε Κιθαιρων
Εσσεται· ευαγεων δε κỳ ευαγεεσσι μελοιμην.
Ως αρ' εφη. Λητω δε μετατροπος αυθις εχωρει.
Αλλ' οτ' Αχαιιαδες μιν απηρνησαντο πολης   100

into the sea at the distance of a few leagues from the sacred city. History of Ancient
Greece. V. 1. C. iii.

* The vile woman is Niobe, whose story as well as that of Pytho, or Python, Sculptors
as well as Poets have laboured in all ages to adorn. See Ovid. Metamorph. L. VI.
V. 146, & seq.

R   But

But thefe, againſt her tender ſuit combine,
Nor grant admiſſion to the Pow'r divine ;
Not ev'n high Helice *, whoſe blooming charms
Won mighty Neptune to her tender arms ;   170
Nor humble Bura †, riſing near the flood,
Where great Dexamenus his oxen ſtood
In lofty ſtalls.   Latona turns with ſighs
To bleak Theſſalia's realms and colder ſkies.
But there Lariſſa flies th' approaching God,   175
Anaurus' waves, and all the rocks that nod
On Pelion's brows ; nor Peneus dares abide,
But rolls thro' Tempe's vale a ſwifter tide ‡.
And thou, fierce Juno, ſtill with rage poſſeſt,
Remain'ſt unmov'd ; no pity touch'd thy breaſt,   180

Ερχομενην, Ελικη τε Ποσειδαωνος εταιρη,
Βυρα τε, Δεξαμενοιο βοοςασις Οινιαδαο,
Αψ δ' επι Θεσσαλιην ποδας ετρεπε. φευγε δ' Αναυρος,
Και μεγαλη Λαρισσα, κ̀ αἱ Χειρωνιδες ακραι·
Φευγε δε κ̀ Πηνειο; ελισσομενος δια Τεμπεων.   105
Ηρη, σοι δ' ετι τημος ανηλεες ητορ εκειτο.
Ουδε κατεκλασθης τε κ̀ ακτισας, ἡνικα πηχεις

* Helice a city of Bœotia.   The Scholiaſt.
† Bura a city of Achaia, inhabited by the Centaur Dexamenus.   Idem.
‡ This circumſtance is properly introduced.   Ælian, in his deſcription of this valley,
ſays the Peneus flows ὀαζν ὀαιν, ſmooth as oil

When

When thus the Goddefs mourn'd with plaintive fighs,
With out-ftretch'd arms, and with heart-rending cries.
Ye daughters of Theffalian floods entreat
Your aged Sire, low bending at his feet,
To ftop the mighty wave ; O grafp with care   185
His hoary beard, and urge him to prepare
His water to receive th' immortal fon
Of thund'ring Jove.   Ah ! why fhould Peneus run
More fwift than win'try winds ? Thy flight is vain ;
Nor canft thou here a glorious prize obtain,   190
As in th' Equeftrian ftrife.   O father fay,
Have thy fwift ftreams thus ever roll'd away ?
Or does Latona's pangs encreafe thy fpeed
To fly from her diftrefs ? In time of need,
Alas ! he hears me not.   Where fhall I turn ?   195
And where, unhappy ! fhall thy fon be born ?

Ἀμφοτεϱυς ὀϱεγυσα, ματην ἐφθεγξατο τοια.
Νυμφαι Θεσσαλιδες, ποταμυ γενος, εἰπατε πατϱι
Κοιμησαι μεγα χευμα· πεϱιπλεξασθε γενειω,   110
Λισσομεναι τα Ζηνος ἐν ὑδατι τεκνα τεκεσθαι.
Πηνειε Φθιωτα, τι νυν ἀνεμοισιν ἐϱιζεις ;
Ὦ πατεϱ, ὐ μην ἱππον ἀεθλιον ἀμφιϐεϐηκας.
Ἡ ῥα τοι ὦδ᾽ αἰει ταχινοι ποδες ; ἠ ἐπ᾽ ἐμειο
Μυνοι ἐλαφϱιζυσι ; πεποιησαι δε πετεσθαι   115
Σημεϱον ἐξαπινης ; ὁδ᾽ ανηκοος. ὠ ἐμον ἀχθος,
Ποι σε φεϱω ; μελεοι γαϱ ἀπειϱηκασι τενοντες.

R 2   My

My ftrength decays; to Pelion * I'll repair,
The bridal bed of Philyre † the fair.
Stay, Pelion, ftay. A Goddefs afks no more
Than to the lionefs you gave before;   200
Oft on thy cliffs fhe bears her favage young
With dreadful yells, and with fierce anguifh ftung.

   Sad Peneus wept, and anfwered thus with fighs:
A mightier God, Neceffity denies
Thy pray'r; O pow'r diftrefs'd, elfe foon fhould I   205
Relieve thy woes, with thy requeft comply,
And grant the boon to other births I gave,
That oft were wafh'd in my refrefhing wave.
The queen of heav'n on Peneus bends her eyes,
And utters furious threats amid the fkies;   210

Πηλιον ω̈ Φιλυρης νυμφηιον, αλλα συ μεινον·
Μεινον, επει κ̓ Θηρες εν ε̈ρεσι πολλακι σειο
Ωμοτοκϗς ωδινας απηοεισαντο λεαιναι.   120
Την δ' αρα κ̓ Πηνειος αμειϐετο δακρυα λειϐων,
Λητοι, Αναγκαιη μεγαλη Θεος. ἐ γαρ εγωγε
Ποτνια σας ωδινας αναινομαι· οιδα κ̓ αλλας
Λϗσαμενας απ' εμειο λεχωϊδας. αλλα μοι Ηρη
Δαψιλες ηπειλησεν. απαυγασαι οιος εϟεδρος   125

   * Pelion, a mountain of Theffaly.
   † The Amour of Saturn with Philyre on mount Pelion produced the Centaur Chiron. Scholiaft.

Lo!

Lo! from yon hill a champion fierce and dread
Frowns ftern deftruction on my wretched head;
And could with cafe my fable deeps o'erturn,
Subvert my ftreams, and dry my fruitful urn.
All ftrife is vain; fay will it pleafe thy foul,   215
That Peneus perifh, and no longer roll
His fwelling ftreams? Th' avenging hour may come;
But, in thy caufe, I'll brave the dreadful doom;
Tho' my fhrunk waves for ever ceafe to flow,
And I be nam'd the meaneft flood below;   220
Behold, approach, Ilythia's aid invoke.
He ftopt his rapid current as he fpoke.
But Mars perceiv'd; from their foundations tore
Pangæus' hills *, and in his arms upbore

Ουρεος εξ υπατυ σκοπιην εχει, ος κε με ρεια
Βυσσοθεν εξερυσειε. τι μησομαι; η απολεσθαι
Ηδυ τι τοι Πηνειον; ιτω πεπρωμενον ημαρ.
Τλησομαι εινεκα σειο, κ) ει μελλοιμι ροαων
Διψαλεην αμπωτιν εχων αιωνιον ερρειν,   130
Και μονος εν ποταμοισιν ατιμοτατος καλεεσθαι.
Ηνι δ' εγω· τι περισσα; καλει μονον Ειληθυιαν·
Ειπε, κ) ηρωησε μεγαν ροον. αλλα οι Αρης
Παγγαιυ προθελυμνα καρηατα μελλεν αειρας

* Pangæus, a mountain of Thrace.

                                                           The

The rocky mountain, an enormous load !   225
To choak the fountains, and o'erwhelm the flood.
His voice like thunder founds ; the fpear and fhield,
Together ftruck, more dreadful murmurs yield:
When trembling Offa * heard, ftrange horrors fill
Cranonia's field, high Pindus' diftant hill,   230
And fhook Theffalia to her fartheft bound.
As Ætna's inmoft caverns under-ground
Roar horrible with floods of rolling fire,
And to the centre fhake ; when fierce with ire,
Briareus turns beneath the mountain's height,   235
And from his fhoulders heaves th' incumbent weight ;

Εμϐαλεειν δινησιν, αποκρυψειν δε ρεεθρα.   135
Τψοθε δ' εσμαραγησε, κ̣ ασπιδα τυψεν ακωκη
Δ̇κρατος· η δ' ελελιξεν ενοπλιον. ετρεμε δ' Οσσης
Ουρεα, κ̣ πεδιον Κρανωνιον, αι τε δυσαεις
Εσχατιαι Πινδοιο· φοϐω δ' ωρχησατο πασα
Θεσσαλιη. τοιος γαρ απ' ασπιδος εϐραχεν ηχος.   140
Ως δ' οποτ' Αιτναικ ορεος πυρι τυφομενοιο
Σειονται μυχα παντα, κατκδαιοιο γιγαντος
Εις ετερην Βριαρηος επωμιδα κινυμενοιο,
Θερμαυςραι τε βρεμκσιν υφ' Ηφαιςοιο πυραγρης
Εργα θ' ομκ, δεινον δε πυρικμητοι τε λεϐητες   145

* Offa, a mountain in Theffaly.

Forge,

Forge, tripods, tongs, the caldron's mighty round,
And all the works of Vulcan ſtrike the ground
With mingled claſh : ſuch and more hoarſe alarms
Sprung from th' immortal powres' diſcordant arms.　　240
　　But Peneus, unappall'd retires no more,
Collects his rolling waters, as before,
And ſtands unmov'd; till thus Latona ſpoke :
Retire in peace, nor yon fierce Gods provoke :
Thou ſhalt not ſuffer, tho' my lot be hard ;　　245
Nor thy compaſſion want its due reward.
　　Then, o'er the main to diſtant iſles ſhe goes,
Struck with new pangs, inextricable woes,
But ſtill without ſucceſs ; nor aid is found
Among the Echinades * for ports renown'd ;　　250

Καὶ τρίποδες ϖιπτοντες ἐπ᾽ ἀλληλοις ἰαχευσι·
Τῃμος ἐγεντ᾽ ἀραϐος σακεος τοσος εὐκυκλοιο.
Πηνειος δ᾽ ἐκ αὐθις ἐχαζετο, μιμνε δ᾽ ὁμοιως
Καρτερος ὡς ταπρωτα. Θοας δ᾽ ἐςησατο δινας,
Εἰσοκε οἱ Κοικῃῖς ἐκεκλετο, Σωζεο χαιρων,　　150
Σωζεο· μη συγ᾽ ἐμειο ϖαθης κακον εἰνεκα, τησδε
Αντ᾽ ἐλεημοσυνης. χαριτος δε τοι ἐσσετ᾽ ἀμοιϐη.
Η, κ᾽ ϖολλα ϖαροιθεν ἐπει καμεν, ἐςιχε νησες
Εἰναλιας. αἱ δ᾽ ὐ μιν ἐπερχομενην ἐδεχοντο,

* The Echinades were ſmall Iſlands at the mouth of the river Achelous lying between Leucas and Cephallenia on the one hand, and the gulph of Corinth on the other. Pliny l. ii.

I

Nor dares Corcyra's hofpitable coaſt *
Receive the pow'r, along the billows toſt.
For Iris dreadful ſtands in open ſight,
And pours her threats from Mima's lofty height :
Before her wrath the crowding iſlands fled,   255
And fought the neareſt rivers friendly bed.
Latona turns to Merop's ancient feat †,
The Coan iſle, Chalciope's retreat ‡ ;

Ου λιπαρον νηεσσιν Εχιναδες ορμον εχυσαι,   155
Ουδ' ητις Κερκυρα φιλοξεινωτατη αλλων.
Ιρις επει πασησιν εφ' υψηλοιο Μιμαντος
Σπερχομενη μαλα πολλον απετραμεν. αι δ' ιφ' ομοκλης
Πασσυδιη φοβεοντο κατα ροον ηντινα τετμοι.
Ωγυγιην δ' ηπειτα Κοων Μεροπηιδα νησον   160

L. ii. C. 85. fays they were gradually formed by the flime of the river. Spanheim obferves that from this paſſage only, we know they had good harbours.

  * The hoſpitality fhown to Ulyſſes as deſcribed in the Odyſſey merited this epithet.

  † The Scholiaſt fays that Cos was called the Meropian iſle, either becaufe it was ruled
by king Merops, or becaufe it was colonized by the Meropes. Hyginus fays that the Meropes were ſo called from their king, and that Cos was his daughter. It is thus that the
Abantes, the inhabitants of Eubœ were denominated from their King Abas, as we learn
from the Scholiaſt on the fecond book of Iliad, V. 536. And Thucydides tells us that, before the Trojan war, the Greeks were not known by any general name, but diſtinguiſhed
by various particular denominations. The Iſle of Cos was ſituated on the coaſt of Aſiatic
Doris, at the entrance of the Ceramic gulph. It produced excellent wine, and was the
birth place of Hippocrates, the father of phyſic, and Appelles the greateſt of painters.

  ‡ Chalciope was a Coan Nymph, and the mother of Eurypylus, king of the Iſland,
which is called by Homer, the city of Eurypylus, Iliad ii. V. 677.

But

But Phœbus ſtops her courſe, and thus relates,
With awful voice, th' irrevocable fates.   260
　O Goddeſs, I nor envy nor diſdain
Theſe flow'ry ſhores, and yonder fertile plain,
But here thou bear'ſt me not; Apollo ſeᴗs
A future God appear by Fate's decrees,
The mightieſt prince of Soter's * royal race,   265
To rule this favour'd iſle, his native place.
To him the willing world ſhall tribute bring;
Green iſles and inland ſtates obey the King,
And bow before him in ſuccceding times;
His pow'r extending from yon' eaſtern climes,   270
To diſtant ſhores, where Sol deſcending leads
Beneath the weſtern waves his weary'd ſteeds.

Ικετο, χαλκιοπης ιερον μυχον ἡρωïνης.
Αλλα ἑ ϖαιδος ἱρυκεν ἑπος τοδε, Μη συ γε μητερ
Τη με τεκοις. ἐτ' ἐν ἐπιμεμφομαι, ἠδε μεγαιρω
Νησον, ἐπει λιπαρη τε κỳ εὐῥοτος, εἰ ιυ τις ἀλλη·
Αλλα οἱ ἐκ μοιρεων τις ὀφειλομενος ϑεος ἀλλος   165
Εϛι, σαωτηρων ὑπατον γενος· ᾧ ὑπο μιτρηϝ
Ιξεται ἐκ ἀεκωσα Μακηδονι κοιρανεεσθαι,
Αμφοτερη μεσογεια, κỳ αἱ ϖελλαγεσσι καϑεκται·
Μεχρις ἐπω ϖερατη τε, κỳ ὁπποθεν ὠκεες ἱππι

* The firſt Ptolemy, and by far the greateſt of that race, was denominated σωτηρ, the Saviour. Callimachus' court flattery to his patron Ptolemy Philadelphus, does not hinder him from ſaying ὁ δι ειοιται τθια πατρος, He ſhall tread in his father's footſteps.

S   From

From Macedonia comes the man divine,
And in the fon the father's virtues fhine.
The glorious prince fhall be my future care,   275
And I the great companion of his war *,
When o'er the Celtic fhores, with wild alarms,
Gigantic nations clafh barbarian arms.
The laft of Titan's fons, a furious throng!
From th' utmoft Weft fhall fwiftly pour along,   280

Ηελιον φορεƞσιν. ο δ' εισεται ηθεα πατρος.   170
Και νυ ποτε ξυνος τις ελευσεται αμμιν αεθλος
Τςατον, οπποτ' αν οι μεν εφ' Ελληνεσσι μαχαιραν
Βαρβαρικην κ Κελτον αναςησαντες αρηα
Οψιγονοι Τιτηνες αφ' εσπερƞ εσχατοωντος

* The war in which Ptolemy Philadelphus and Apollo were companions was the invafion of Europe by the Gauls, whofe main object was to plunder the Delphic temple.
This memorable expedition, its caufes and its confequences had been explained by many
ancient writers, Greek and Latin, whofe works are now loft.   Demetrius of B zantium
had treated this fubject in thirteen books, which were highly praifed by the beft critics.
Diogenes Laertius in vita Demetrii Phalerii.   Callifthenes of Sybaris had written ftill
more copioufly on the fame fubject. Stobaeus Sermon. 98.   And Eratofthenes, libra-
rian to Ptolemy Euergetes and his immediate fucceffor, compofed a hiftory of the Gallic
expedition far furpaffing the two former works in bulk as well as in value.   The
fame illuftrious theme was adorned by Terentius Varro, the moft learned of the Romans whofe work fubfifting in the time of St. Jerom, was too faftidioufly rejected by that
Father in his commentary on the Epiftle to the Galatians (a fmall remnant of the Gauls)
Jerom difdaining to employ Varro's information, left (fays he) I fhould introduce an
uncircumcifed heathen into the temple of God.   A fmall wreck of this important part
of hiftory is preferved in Polybius, Livy, Juftin, Paufanias (in Phocic) and the prefent
hymn of Callimachus.

And,

And, rufhing dreadful, Grecian plains o'erflow,
Thick as the driving rain, or falling fnow;
Or num'rous as yon' filver lamps of night,
That fill their urns with Jove's ætherial light.
From Locrian forts and undefended towns, 285
From Delphic mountains, and Criflæan downs,
From all the midland cities far around,
Deep groans fhall iffue; when along the ground,
Wide wafting flames devour the rip'ning grain,
And all the labours of th' adjoining fwain. 290
Nor thefe fhall hear alone the fierce alarms
Of hoftile armies, fheath'd in fhining arms
Around my temple; but with terror view
Th' impetuous Gauls their impious courfe purfue,
With bloody faulchions, belts and bucklers ftain 295
My holy tripods, and my cave profane,

Ρωωνται, νιφαδεσσιν εοικοτες, ἠ ἰσαριθμοι 175
Τειρεσιν ἡνικα πλειςα κατ' ἠερα βκκολεονται·
Φρκρια κ̅ κωμαι Λοκρων, κ̅ Δελφιδες ἀκραι,
Και πεδια Κριςσαια, κ̅ ἠπειροιο πολυες
Αμφιπεριςεινωνται. ἰδωσι δε πιονα καρπον
Γειτονος αἰθομενοιο κ̅ κκετι μουνον ἀκκη, 180
Αλλ' ἠδη περι νηον ἀπαυγαζοιντο φαλαγγες
Δυσμενεων· ἠδη δε παρα τριποδεσσιν ἐμειο
Φασγανα κ̅ ζωςηρας ἀναιςεας, ἐχθομενας τε
S 2 For

For which fierce war fhall rage, at my command,
And wreak my vengeance on th' unhallow'd band.
Of conquer'd armour, half fhall deck my fhrine,
And half, the prize of valour, fhall be thine,   300
Illuftrious prince ! when midft attacks and fire,
On Nilus banks * the vanquifhed hofts expire.
Thus fate foretells the glory thou fhalt gain,
O Philadelphus ! in thy wondrous reign,
For which, immortal King, thou ftill fhalt pay   305
Unceafing honours to the God of day ;
And future ages to the ftars fhall raife
Apollo's name, and Philadelphus' praife,

Ασπιδας. αἱ Γαλατησι κακην ὁδον ἀφρονι φυλῳ
Στησονται· τεων αἱ μεν ἐμοι γερας, αἱ δ' ἐπι Νειλῳ   185
Εν πυρι τὰς φορεοντας ἀποπνευσαντας ἰδὰσαι,
Κεισονται, βασιληος ἀεθλια πολλα καμοντος
Εσσομεναι· Πτολεμαιε, τα τοι μαντηϊα φαινω.
Αἰνησεις μεγα δη τι τον εἰσετι γαςερι μαντιν

* On Nilus banks the vanguifhed hofts expire] The Scoliaft relates the hiftory in few words as follows. " Brennus, King of the Gauls, having affembled his countrymen marched to plunder the Delphic treafure. Apollo waited the approach of the enemy; and when they advanced to the affault, deftroyed the greateft part of them by a ftorm. Antigonus, a friend of Ptolemy Philadelphus, hired the remainder for the fervice of that Prince. But the Gauls, ftimulated by avarice, confpired againft their mafter. Ptolemy, therefore, apprized of their perfidy, conducted them to the Sebennytic mouth of the Nile, and there drowned them."

Both

Both yet unborn; thy pow'r, O mother join,
Fulfil the Fates, and aid my great defign.   310
An ifle there is yet unconfined and free,
With feet unfix'd amid the rolling fea,
To mariners well-known; it wanders wide,
Now here, now there, before the driving tide,
And yields, and fhakes, like pliant Afphodel,   315
As eaft or weftern winds the floods impel:
There fhall thy labours end.   The facred earth
Will grant relief, and aid my glorious birth.

As Phœbus fpoke, th' obedient ifles gave way,
Forfook the fhores, and floated o'er the fea,   320
Returning to their feats.   Not long before
Th' Afterian ifle had left Eubœa's fhore,
And, at the voice divine, came flowly down,
To view the Cyclades óf great renown,

Τςερον ήματα παντα· συ δε ξυμβαλλεο μητερ·   190
Εςι διειδομενη τις εν υδατι νησος αραιη,
Πλαζομενη πελαγεσσι· ποδες δε οι υχ ενι χωρω,
Αλλα παλιρροιη επινηχεται, ανθερικος ως·
Ενθα νοτος, ενθ' ευρος, οπη φορησι θαλασσα·
Τη με φερσις· κεινην γαρ ελευσεαι εις εθελσαν.   195
Αι μεν τοσσα λεγοντος απετρεχον ειν αλι νησοι.
Αςεριη φιλομολπε, συ δ' Ευβοιηθε κατηεις
Κυκλαδας οψομενη περιηγεας, ὁ τι παλαιον,

                                                   Encumber'd

Encumber'd oft by dank fea-weeds, that fprung   325
From rough Geræftus, and around her hung.
Full in the midft fhe ftood ; beheld with grief
Latona's dreadful pangs, and no relief.
At her command a fiery torrent roar'd
Around the fhores, the crackling weeds devour'd,   330
Prepar'd the facred ifle, and clear'd the fkies ;
While thus imperial Juno fhe defies.

Difcharge thy vengeance on Afteria's head ;
Thy frowns I reck not, nor thy threatnings dread ;
Come, Goddefs, come ; my fav'ring fhores afcend :   335
She heard, obey'd, and there her wand'rings end.
By deep Inopus * (whofe dark fountains boil
Still moft impetuous, when th' o'erflowing Nile

Αλλ' ετι τοι μετοπισθε Γεραιςιον ειπετο φυκος·
Εξης δ' εν μεσσησι. κατοικτειρασα δε Λητω,   200
Φυκος απαν κατεφλεξας· επει περικαιεο πυρι,
Τλημον' υπ' ωδινεσσι βαρυνομενην οροωσα·
Ηρη τατο με ρεξον ο τοι φιλον. ἀ γαρ απειλας
Υμετερας εφυλαξα· περα, περα εις εμε Λητοι.
Εννεπες. η δ' αρρητον αλης απεπαυσατο λυγρης·   205
Ιζετο δ' Ινωποιο παρα ροον, οντε βαθιςον
Γαια τοτ' εξανιησιν, οτε πληθοντι ρεεθρω.

† Inopus was the only river in Delos. It alternately fwelled and ebbed, and at the fame time as the Nile, which gave rife to the opinion of the fubterranean communication between them.

From

From Æthiopia's rocks defcends amain,
And fpreads a fudden deluge o'er the plain)
Soft fhe reclin'd the crowded zone unbound,
And dropt her fainting limbs along the ground.
Againft a fhading palm her fhoulders reft;
But racking pangs diftend her lab'ring breaft;
Her body bath'd in fweat, with deep'ning groans,
And painful fobbings, thus fhe pour'd her moans.
   Why, why, my Son, doft thou with anguifh fill
My tortur'd heart with pangs increafing ftill?
For thee, for thee, I fought the wat'ry plain;
For thee, this ifle receiv'd me from the main:
Haft thou no pity for heart-rending throes?
O fpring to light, and eafe thy mother's woes!
   But Iris mounts, all trembling to reveal
The fatal news, fhe could no more conceal;

340

345

350

Νειλος ἀπο κρημνοιο κατερχεται Αἰθιοπηος,
Λυσατο δε ζωνην, ἀπο δ' ἐκλιθη ἐμπαλιν ὠμοις
Φοινικος ποτι πρεμνον, ἀμηχανιης ὑπο λυγρης
Τειρομενη· νοτιος δε δια χροος ἐρρεεν ἱρως.
Εἰπε δ' ἀλυσθμαινυσα, Τι μητερα κυρε βαρυνεις;
Αὐτη τοι, φιλε, νησος ἐπιπλωυσα θαλασση.
Γεινεο, γεινεο κυρε, κ) ἠπιος ἐξιθι κολπυ.
Νυμφα Διος βαρυθυμε, συ δ' ἐκ ἀρ' ἐμελλες ἀπυςος
Δην ἐμεναι· τοιη σε προσεδραμεν ἀγγελιωτις.

210

215

To

To wrathful Juno told the tale with tears,   555
With broken accents and uneafy fears.
Majeftic Juno, fpoufe of thund'ring Jove,
Great Queen of heav'n, and mightieft Pow'r above;
Thy faithful Iris, all the Gods are thine,
Nor dread the wrath of other hands divine;   360
But one prefumptuous ifle refifts thy pow'r,
And aids Latona in the dang'rous hour.
From her approach the reft abhorrent turn'd,
Nor durft receive her when thy fury burn'd.
But vile Afteria, whom the furges fweep   365
Around the fhores, invited from the deep
Thy hated foe.   Her crimes I thus make known;
But ftill, bleft Goddefs, be thy favour fhown

Εἶπε δ᾽ ἐτ᾽ ἀσθμαινυσα, (φοβω δ᾽ ἀνεμισγετο μυθος)
Ηρη τιμηεσσα, πολυ πρυχυσα θεαων,
Ση μεν εγω, σα δε παντα· συ δε κρεισσα καθησαι
Γνησιη ἐλυμπ̄οιο· κὴ ὑ χερα δειδιμεν ἀλλην   220
Θηλυτερην. συ δ᾽ ἀνασσα τον αιτιον εισεαι οργης.
Λητω τοι μιτρην ἀναλυεται ἐνδοθι νησυ.
Αλλαι μεν πασαι μιν ἀπεσυγον, ἀδ᾽ ἐδεχοντο·
Αςεριη δ᾽ ὀνομαςι παρερχομενην ἐκαλεσσεν,
Αςεριη ποντοιο κακον σαρον· οἰσθα κὴ αὐτη.   225
Αλλα φιλη, δυνασαι γαρ, ἀμυνειν ποτνια δυλοις
Υμετεροις, οἱ σειο πεδον πατευσιν ἐφετμη.

           T' obedient

T' obedient pow'rs, that from thefe fields of air
Walk o'er the world, and thy dread mandates bear.   370
    She faid, and hafty funk beneath the throne,
That bright with radiant gold refplendent fhone :
As at Diana's feet a fav'rite hound
In filence liftens to the diftant found
Of pafling game ; and tho' foft flumbers creep   375
O'er his keen fenfes, only feems to fleep,
Impatient waits the whifpers of her voice,
Erects his ears, and ftarts at ev'ry noife,
So fat Thaumantia *, fill'd with deep regret,
Nor left her place beneath the facred feat ;   380
And ev'n when fleep, on downy pinions, came
To fhed foft dews o'er all her weary'd frame,
On Juno's throne her beauteous head reclin'd,
And fcarcely flumb'ring, wak'd with ev'ry wind ;

Η, κỳ ὑπο χρυσειον ἐδεθλιον ἱζε, κυων ὡς
Αρτεμιδος, ἡτις τε θοης ἐτε παυσεται ἀγρης,
Ιζει θηρητειρα· παρ' ἰχνεσιν ἐκατα δ' αὐτης   230
Ορθα μαλ' αἰεν ἑτοιμα θεης ὑποδεχθαι ὁμοκλην.
Τη ἰκελη Θαυμαντος ὑπο θρονον ἰζετο κωρη.
Κεινη δ' ἐδεποτε σφετερης ἐπιληθεται ἑδρης,
Οὐδ' ὁτε οἱ ληθαιον ἐπι πτερον ὑπνος ἐρεισει·
Αλλ' αὐτε μεγαλοιο ποτι γλωχινα θρονοιο   235

* Iris, the daughter of Thaumas.

T   Nor

Nor loos'd the winged fandals, nor unbrac'd   385
The circling zone that bound her tender waift;
Left fome unthought of meffage, giv'n in hafte,
Might claim her fpeed. But other cares engage
Th' imperial Queen, and thus fhe vents her rage.

     Ye fecret paramours, that bring difgrace   390
On faithlefs Jove! bear your detefted race
For ever thus, on barren rocks reclin'd,
More wretched than the worft of human-kind;
Or like the unwieldy whale in wat'ry caves;
Or fpawn your brood amid the whelming waves.   395
But this contents; nor let Afteria dread
My fudden wrath on her offending head;
For thefe unfertile fhores can only fhew
Poor entertainment to my hated foe,

Τυτθον αποκλινασα καρηατα μεχριος ευδει.
Ουδεποτε ζωνην αναλυεται, ‘υδε ταχειας
Ενδρομιδας· μη οἱ τι κ͜ αιφνιδιον επος ειπη
Δεσποτις. ἡ δ̓ αλεγεινον αλαςησασα ϖροσηυδα,
Ουτω νυν, ω Ζηνος ονειδεα, κ͜ γαμηοισθε   240
Λαθρια, κ͜ τικτοιτε κεκρυμμενα. μηδ̓ οθι φωκαι
Δυςοκεες μογευσιν αλετριδες, αλλ̓ οθι δειλαι
Εἰναλιαι τικτυσιν ενι σπιλαδεσσιν ερημοις.
Αςεριη δ̓ ‘υδεν τι βαρυνομαι εινεκα τησδε
Αμπλακιης, ‘υδ̓ ες-ιν οπως αποθυμια ρεξω   245
                              Her

Her pangs to foften, and her grief t' affuage. 400
Afteria's virtue has difarm'd my rage ;
She fought the feas to fhun th' embrace of Jove,
Refus'd my bed, and hence enjoys my love.
Scarce had fhe fpoke when Phœbus tuneful fwans *,
From rich Pactolus, and Mæonia's plains, 405

Τοσσαδε οἱ. μαλα γαρ τε κακως ἐχρισσατο Λητοι.
Αλλα μιν ἐκπαγλον τι σεбιζομαι, ἐνεκ' ἐμειο
Δεμνιον ἐκ ἐπατησε, Διος δ' ἀνθειλετο ποντον.
Η μεν ἐφη κυκνοι δε θεα μελποντες ἀοιδοι
Μηονιον Πακτωλον ἐκυκλωσαντο λιποντες 250

* In afcribing mufical power to fwans, Callimachus follows the ftream of ancient authority poets, hiftorians, and philofophers. Yet, if we admit for an univerfal and unalterable maxim, that the animal creation muft be uniform in the exercife of its faculties, ftrictly defined by nature, modern obfervation may be juftly employed to refute ancient authorities; efpecially fince this authority, though general, is not univerfal among the ancients themfelves, Ælian (de Natur. Anim. l. ii. c. 32. and Hift. var. l. iii. c. 14.) doubts; Pliny (Nat. Hift. x. 23.) denies ; and Lucian (de Electro) turns into redicule, the vocal power of fwans. To balance their incredulity, feveral moderns of great name, have maintained a firm belief in the ancient creed, and endeavoured to confirm it by new obfervations and experiments. In 1545, Leland the antiquarian publifhed his κυκνα αϲμα, or fwan's fongs. Olaus Magnus, in his hiftory of northern nations, maintains that fwans fing, and afcribes the fweetnefs of their modulation to their long and winding necks. The northern hunters, he fays, well know how much the fwan is delighted with mufic; fince by means of the harp and pipe, they allure them to fhore. Thomas Bartholinus, Olaus Wornius, and the great naturalift Aldrovandus in his ornithology, maintain the fame opinion, and adduce many teftimonies of thofe who fay they have heard the melody of fwans. It is certain that this bird was not only confecrated to Apollo, the God of harmony, by the Greeks; but was likewife em-

ployed

Sev'n times, on fnowy pinions, circle round
The Delian fhores, and fkim along the ground :
The vocal birds, the fav'rites of the Nine,
In ftrains melodious, hail the birth divine.
Oft as they carol on refounding wings,   410
To footh Latona's pangs ; as many ftrings
Apollo fitted to the warbling lyre,
In after-times ; but e'er the facred choir
Of circling fwans another concert fung
In melting notes, the pow'r immortal fprung   415
To glorious birth.   The Delian nymphs around
Rife from the flood, in ftrains divine refound
Ilythia's praife ; triumphant fongs afpire,
And the rejoicing Æther feems on fire.

Εβδομακις περι Δηλον. επηεισαν δε λοχειη
Μυσαων ορνιθες, αοιδοτατοι πετεηνων.
Ενθεν ο παις τοσσασδε λυρη ενεδησατο χορδας
Υςερον, οσσακι κυκνοι επ' ωδινεσσιν αεισαν.
Ογδοον υκ ετ' αεισαν, ο δ' εκθορεν. αι δ' επι μακρον   255
Νυμφαι Δηλιαδες ποταμυ γενος αρχαιοιο,
Ειπαν Εληθυιης ιερον μελος· αυτικα δ' αιθηρ
Χαλκεος αντηχησε διαπρυσιην ολολυγην.

ployed as the hieroglyphic of mufic, among the Egyptians. This latter circumftance
affords a ray of light ; fince not a few points in Grecian mythology, may be re-
ferred to the error of taking in a literal fenfe, the Egyptian hieroglyphics, which
like all allegorical paintings were barely metaphors.

                                                        Jove

Jove footh'd his angry queen ; fhe dropt her fcorn,   420
And felt the gen'ral joy when Sol was born.
   Then, happy Delos ! thy foundations chang'd
To golden columns in bright order rang'd ;
On that bleft day thy circling lake became
Of liquid gold, and feem'd a moving flame :   425
On golden branches golden olives roll'd,
And deep Inopus flow'd in waves of gold.
Then lifting from the fhining foil you preft
With arms encircling, to your fnowy breaft
The new-born God, and thus with pleafure fpoke :   430
On thee, proud earth, unnumber'd altars fmoke ;
On thee fair cities, mighty ftates are feen ;
Thy fhores are fertile, and thy fields are green :
Thy thronging iflands countlefs numbers yield,
Whilft I lie wafte with all my plains untill'd.   435

Οὐδ' Ἡρη νεμεσησεν, ἐπει χολον ἐξελετο Ζευς,
Χρυσεα τοι τοτε παντα θεμειλια γεινετο Δηλε.   260
Χρυσω δε τροχοεσσα πανημερος ἐῤῥεε λιμνη,
Χρυσειον δ' ἐκομισσε γενεθλιον ἑρνος ἐλαιης.
Χρυσω δε πλεμμυρε βαθυς Ινωπος ἐλιχθεις.
Αὐτη δε χρυσεοιο ἀπ' ἠεος εἱλεο παιδα,
Εν δ' ἐβαλευ κολποισιν· ἐπος δ' ἐφθεγξαο τοιον,   265
Ω μεγαλ', ὠ πολυβωμε, πολυπτολι, πολλα φερεσα,
Πιονες ἠπειροι τε κ᾽ αἱ περιναιετε νησοι,

                                                        But

But since Apollo deigns to take my name,
The pow'r will bless, and grant me greater fame
Than all the world receives from Gods beside :
More than from Neptune the Cenchræan tide ;
More than Cyllene's hill, or Creta's plains,   440
From Hermes one, and one from Jove obtains.
By Phœbus lov'd, my station here I'll keep,
And float no more amid the stormy deep.

  So saying, she display'd her sacred breast,
Which, with his lips, the smiling infant prest,   445
And suck'd ambrosial juice ; from whence the name
Of isle most holy consecrates thy fame,
O glorious nurse ! and hence thou ne'er shalt feel
The force of stern Belona's vengeful steel ;
Nor here shall Pluto spread his dark domain,   450
Nor Mars impetuous thunder o'er thy plain.

Αὔτη ἐγω τοιηδε δυσηροτος· ἀλλ᾽ ἀπ᾽ ἐμειο
Δηλιος Απολλων κεκλησεται. ὐδε τις ἀλλη
Γαιαων τοσσονδε θεω πεφιλησεται ἀλλω·   270
Οὐ Κερχνις κρειοντι Ποσειδαωνι Λεχαιω,
Οὐ παγος Ερμειη Κυλληνος, ἠ Διῖ Κρητη,
Ως ἐγω Απολλωνι· κỳ ἐσσομαι ὐκ ἐτι πλαγκτη.
Ωδε συ μεν κατελεξας· ὁ δε γλυκυν ἐσπασε μαζον.
Τω κỳ νησαων ἀγιωτατη ἐξετι κεινυ   275
Κληζῃ, Απολλωνος κυροτροφος. ὐδε σ᾽ Ευυω,

                                                                      But

But tithes, and firſt-fruits * each revolving year,
From diſtant climes ſhall on thy ſhores appear,

Οὐδ' Αἴδης, ἐδ' ἵπποι ἐπιςειδυσιν Αρτος·
Αλλα τοι ἀμφιετεις δεκατηφοροι ἀιεν ἀπαρχαι

* Tithes and firſt fruits.] The revenues levied by Delos on the ſuperſtition of
the ancient world were the ſource of all the advantages of that favoured iſland ;
which, in the words applied by Lucian to the territory of Delphi, flouriſhed
in rich luxuriance under the culture of the God. Lucian Phalar. ii. Cecrops
king of Attica, or his ſon Eryſichthon, laid the foundations of the temple, about
200 feet from the ſhore, (Tournefort t. 1. p. 300) and ſucceeding princes and re-
publicks continued to embelliſh it for upwards of two thouſand years; a vaſt ſpace
of time in the hiſtory of the world, during which Apollo's temple was held in awful veneration. The ſtatue of the God adorned the middle of the temple, holding in
one hand a bow, and in the other the images of the three Graces, each diſtinguiſhed
by an inſtrument of Muſic. At the foot of the ſtatue ſtood the famous altar, formed
from the horns of the wild goats of mount Cynthus, the firſt trophies of Diana's
archery, and artfully interwoven into an elegant ſtructure by the playful ingenuity of
young Apollo. It was this cubical altar which, when Delos was afflicted by the peſtilence, the Oracle commanded the Delians to *double*. Plato who with the fire of the
poet, united the patient ſagacity of the Geometer, doubled the cube, ſolved the pro-
blem, and gave birth to the ſolid geometry ; exhorting his countrymen to reſpect
the admonitions of the oracle, who in this memorable reſponſe, commanded them to
forſake their miſerable diſputes of intereſt and ambition, and to taſte the ineſtimable
charms of ſcience. The golden palm tree was the copy of that whoſe ſpreading
branches had hoſpitably received Latona fainting under the pains of parturition. Every
object of Delos announced the holy land, to which ſolemn deputations were ſent
every fifth year in the ſpring, from the various ſtates and colonies of Greece, ſo widely
diffuſed over the ancient world. Theſe deputations were called θιωραι; the veſſels
which conducted them, θιωρήδες; and the perſons ſent θιωροι; words denoting the ſacred
miniſtry in which they were employed. When the ſeaſon of the feſtival approached,

the

And ev'ry flate beneath the morning ray,
The ftar of ev'ning, or meridian day,   450
Shall join the myftic dance ; ev'n thofe renown'd
For length of days, fhall tread the hallow'd ground
From Hyperborean fhores * ; by whom are born
The firft ripe ears and fheaves of yellow corn.

Πεμπονται. πασαι δε χορυς αναγυσι πολη̣ες,
Αἱ τε προς ἠοιην, αἱ Ϟ' ἑσπερον, αἱ τ' ανα μεσσην   280
Κληρυς ἑςησαντο, ϰ̇ οἱ καθυπερθε βορειης
Οἱκια Ϟινος ἑχυσι, πολυχρονιωτατον αἱμα.

the fhores of Delos, and its neighbouring ifles were crowded with fhips or gallies
fplendidly equipped, fhining with gold and purple, and whofe gilded oars, moving to the
found of mufic, reflected the rays of the Sun.   Each veffel contained its offering to the
Delian temple; and each contained, what was far more precious, a chorus of Grecian
boys and girls, whofe varied dances, defcriptive of the hiftory of Latona and her divine
children, formed the greateft ornament of the feftival.

     * Hyperborean fhores]   Spanheim on this occafion pours forth a profufion of learn-
ing, and mixes conjectures with facts. We know from Herodotus, that the Hyperboreans
or Arimafpi a northern nation, fent deputations to Delos ; but that the laft deputies fent thither having died in the ifland, the Hyperboreans thenceforth contented themfelves with
delivering their prefents on the frontiers of their country to a nation near the Scythians.
(Herodot. VI. 33.)   The Scythians delivered them to the Pelafgi of Epirus, who fent
them acrofs Greece to Eubæa, from whence they were conveyed to Tenos, and finally
delivered by the Tenians to the priefts of Delian Apollo.   The names of the firft
Hyperborean deputies, Upis Hecaerge and Loxo, if not Hellenized by Callimachus,
betray a Grecian extraction, and would prove that the Hyperboreans were an obfcure
but adventurous, colony of Greeks, who had fettled on fome remote fhore of the
north.

And the Pelaſgi, from Dodona's ſhores,   460
Shall firſt receive the conſecrated ſtores ;
The race, that nightly reſt along the ground,
Attentive to the caldron's myſtic ſound * ;
Conſign'd by them the grateful off'rings fill
The Melian city, and the ſacred hill :   465
From whence they paſs to fair Lilantia's land,
And from Eubœa reach thy neighbouring ſtrand.
But Upis bright, and Hecaërge kind,
And Loxo daughters of the Northern wind,

Οἱ μεντοι καλαμην τε κỳ ἱερα δραγμᾶτα πρωτοι
Αςαχυων φορευσιν· ἁ Δωδωνηθε Πελασγοι
Τ'ηλοθεν ἐκβαινοντα πολυ πρωτιςα δεχονται   285
Γηλεχεες θεραποντες ἀσιγητοιο λεβητος.
Δευτερον ἱερον ἀςυ, κỳ ὖρεα Μηλιδος αἰης
Ερχονται· κειθεν δε διαπλωυσιν Αβαντων
Εἰς ἀγαθον πεδιον Ληλαντιον. ὐδ' ἐτι μακρος
Ο πλοος Εὐβοιηθεν· ἐπει σεο γειτονες ὁρμει.   290
Πρωται τοι τα δ' ἐνεικαν ἀπο ξανθεν Αριμασπων
Οὐπις τε, Λοξω τε, κỳ εὐαιων Εκαεργη,

* The Caldron's myſtic ſound.] This refers to the brazen kettles of Dodona, the moſt probable account of which is, that they were ſo formed and arranged that by ſtriking one of them the ſound communicated to the reſt: (Demon apud Suidam) by which means they made a continual noiſe; and thence a great talker was called proverbially, εκδωνῳ χαλκος, a Dodonean kettle.

U   With

With pious hands the firſt ripe off'rings bore   470
To Delos' iſle, from th' Arimaſpian ſhore
Fair youths attending, that return'd no more,
But here were bleſs'd ; and hence each hallow'd name
Shall ever flouriſh in immortal fame.
For when the Delian nymphs, a beauteous throng!   476
With am'rous throbbings hear the nuptial ſong ;
The joyful bridegroom hails the bliſsful morn,
Whilſt from his face the virgin down is ſhorn ;
The bluſhing bride, with equal ſpeed, prepares,
And from her head divides the votive hairs ;   480
The firſt is ſacred to the youths divine,
The beauteous locks adorn the virgin's ſhrine *.

From thee, fair Delos, ſweet perfumes aſcend ;
Still, at thy feet, encircling iſlands bend ;

Θυγατερες Βορεαο, κỳ αρσενες οἱ τοτ' αριςοι
Ηϊθεων. ὐδ' οἱγε παλιμπετες οικαδ' ἱκοντο·
Εὐμοιροι δ' ἐγενοντο, κỳ ακλεες ὐποτ' εκεινοι.   295
Ητοι Δηλιαδες μεν, ὁτ' εὐηχης ὑμεναιος
Ηθεα κυρααν μορμυσσεται, ἡλικα χαιτην
Παρθενικαι, παιδες δε θερος το πρωτον ἰυλῳ
Αρσενες ηϊθεοισιν ἀπαρχομενοι φορευσιν.
Αςεροιη θυεσσα, σε μεν περι τ' αμφι τε νησοι   300

* Virgins ſhrine.]   Theſe circumſtances are likewiſe related by Herodotus. L. IV.
C. 34.

                                                        To

To folemn fongs their verdant heads advance, 485
And feem to move, as in the mazy dance;
When ev'ning Hefper darts his rays around
Thy flow'ry fhores; and brightens at the found.
By chofen youths the lofty lays are fung
That flow'd from Lycian Olens * tuneful tongue, 490
An ancient feer; fair virgins dance around,
And fhake, with choral feet, the folid ground.
Bright Venus, lift'ning to the hymns divine,
The nymphs with garlands deck her ancient fhrine,
By Thefeus rais'd †; when with the fons of Greece 495
From Cretan plains he gain'd the fhores in peace;

Κυκλον εποιησαντο, κ̀ ὡς χορον ἀμφεβαλοντο,
Οὐτε σιωπαλην, ἐτ' ἀψοφον. ἑλος ἐθειραις
Εσπερος ἀλλ' αἰει σε καταβλεπει ἀμφισβητον.
Οἱ μεν ὑπαειδεσι νομον Λυκιοιο γεροντος,
Ον τοι ἀπο Ξανθοιο θεοπροπος ἡγαγεν Ὡλην· 305
Αἱ δε ποδι πλησσεσι χορητιδες ἀσφαλες ἑδας;
Δη τοτε κ̀ ϛεφανοισι βαρυνεται ἱσον ἀγαλμα
Κυπριδος ἀρχαιης ἀριηκοον· ἡν ποτε Θησευς
Εἱσατο συν παιδεσσιν, ὁτε Κρητηθεν ἀνεπλει.

---

* Lycian Olen was the moft ancient of all the Greek Poets, prior not only to Homer but to Orpheus. He compofed hymns for the priefts of Delphi and Delos. Paufan. in Phocic. & Bœotic.

† The Athenians never failed to diftinguifh themfelves on every occafion of piety as well as patriotifm. Thefeus failed to Delos, and returned thanks for the fuccefs of

Return'd in triumph o'er the briny main,
From fell Pafiphaës monftrous offspring flain;
For Venus guided thro' the maze beneath,
The winding lab'rinth, and the den of death.   500
Hence beauteous Queen, he led the choir around
Thy facred altars, to the folemn found
Of melting lyres; and here the Athenians fent,
In grateful memo'ry of this fam'd event,
The fhrouds and tackling to the God of day,
That ftill remain, nor fhall with time decay.

And fince, Afteria, thy bright fhores are crown'd
With fmoking altars, and with hymns refound,
What mariners, when fwift-wing'd veffels keep
Their courfe by thee, along th' Ægean deep,   510

Οἱ χαλεπον μυκημα κỳ ἀγριον ὑια φυγοντες   310
Πασιφαης, κỳ γναμπτον ἑδος σκολι8 λαβυρινθ8,
Ποτνια σον περι βωμον ἐγειρομεν8 κιθαρισμ8
Κυκλιον ὠρχησαντο· χορε8 δ᾽ ἡγησατο Θησευς.
Ενθεν ἀειζωντα Θεωριδος ἱερα Φοιβῳ
Κεκροπιδαι πεμπ8σι τοπηϊα νηος ἐκεινης.   315
Αϛεριη πολυβωμε, πολυλλιτε, τις δε σε ναυτης

his Cretan expedition, the deftruction of the fierce Minotaur and the delivery of Athens from a cruel and ignominious tribute.

Tum pendere pœnas
Cecropidae juffi, miferum! *feptena* quotannis Corpora natorum, **VIRGIL.**

But here fhall ftop, and furl their fwelling fails,
Tho' bent on fpeed, and borne by driving gales ?
Nor fhall return, till circling o'er the ground,
They fhape the maze, and the ftruck altar found
With myftic blows, nor till at they command,   515
With arms averted, as the rites demand,
They bite the facred olive *. Thus the god,
O Nymph of Delos, in thy bright abode,
Was entertain'd ; and thus Apollo fpent
His infant-years in mirth and fweet content.   520

    Hail ! fair Afteria, girt with ifles around,
Like Vefta † ftationed, and for peace renown'd ;

Εμπορος Αιγαιοιο παρηλυθε νηϊ θεεση ;
Οὐχ ἕτω μεγαλοι μιν ἐπιπνειεϲιν ἀηται,
Χρειω δ' ὁττιταχιϲον ἀγει πλοον· ἀλλα τα λαιφη   320
Ωκεες ἐϲειλαντο, κὴ ἒ παλιν αὐθις ἐθησαν
Πριν μεγαν ἠ σεο βωμον ὑπο πληγησιν ἐλιξαι
Ρησσομενον, κὴ πρεμνον ὀδακτασαι ἁγνον ἐλαιης,
Χειρας ἀποϲρεψαντας. ἁ Δηλιας εὑρετο νυμφη
Παιγνια κυριζοντι κὴ Απολλωνι γελαϲυν.

* They bite the facred olive.] Thefe extraordinary ceremonies were practifed in
imitation of the fimple fports or amufements that diverted Apollo and Diana in their
youth; ceremonies ludicrous indeed, yet not therefore inconfiftent with the genius of
Grecian fuperftition.

† Delos is called the Vefta of the ifles for two reafons, its immobility or tranquillity,
and its occupying the center of the Cyclades.

St.t

Hail Phœbus ! Guardian of thy facred fhore;
And hail the Goddefs *, whom Latona bore !

Ιϛιη ὠ νησων, εὑεϛιε, χαιρε μεν αὑτη,　　　　　　325
Χαιροι δ᾽ Απολλων τε, κỳ ἡν ἐλοχευσατο Λητω.

Stat vi terra fua, vi ftando vefta vocatur.　Ovid.

Vefta, whether taken to denote the Earth, as above; or to denote the Element of Fire, as in another paſſage of the fame author;

Nec tu aliud Veftam, quam vivam intellige flammam, ftill occupied the center according to the mythological philofophy.

　　　　ἡ μεσον ειχον εχει πυρος αεναοιο μιγεν.　Orpheus.

*　The Poet concludes very properly with this addrefs to Diana, left that jealous god-defs, as fhe is more than once defcribed in thefe hymns, fhould have been offended at his negleét.

END OF THE HYMN TO DELOS.

THE FIFTH HYMN

OF

CALLIMACHUS.

ON

THE BATHING OF PALLAS *.

Come forth, come forth †, ye virgins, and prepare
The bath for Pallas with afsiduous care :

Οσσαι λωτροχοοι τας Παλλαδος, ἐξιτε πασαι,
Εξιτε. ταν ἱππων ἀρτι φρυασσομεναν

---

* On the bathing of Pallas.] The Greeks inhabiting a warm climate, and being unacquainted with the ufe of linen, had recourfe to bathing as efsential to cleanlinefs and health.
A practice which they found to be ufeful and agreeable to themfelves, they naturally tansfered to their Gods: for as Ariftotle juftly obferves in the firft book of his Politicks,
" men having made the Gods after their own image, naturally afcribe to thofe etherial beings,
their own cuftoms and manners." Criticks who look for hidden myfteries and a double
meaning in the rites of heathen mythology, confider thefe ceremonial wafhings as fymbolical and figurative : and regard fuch external purifications as mere types of that inward
purity, which religion fo powerfully recommends. Spanheim thinks that in the bathing of
Pallas, he fees evident traces of the Mofaic inftitutions. He refers to Numbers viii. 7.
" And thus fhalt thou do unto them (the Levites) to cleanfe them: fprinkle water of purifying

The Goddefs comes; from yon' ætherial meads
I hear the fnorting of her fiery fteeds.

Ταν ἱεραν ἐτακυσα, κ̣ α̣ ϑεος εὐτυχος ἐρπει·

ing upon them and let them fhave all their flefh, and let them wafh their cloaths, and fo make themfelves clean." And to Ifaiah li. 11. " Depart ye, Depart ye, go ye out from thence, touch no unclean thing: go ye out of the midft of her: be ye clean that bear the veffels of the Lord." But it is to be obferved, that it is a very different thing to require cleanlinefs in them who officiate at the altar, and to fuppofe that the Gods themfelves, as well as their minifters, require being purified by ablutions. In the text above quoted, the Levites are commanded not only to wafh with water but to fhave their flefh: and the latter cuftom prevailed alfo among the ancient Egyptians, as appears from the figures of the Egyptian priefts delineated by M. Bruce. The heads of the figures difcovered among the ruins of ancient Thebes are clofely fhaven; but hair forms a diftinguifhing ornament of the Grecian divinities, male and female. Pallas was not only to be wafhed, but anointed; but the practice of anointing, as we are told by Jofephus, De Bell. Jud. ii. C. VII. and by Porphyry (De Abf. l. iv. p. 383), was ftrongly condemned by the Effenians, the pureft and moft fpiritual fect of the Jews. Pallas, alfo, as we are told in this hymn, practifed the gymnaftic exercifes, which all freeman were commanded to practice in moft Grecian republics, as we learn from Ariftotle; and in which even women are enjoined to participate by the laws of Lycurgus and of Plato. Still faithful to their principles, the Greeks, in the pithy language of Ariftotle, which often contains a fcience in a fentence, " continually transferred human cuftoms to the Gods;" believing that by exercifes which they found beneficial to themfelves even Minerva might embellifh her beauty, and fortify her ftrength. By this we do not mean that the heathen mythology was intirely the work of fancy: its foundation was doubtlefs laid in philofophical doctrines, and in ancient traditions derived from thofe great events recorded in the books of Mofes. But the fuperftructure ill correfponded with the foundation; and in endeavouring to reduce this fanciful fuperftructure to the regularity of a fixed plan, men of more learning than judgment bewilder their readers and themfelves.

    † Come forth, Come forth.] In commands, particularly relating to the fervice of the

Come forth, come forth, ye brown Pelafgian maids; 5
For bright Minerva never feeks the fhades,
Nor bathes her limbs in the refrefhing flood,
Till from her fteeds fhe wafh the duft and blood:
Not tho' th' immortal arms, as once before,
Were ftain'd with flaughter'd giants reeking gore. 10

Σεσθε νυν, ω ξανθαι, σεσθε Πελασγιαδες.
Ου ποκ' Αθαναια μεγαλως απενιψατο παχεις, 5
Πριν κονιν ιππειαν εσελασαι λαγονων·
Ουδ' οκα δη λυθρω πεπαλαγμενα παντα φεροισα
Τευχεα των αδικων ηνθ' απο γηγενεων.

Gods, thofe repetitions and reduplications of words are common among the poets, Greek and Latin, particularly in the choral fongs of the Greek Tragedians.

Ye Virgins] Minerva the patronefs of purity was to be ferved by virgins only. But thefe Virgins continued to be prieftefles of the Goddefs only untill they attained the marriageable age. Paufan. L. VII. p. 451. They then cut off a lock of their hair, and dedicated it as a peace offering in the temple of Minerva.

———————hic more parentum
Jafides, thalamis fibi cafta adolefceret ætas,
Virgineas libare comas, primofque folebant
Excufare toros, Theb. II. V. 252.

Ver. 10. Were flained with flaughterd Giants recking gore] This circumftance is introduced with great propriety, Minerva being faid to have gained the αρενα or firft prizes of valour in the glorious victory of the Gods over the earth-born Giants. Phurnutus p. 189. To which Horace alludes in thefe beautiful lines.

Quid Rhaecus, evulfisque truncis
Enceladus Jaculator audax
Contra fonantem Palladis aegida
Poffent ruentes? Hor. Carm. liii. Od. 4.

X   No

Nor till, unloofing from the car, fhe lave
The courfer's panting fide in ocean's wave,
And cleanfe their mouths that gather'd foam diftains,
When bounding fwift, they fhake the flowing reins.
Come forth, ye nymphs; no precious ointments bring   15
(I hear the wheels around her axles ring)
Nor oils, in alabafter * fmooth, prepare;
Nor oils, nor unguents are Minerva's care;
She needs no glafs; her eyes are ever bright,
Nor when the Phrygian youth on Ida's height,   20

Αλλα πολυ πρατιςον ὑφ' ἁρματος αὐχενας ἱππων
Λυσσαμενα, παγαις ἐκλυσεν Ωκεανω   10
Ιδρω κ̓ ῥαθαμιγγας· ἐφοιβασεν δε παγεντα
Παντα χαλινοφαγων ἀφρον ἀπο ςομᾳτων.
Ω ἰτ' Αχαιιαδες· κ̓ μη μυρα, μηδ' ἀλαβαςρως
(Συριγγων ἀιω φθογγον ὑπαξονιων)
Μη μυρα λωτροχοοι τᾳ Παλλαδι, μηϸ' ἀλαβαςρως;   15
(Οὐ γαρ Αθαναια χριματα μικτα φιλει)

No precious unguents bring] Athenaeus L. XV p. 687, obferves that Sophocles in a Tragedy, called the Cretans, now loft, introduces Venus with her perfumes and her look-ing Glafs, but Minerva anointed with oil only, after performing the gymnaflic exercifes. All the retinue of Venus delight *in mixt unguents* χρματα μικτα; but it became not the purity of Pallas to employ thofe pernicious drugs, which beaux and fine ladies are often *obliged* to make ufe of.

Alabafter. V. 17] Unguents, fays Pliny, are beft preferved in alabafter. Plin l. XIII. C. 2. Her eyes are ever bright] γλαυκωπις Αθηη alluding to the bright blue eyes properly fcribed to the Goddefs of wifdom, the eye being the Index of the mind.

Misjudged

Misjudg'd the ſtrife, did mighty Pallas gaze
On poliſh'd braſs, or Simois' wat'ry maze ;
Nor Jove's imperial queen : but Venus fair
Fond ſeiz'd the charm, and oft replac'd her hair.
Whilſt Pallas drove around, and urg'd her ſteeds,   25
Like Leda's offspring on Eurotas' meads ;
Then o'er her limbs ſhe pour'd ambroſial oil,
The produce of her garden's fertile ſoil.

Οἴσετε· μηδὲ κατοπτριν. ἀεὶ καλον ὄμμα το τῆνας.

  Οὐδ' ὁκα ταν Ιδαν Φρυξ ἐδικαζεν ἐριν,

Οὐδ' ἐς ὀρειχαλκον μεγαλα Θεος, ἐδε Σιμουντος

  Εϐλεψεν διναν ἐς διαφαινομεναν·   20

Οὐδ' Ηρη· Κυπρις δε διαυγεα χαλκον ἐλοισα,

  Πολλακι ταν αὐταν δις μετεθηκε κομαν.

Α δε, δις ἐξηκοντα διαθρεξασα διαυλῶς,

  Οἷα παρ' Εὐρωτα τοι Λακεδαιμονιοι

* On poliſhed braſs] The ὀρειχαλκος, or mountain braſs. This was the only artificial looking glaſs, till luxury introduced mirrors of ſilver, which Pliny refers to the age of Pompey. But golden ones were known in Aſia long before. In the Troades of Euripides. v. 1107, Helen is ſaid to have brought from Troy

  χρυσια δε ιοπτρα παρθενων

  χεριας;—

    Golden looking glaſſes,

  The ornaments of girls.

V. 28. * She poured ambroſial oil.] The ancients rubbed with oil both before, and after, their exerciſes. Galen de ſanit. tuend. ii. 4 and 7. defends this practice, and the uſe of oil in general, againſt Archidamus, who preferred dry frictions.

Behold,

Behold, ye nymphs, the blufhing morn arife
More bright than rofes' or pomegranates' dyes ;   30
Bring forth the facred oil that Caftor us'd,
And o'er Alcides manly ftrength diffus'd :

Αςερες, ἐμπεραμως ἐτριψατο λιτια λαβοισα   25
Χριματα, τας ἰδιας ἐκγονα φυταλιας.
Ω κωραι, το δ᾽ ἐρευθος ἀνεδραμε πρωϊον, οἱαν
Η ῥοδον ἠ σιβδης κοκκος ἐχει χροιαν.
Τῳ κ̀ νυν ἀρσεν τε κομισσατε μηνον ἐλαιον,
Ω Καςωρ, ᾡ κ̀ χριεται Ηρακλεης·   30

Pomegranates' dyes. V. 30] In former times they dyed fcarlet with the fruit of the
Pomegranate. Peacham on drawing.
        V. 30. Behold, ye nymphs, the blufhing morn arife
            More bright then rofes or pomegranates' dyes.]
    I have taken this paffage in the fenfe in which it is underftood by all thofe who have
tranflated or commented Callimachus. Yet an attentive confideration of the words in
the original would incline me to affign to them a ftill more poetical meaning. The poet
fays that "Minerva inftead of embellifhing her charms by mixed unguents applied by the
affiftance of her looking glafs, drove 24 miles at full fpeed, and then fkilfully employed
for her perfon, oil only, the native fruit of her own plantation. In confequence of which
the morning red fprung up, rivalling the beauty of the rofe or pomegranate. Therefore
bring with you oil only." Callimachus, who has been obferved, even in his hymns to admit
ftrokes of fatire, perhaps intended a leffon to the court ladies of Alexandria, and might
poffibly have in view a paffage in the Vth book of Xenophon's Memorabilia; in which
exercife is faid to be the beft embellifher of beauty. " Ifchomachus, as Socrates tells us
in that paffage, had married a very young wife, whom he obferved one day with her
face painted, and with high-heeled fhoes to make her appear taller. Ifchomachus, who
is defcribed as a man of great prudence, chid her with feverity for thefe impertinent
follies. Could fhe imagine to pafs fuch filly deceits on a man well acquainted with her,
                                                                                            and

Bring forth the comb, that fhines with yellow gold,
To fmooth her hairs, and curl each beauteous fold.
    Come forth, Minerva; lo! thy virgins wait;   35
Aceftor's offspring ftand before the gate,
And bear Tydicles' fhield with holy hands,
As once the good Eumedes gave commands.

Οισετε κỳ κτενα οἱ παγχρυσεον, ὡς ἀπο χαιταν
    Πεξηται, λιπαρον σμασαμενα πλοκαμον.
Εξιθ᾽ Αθαναια· παρα τοι καταθυμιος ἰλα,
    Παρθενικαι μεγαλων παιδες Ακεςοριδαν.
Ω Ἀανα, φερεται δε κỳ ἁ Διομεδεος ἀσπις,   35
    Ως ἑθος Αργειων τητο παλαιοτερον

and who faw her daily. If fhe wifhed to have a brighter complexion, why did fhe not
weave at her loom, ftanding up-right! This, and fuch exercifes would ftrengthen her
conftitution, and give her a natural bloom, which the moft exquifite paint could not imitate."

    Aceftor's offspring V. 36] In Greece particular families, or tribes, were frequently
dedicated to the miniftry of particular divinities. We are told by the fcholiaft that the
Aceflorides were an illuftrious family at Argos, from which only the virgins, who ferved
Minerva in this ceremony, could lawfully be chofen.

    And bear Tydides' fhield V. 37] Ulyffes and Diomede were the favourite heroes of Mi-
nerva. Dr. Dodd quotes with propriety as illuftrative of this paffage the following beautiful lines.

            But Pallas now Tydides' foul infpires,
            Fills with her force, and warms with all her fires:
            Above the Greeks his deathlefs fame to raife,
            And crown her hero with diftinguifhed praife.
            High on his helm celeftial lightning's play
            His beamy fhield emits a living ray :

                                            The

Thy favour'd prieft; for when bad men combin'd
Againft his life, he fled, nor left behind   40
Thy facred image, which, with pious toil,
He plac'd on lofty Creon's rocky foil;
On Creon's pointed cliffs, renown'd in fame,
And call'd Palladian from thy facred name.
  Come forth, Minerva; from whofe golden helm   45
Red lightning glances on th' unhallow'd realm:

Εὐμήδης ἐδίδαξε, τεῒν κεχαρισμένος ἱρευς·
Ὅς ποτε βαλευτον γνας ἐπι οἱ θανατου
Δαμον ἑτοιμαζοντα, φυγα τεον ἱρον ἀγαλμα
Ωιχετ' ἐχων, Κρειον δ' εἰς ὁρος ᾠκισατο,   .   40
Κρειον ὁρος· σε δε, δαιμον, ἀπορρωγεσσιν ἐθηκεν
Εν πετραις, αἱς νυν ἐνομα Παλλατιδες.
Εξιθ' Αθαναια περσεπτολι, χρυσεοπηληξ,
Ιππων κ σακεων ἀδομενα παταγῳ.

    The unweary'd blaze inceffant ftreams fupplies
    Like the red ftar that fires th' autumnal fk'e
    When frefh he rears his radiant orb to fight,
    And bathed in ocean fhoots a keener light.
Such was the famous fhield of the hero, who removed the famous Palladium from Troy,
and was rewarded with immortallity as Pindar tells us by his almighty patronefs.
    Διομηδεα δε αμβροτον
    Ξανθη ποτε γλαυκωπις εθηκε θεον
  The fair-haired blue-eyed Minerva formerly made Diomede an immortal God. His
worfhip therefore was naturally joined to that of Minerva herfelf, by the grateful partiality of his Argive countrywomen.

Come

Come forth, Minerva; pleas'd with wars' alarms,
The bounding courfer, and the clang of arms.
This day, ye maids, the cleanfing water bring,
Not from the river, but the chryftal fpring.
This day, ye maids, at Piyfadea fill
The brazen urn, or Amymone's rill:
For Inachus, from yon' green mountain pours
His waters, bright with gold, and gay with flow'rs
To fill the bath. Pelafgian! fly from harms,
Nor unpermitted view Minerva's charms;

50

55

Σαμερον ὑδροφεροι μη βαπτετε· σαμερον Αργος   45
   Πινετ' απο κραναν, μηδ' απο των ποταμων.
Σαμερον αἱ δωλαι τας καλπιδας ἡ 'ς Φυσαδειαν,
   Η ἑς Αμυμωνην οἱσετε ταν Δαναω.
Και γαρ δη χρυσῳ τε κ᾽ ανθεσιν ὑδατα μιξας
   Ηξει φορβαιων Ιναχος ἑξ ορεων,   50
Τᾳ 'θαιᾳ το λοετρον αγων καλον. αλλα, Πελασγε,
   Φραζεο μ' ἑκ εθελων ταν βασιλειαν ἰδης.

V. 55.   Pelafgian fly from harms
       Nor unpermitted view Minerva's charms.]
   The divinities of Greece fhewed themfelves only to favoured perfons; all others who
beheld them, even though involuntarily, fuffered grevioufly for this unintentional offence.
Such is the general doctrine, which is proved by a great variety of concurring paffages.
The injuftice and cruelty of this law appears the more evidently, when it is confidered that
Gods could render themfelves invifible whenever they pleafed (Homer paffim) They
therefore voluntarily furnifh to men an opportunity of commiting an unvoluntary
crime, which is punifhed by fome *dreadful* calamity; for Tirefias who was punifhed

Left, from your blind-ftruck eyes, fhe fnatch away
The tow'rs of Argos, and the golden day.
Come forth, Minerva; while to nymphs I fing
A tale renown'd, and ftrike the vocal ftring.   60

 Attend, ye maids.—A nymph of Thebæ's town,
Tirefias' mother, from Minerva won
Diftinguifh'd love.   The facred pair were join'd
In friendfhip fweet, the union of the mind.
And, when the pow'r to Thefpis urg'd her fteeds,
To Haliartus, o'er Bœotias meads,
Or Coronea, by Curalius' flood,
Where, near a breathing grove, her altar ftood;

Ὁς κεν ἰδῃ γυμναν ταν Παλλαδα ταν πολιᾶχον,
 Τὠργος ἐσοψειται τᴚτο πανυϛατιον.
Ποτνι Ἀθαναια, συ μεν ἔξιθι· μεσφα δ᾽ ἐγω τι   55
 Ταις δ᾽ ἐρεω. μυθος δ᾽ ᴚκ ἐμος, ἀλλ᾽ ἑτερων.
Παιδες, Ἀθαναια νυμφαν μιαν ἐν ποκα Θήβαις
 Πᴚλυ τι κϳ περι δε φιλατο ταν ἑτεραν,
Ματερα Τειρεσιαο, κϳ ᴚποκα χωρις ἐγεντο·
 Ἀλλα κϳ ἀρχαιων εὐτ᾽ ἐπι Θεσπιεων,   60
Ἡ ᾽πι Κορωνειας, ἠ εἰς Ἁλιαρτον ἐλαυνᵉι
 Ἱππᴚς, Βοιωτων ἐργα διερχομενα,
Ἡ ᾽πι Κορωνειας, ἱνα οἱ τεθυωμενον ἀλσος
 Και βομοι ποταμῳ κεῖντ᾽ ἐπι Κᴚραλιῳ·

with blindnefs only, was confidered as meeting with a treatment uncommonly mild, pro-
ceeding from the partiality of Minerva for his mother.

               Still

Still in the car the nymph attending rode.
Nor dance, nor focial converfe pleas'd the God,　　70
Unlefs her dear Chariclo led the way :
But fhe, with many tears, muft fhortly pay
For Pallas' love, and woes attend behind.
For when the pair their fhining veils unbind
To bathe their limbs in Hippocrene's rills　　75
(That foftly flow from Heliconian hills)
At mid-day, when no breath was heard around,
Nor from the mountain came the ftilleft found.
At mid-day bathing, when the fun was bright,
And filence reign'd, as at the noon of night.　　80
The firft foft down juft rifing on his face,
Tirefias then with hounds approach'd the place,

Πολλακις ἁ δαιμων μιν ἑῳ ἐπεβασατο διφρῳ.　　65

　Οὐδ' ὀαροι νυμφαν ἐδε χοροςασιαι

Αδειαι τελεθεσκον, ὁτ' ἐχ ἀγειτο Χαρικλω.

　Αλλ' ἐτι κ̑ τηναν δακρυα πολλ' ἐμενε,

Καιπερ Αθαναια καταθυμιον εὐσαν ἑταιραν.

　Δη ποτε γαρ πεπλων λυσαμενα περονας,　　70

Ιππω ἐπι κρανα Ελικωνιδι καλα ῥεοισα

　Λωντο· μεσαμβρινα δ' εἰχ ὀρος ἀσυχια.

Αμφοτεραι λωοντο, μεσαμβριναι δ' ἐσαν ὡραι·

　Πολλα δ' ἀσυχια τηνο κατειχεν ὀρος.

Τειρεσιας δ' ἐτι μενος ἁμαι κυσιν, αρτι γενεια　　75

Υ　　　　　　　　　To

To quench his thirſt in the refreſhing ſtreams,
And undeſign'd beheld their naked limbs:
Ah! luckleſs youth; for thus Minerva ſpoke,   85
Tho' ſoft'ning pity ſmooth'd her angry look.

 Euerus' ſon! what unpropitious God
Has led thy ſteps to this retired abode?
Some dæmon urg'd thee, this unhappy day;
Doom'd hence no more to bear thy ſight away.   90

 She ſaid: thick darkneſs inſtant veil'd his eyes;
Amaz'd he ſtood, and ſpeechleſs with ſurprize:
Black horror chill'd his limbs: his mother mourn'd
With rage and grief, and furious thus return'd.

 What haſt thou done? Is this Minerva's love?   95
And this the kindneſs of the God's above?

Περκαζων, ἱερον χωρον ἀνεϛρεφετο,
Διψασας δ' ἀφατον τι, ποτι ῥοον ἠλυθε κρανας,
 Σχετλιος· ὐκ ἐθελων δ' εἰδε τα μη θεμιδες.
Τον δε χολωσαμενα περ, ὁμως προσεφασεν Αθανα,
 Τις σε, τον ὀφθαλμως ὐκ ἐτ' ἀποισομενον,   80
Ω Εὐηρειδα, χαλεπην ὁδον ἀγαγε δαιμων;
 Α μεν ἐφα, παιδος δ' ὀμματα νυξ ἐβαλεν.
Εϛαθη δ' ἀφθογγος· ἐκολλασαν γαρ ἀνιαι
 Γωνατα, κ̀ φωναν ἐσχεν ἀμηχανια.
Α νυμφα δ' ἐβοησε, Τι μοι τον κωρον ἐρεξας   85
 Ποτνια; τοιαυται δαιμονες ἐϛε φιλαι;

My

My Son's bright eyes thou haft for ever clos'd,
Becaufe he faw thy beauteous limbs expos'd.
Since he no more beholds ætherial day,
No more my feet on yonder mountain ftray;   100
Since he no more this happy fcene fhall view,
Ye pendant rocks! Ye falling rills adieu!
Ah! wretched mother; more unhappy fon!
Revengeful Goddefs! What could he have done?
Thy worthlefs goats and hinds were once his prize;   105
For which, unpitying pow'r, you feiz'd his eyes!
  She faid: with circling arms embrac'd her fon,
And pour'd her forrows, helplefs and undone,
As for her young fad Philomel complains,
In mournful notes, and melancholy ftrains.   110
At her diftrefs Minerva's eyes o'erflow,
And thus fhe footh'd her lov'd Companion's woe.

Ομματα μοι τȣ παιδος αφειλεο. τεκνον αλαϛε
  Ειδες Αθȥναιας ϛȥθεα κȣ λαγονας·
Αλλ' ȣκ αελιον παλιν οψεαι· ω εμε δειλαν.
  Ω ερος, ω Ελικων ȣκ ετι μοι παϛιτε.   90
Η μεγαλ' αντ' ελιγων επραξαο· δορκας ολεσσας,
  Και προκας ȣ πολλας, φαεα παιδος εχεις.
Α μεν επ' αμφοτεραισι φιλον περι παιδα λαϐοισα
  Ματηρ μεν γοερων οιτον αȥδονιδαν
Αγε βαρυ κλαιȣσα. θεα δ' ελεȥσεν εταιραν,   95
                Y 2   Recal

Recal thefe hafty words, O Nymph divine;
Thy fon is blind, but not by my defign.
The pow'rs of heav'n delight not to deftroy,   115
Nor fnatch the light from ev'ry beauteous boy:
Charge not, my friend, this dire mifchance on me;
For ev'ry man, by Saturn's ftern decree,

Και μιν Αθαναια προς τοδ' ελεξεν επος,
Δια γυναι, μ3τα παντα βαλευ παλιν οσσα δι οργαν
Ειπας. εγω δ' ντοι τεκνον εθηκ' αλαον.
Ου γαρ Αθαναια γλυκερον πελει ομματα παιδων
Αρπαζειν· Κρονιοι δ' ωδε λεγοντι νομοι.   100

For every man by Saturn's ftern decree.] This circumftance is worthy of obfervation. It is not Minerva herfelf but the laws of Saturn κρ1ιο1 ιομοι that punifhed Tirefias. If the doctrine ftated in the former note were founded on the divine maxims of heathen antiquity, and thefe maxims themfelves were indeed derived, as Spanheim and others think, from a more venerable fource, (referring to Exodus xix. and xx. and xx. and xxi. &c.) our ferious thoughts will teach us that thefe heaven-fprung laws might be founded on the falutary principle of inculcating reverence and refignation; duties which obfervation and reflection, that is, the knowledge of nature and of ourfelves, continually and powerfully inculcate on the wife, but which the bulk of mankind can only be taught by the ftrong impreffions of terror. The propriety of enforcing them in this manner on the Egyptians, among whom Ptolemy had introduced the rites of Grecian fuperftition, is fufficiently evident; and Callimachus, who may be regarded as the Poet laureat, both of Ptolemy Philadelphus, and of his fucceffor Ptolemy Euergetes, could not better pay his court, than by ftrengthening the foundation of a religious worfhip, which thofe enlightened princes regarded as intimately connected with the ftability of their royal authority.

That,

That, unpermitted, views the pow'rs divine,
Still makes atonement with an ample fine.   120
Before his birth, bright Nymph, the Parcæ spun
This fatal thread for thy much-favour'd Son.
Mourn not, Tiresias, tho' thy lot be hard,
But for the deed receive a great reward.
What Hecatombs would fair Cadmeïs burn?   125
Nor more would wretched Aristæus mourn
In after-times, when young Actæon dies;
Could he return with only lofs of eyes.
For tho' Diana's fav'rite in the chace,
And fkill'd, with her, to hunt a favage race;   130
Yet when the Youth, unwilling, tempts her wrath,
And undefign'd beholds her in her bath,

Ος κε τιν' αθανατων οκα μη θεος αυτος εληται,
Αθρηση, μισθω τετον ιδειν μεγαλω.
Δια γυναι, το μεν ε παλιναγρετον αυθι γενοιτο
Εργον· επει μοιραν ωδ' επενευσε λινα,
Ανικα τοπρωτον νιν εγειναο· νυν δε κομιζευ,   105
Ω Ευηιειδα, τελθος οφειλομενον.
Ποσσα μεν α Καδμηϊς εσυτερον εμπυρα καυσει,
Ποσσα δ' Αρισαιος, τον μονον ευχομενοι
Παιδα τον αβαταν Ακταιονα τυφλον ιδεσθαι.
Και τηνος μεγαλας συνδρομος Αρτεμιδος   110
Εσσεται· αλλ' εκ αυτον ο, τε δρομος αι τ' εν ορεσσι
Ρυτευνται ξυναι ταμος εκαβολιαι.

Nor

Nor chace nor fports avail: She gives the word,
And his fierce dogs devour their former Lord.
Thro' lonefome woods the Mother then fhall rove,   135
Collecting his white bones from ev'ry grove,
And call thee bleft, and not like her undone,
That from the hills, receives thy fightlefs fon.
Then weep no more, O moft belov'd of friends ;
A gift more glorious on that Son attends,   140
For great Minerva, from this happy hour,
His breaft irradiates with prophetic pow'r,
Illumes his mind, and grants him greater praife,
Than e'er fhall crown the Seers of future days.
For he fhall mark the wand'ring birds that fly   145
To right, to left, along th' ætherial fky,

Οπποταν εκ εθελων περ ιῃ χαριεντα λοετρα
  Δαιμονος· αλλ' αυται τον πριν ανακτα κυνες
Τυτακι δειπνησευντι. τα δ' υιεος οςεα ματηρ   115
  Δεξειται, δρυμως παντας επερχομενα·
Ολβιςαν ερεει σε κỳ ευαιωνα γενεσθαι,
  Εξ ορεων αλαον παιδ' υποδεξαμεναν.
Ω εταρα, τω μη τι μινυρεο. τῳδε γαρ αλλα
  Τευ χαριν εξ εμεθεν πολλα μενευντι γερα.   120
Μαντιν επει θησω νιν αοιδιμον εσσομενοισιν,
  Η μεγα των αλλων δη τι περισσοτερον.
Γνωσειται δ' ερνιθας, ος αισιος, οι τε πετονται

                I   Shall

Shall read their motions, as they fwiftly fpring,
Obferve the flight of each unpros'rous wing,
And utter facred truths, in after-times,
To Cadmus, Thebes, and fam'd Bœotia's climes.   150
A myftic ftaff fhall guide his fteps, and he
Long life and honour'd age obtains from me.
And when he dies, from him alone fhall flow
Prophetic truths in difmal realms below ;
While, ftill-infpir'd, he walks among the dead,   155
And Pluto's felf reveres the mighty fhade.

Ηλιθα, κὴ ποιων ἐκ ἀγαθαι πτερυγες.
Πολλα δε Βοιωτοισι θεοπροπα, πολλα δε Καδμω   125
  Χρησει, κὴ μεγαλοις ὑςερα Λαβδακιδαις.
Δωσω κὴ μεγα βακτρον, ὁ οἱ ποδας ἐς δεον ἀξει,
  Δωσω κὴ βιοτη τερμα πολυχρονιον.
Και μονος, εὐτε θανη, πεπνυμενος ἐν νεκυεσσι
  Φοιτασει, μεγαλω τιμιος ἀγεσιλα.   130

While ftill infpired he walks among the dead.] Homer furnifhes the beft comment
on this paffage.

     Τῳ και τιθημιτι νοεν ποξι περσιφονιια,
     Οιω πιπνυσθαι τοι δι σκιαι αισσυσι.   OdyfT. x. v. 494—5.
     To whom (Tirefias) Perfephone intire and whole,
     Gave to retain th' unfeparated foul,
     The reft are forms, of empty æther made
     Impaffive femblance and a flitting fhade.

Plato in the beginning of the third book of his Republic is very angry with Homer,
not for what he fays of Tirefias, but for his fpeaking honourably of this prophet at the

She spoke, and bow'd her beauteous head, that ftill
Confirms her vows: for by Jove's awful will,
Of all his daughters, Goddeffes in heav'n,
This honour only was to Pallas giv'n;   160
That fhe, with him, might equal glory gain.
No mother bore her with a mother's pain,

Ὡς φαμενα κατενευσε· το δ᾽ εντελες, ᾧ κ᾽ επινευσῃ

Παλλας. επει μωνα Ζευς τογε ϑυγατερων

Δωκεν Αθαναια, πατρωϊα παντα φερεσθαι.

Λωτροχοοι, ματηρ δ᾽ ᾽ͅτις ετικτε θεαν·

Αλλα Διος κορυϕα. κορυϕα Διος ᾧ κ᾽ επινευσῃ,   135

expence of the other fhades—He fays the Poet is blameable for treating the fhades with unjuft raillery, a raillery founded in falfehood, and tending to a hurtful purpofe, fince the belief of it would weak n or deftroy martial fpirit.

  * That fhe with him might. equal glory gain.] Spanheim refers this to the *true light* in the Gofpel, and thinks that this and fimilar opinions were taken from the feptuagint tranflation, made under Ptolemy Philadelphus. But Pindar, above two centuries before, fpeaks of Minerva as fitting at the right hand of the father—and Homer has a paffage in honour of the fame Goddefs, which is faithfully tranflated by Pope.

    Mark well my voice, Ulyffes ftraight replies;
    What need of aids, if favoured by the fkies!
    If fhielded to the dreadful fight we move,
    By mighty Pallas, and by thundering Jove.
    Sufficient they, (Telemachus rejoined,)
    Againft the banded powers of all mankind:
    They hi_h enthron'd above the rolling clouds,
    Whither the ftrength of men, and awe the Gods.

The words, ὑ̣ͅ πη ν ιημσει—"They high enthroned above the rolling clouds"—countenance the opinion of thofe, who think that Pallas in the heathen mythology means the pure ætherial light t. as Jupiter means the æther itfelf.

But her great Father's head ; and hence the God
Still gives, like him, th' irrevocable nod.

But now Minerva comes, nor comes unfeen ;   165
Prepare, ye virgins, to receive your Queen
With acclamations, in this blifsful hour,
With vows and fongs receive th' approaching pow'r.
Hail ! guardian Goddefs, ftill let Argos claim
Thy kind protection, and adore thy name.   170
Whether, bright Queen, thou leadft thy fiery fteeds
From Argos tow'rs along the verdant meads,
Or back to yonder walls thy chariot runs,
Still ftill, defend old Danaus' mighty fons.

Εμπεδον· ωσαυτως ω κεν οι α θυγατηρ.
Ερχετ' Αθαναια νυν ατρεκες· αλλα δεχεσθε
  Ταν θεου, ω κωραι, τωργος οσαις μελεται,
Συν τ' ευαγοριᾳ, συν τ' ευγμασι, συν τ' ολολυγαις.
  Χαιρε θεα, καδευ δ' Αργεος Ιναχιε.   140
Χαιρε κ̔ εξελαοισα, κ̔ ες πολιν αυτις ελασσαις
  Ιππꙅς, κ̔ Δαναων κλαρον απαντα σαω.

Z

THE SIXTH HYMN

OF

CALLIMACHUS.

TO CERES.

THE Bafket fwift-defcending from the fkies,
Thus, thus, ye matrons, let your voices rife :

Τ Ω καλαθω κατιοντος επιφθεγξασθε γυναικες,
Δαματερ μεγα χαιρε, πολυτροφε, πυλυμεδιμνε.

Hymn to Ceres] Among the religious folemnities tranfported from Greece to Alexandria, Ptolemy could not fail to introduce the famous Eleufinian feftival, celebrated
with fuch pomp at Athens, in honour of Ceres; the great benefactrefs of that city;
and through it, as Ifocrates relates, of the other Republics of Greece, and of all the
reft of mankind. "When Ceres wandered over Greece in queft of her daughter
Proferpine, fhe received in Attica the moft hofpitable treatment, and thofe particular
good offices which it is lawful to make known only to the initiated. The Goddefs
was not ungrateful for thofe favours, but, in return conferred on our anceftors, the
two moft valuable prefents which mankind can receive or even Heaven can beftow.
The art of agriculture, which delivered us from the fierce and precarious manner

of

" Hail! Ceres, hail! by thee, from fertile ground
Swift fprings the corn, and plenty flows around."
Ye crouds, yet uninftructed, ftand aloof,   5
Nor view the pageant from the lofty roof,
But on the ground below ; nor matrons fair,
Nor youth, nor virgins, with difhevell'd hair,
Dares here approach : nor let the moifture flow
From fafting mouths to ftain the myftic fhow. 10

Τον καλαθον κατιοντα χαμαι θασσεισθε βεβαλει,
Μηδ᾽ απο τυ τεγεος μηδ᾽ υψοθεν αυγασσησθε.
Μη παις, μηδε γυνα, μηδ᾽ α κατεχευατο χαιταν, 5
Μηδ᾽ ο κ᾽ αφ᾽ αυαλεων ϛοματων πτυωμες απαϛοι.

of life common to us with wild animals; and the knowledge of thofe facred myfteries
which fortify the initiated againft the terrors of death, and infpire them with the
pleafing hopes of an happy immortality. Our anceftors difcovered as much bene-
volence in diffufing thofe advantages as piety in obtaining them—Their humanity
communicated what their virtue had acquired. The myfteries were annually unveiled
to all defirous and worthy of receiving them : and the practife, the means and advantages of agriculture were fpeedily extended over all Greece. I ocrates in panegyric A-
then, Gillies' Tranflation Such is the Athenian legend : and if Ceres, as is generally
fuppofed, denote the fertalizing power of nature, her worfhip muft have been one of the
moft ancient. For Ariftotle in his Ethicks (ad Nicomach. VIII. 9) tells us that the
ancient facrifices, and religious folemnities appear to have taken place after the gather-
ing in of the grain, and confifted in a fort of firft-fruit-offerings to the Gods ; men
having moft leifure at that feafon.

The bafket.] The proceffion of the bafket, a proper emblem of Ceres, was on the
fourth day of the feftival. This holy bafket, or καλαθοι, was carried on a confecrated ve-
hicle, crouds of people fhouting as it went along χαιρ Δημτηρ, Hail Ceres.

           But

But radiant Hefper, from the ftarry fkies,
Beholds the facred bafket as it flies :
Bright Hefper only could perfuade the pow'r
To quench her thirft, in that unhappy hour,
When full of grief, fhe roam'd from place to place,   15
Her ravifh'd daughter's latent fteps to trace.
How could thy tender feet, O Goddefs, bear
The painful journey to the weftern fphere ?
How couldft thou tread black Æthiops burning climes ;
Or that fair foil, in thefe diftrefsful times,   20
Where, on the tree, the golden apple beams,
Nor eat, nor drink, nor bathe in cooling ftreams ?
      Thrice Achelous flood her fteps divide,
And ev'ry ftream that rolls a ceafelefs tide.

Εσπερος, ὁς τε πιειν Δαματεːα μωνος επεισεν,
Εσπερος εκ νεφεων εσκεψατο πανικα νειται·
Αρπαγιμας ὁτ᾽ απυσα μετεςιχεν ἰχνια κωρας,
Ποτνια, πως σε δυναντο ποδες φερεν ἐς τ᾽ επι δυθμας,   10
Ἐς τ᾽ επι τ℘ς μελανας, ϰ᾽ ὁπα τα χρυσεα μαλα ;
Οὐ πιες ℥τ᾽ ἀρ᾽ ἐδες τηνον χρονον, ℥δ᾽ ἐλοεσσω.
Τρις μεν δη διεϐης Αχελωιον αργυροδινην,

      Bright Hefper only would perfuade the power to quench her thirft.] This paffage
has given rife to innumerable conjectures ; of which the moft probable is, that this is
only a poetical mode of faying, that Ceres was fo eager to difcover her daughter, that fhe
drank nothing all day, nor quenched her thirft till the rifing of the evening ftar.

                                                                              Three

Three times she prefs'd the center of that ifle,　25
Where Enna's flow'ry fields with beauty fmile.
Three times, by dark Challichorus, fhe fate,
And call'd the yawning gulph to mourn her fate:
There, faint with hunger, laid her weary'd limbs,
Nor eat, nor drank, nor bath'd in cooling ftreams.　30
　But ceafe, my Mufe, in thefe unhallow'd ftrains,
To fing of Ceres' woes, and Ceres' pains;

Τοσσακι δ' αεναων ποταμων επερασσας εκαςον,
Τρις δ' επι καλλιςης νησυ δραμες; ομφαλον Ενναν,　15
Τρις δ' επι καλλιχορω χαμαδις εκαθισσαο φρητι,
Αυςαλεα, αποτος τε· κ̀ υ̌ φαγες, υδ' ελεεσσω.
Μη μη ταυτα λεγωμες, α δακρυον ηγαγε Δηοι.

The center of that ifle.] Sicily. Enna was called the umbilicus Siciliæ.

To fing of Ceres woes] That the ftory of Ceres feeking her daughter Proferpine contains a philofophical meaning, receives countenance from the orphic fragments. Proferpine is feigned to have been alternately in the fhades with Pluto her hufband and on the earth with Ceres her mother: and to have continued in each habitation fix months. The orphic hymn to Proferpine fpeaks of her as carried to her unvoluntary marriage bed after the autumn, as producing and deftroying all things, as firft fhowing her facred body in the green germs; and concludes, by invoking her to fend forth the fruits of the earth. " Proferpine therefore is explained, to be that power which hides and preferves, during the fix winter months, the germs of vegetable life, notwithftanding their apparent corruption—She goes to Pluto, that is fhe goes under the earth—She appears in the green germs in the fpring, which by the affiftance of Ceres are ripened, and reaped in autumn. The allegory of Proferpine bears a great analogy to that of Pfyche, the moft beautiful of all the Grecian fictions. Latter artifts reprefented Pfyche as a beautiful young girl, but fhe originally meant the butterfly as a fymbol of the Ætherial

Far nobler to refound her facred laws,
That blefs'd mankind, and gain'd their loud applaufe.

Καλλιον, ὡς πολισσιν ἑαδοτα τεθμια δωκε·

principle. This infect, hatched from the egg, is nothing but a grub crawling on the
earth like man in his earthly form. It then degenerates ftill further, into the torpid
Chryfalis, whofe infenfibility prefents an apt reprefentation of Death : while the butterfly
breaking from its dull prifon, and mounting in the air, exhibit a natural image of the
celeftial fpirit burfting from the reftraints of matter, and feeling its native fkies.

Far nobler to refound her facred laws] fo Virgil.

        Mactant lectas de more bidentes

        Legiferae Cereri.

Laws are moft naturally afcribed to Ceres, the inventrefs of agriculture, fince agriculture occafioned the divifion or appropriation of lands, and the appropriation of land
produced the neceffity of laws. The feftival of Ceres called θεσμοφορια denotes this
characteriftic of the Goddefs, meaning the feftival in honour of the eftablifhment of laws.
Spanheim obferves that the feaft of penticoft, or of wheat harveft, has exactly the fame
appellation in Hebrew, in memory of the law giver from mount Sinai; and that laws
engraven on tables of brafs were hung up in the temples of Ceres in Greece; the inftitution of the Gentile nations thus concurring with the evidence of facred fcripture in re-
fering the benefits of legiflation to a divine original. He might have added that before
thefe written laws of Ceres, there exifted others, not lefs facred, the χρονια νομη, the laws
of Saturn, and particularly the θεμιστες διος the laws of Jupiter, fo named from θεμις, his
minifter or meffenger, a moft important perfonage in the polity as well as in the religion
of antiquity, being nothing lefs then a perfonification of diftributive juftice. In all ages
and nations, and under every form of fociety, law, or juftice, is equally worthy of veneration. the great bon and center of attraction, or, as it were the key ftone of the arch,
that fupports the fabrick of focial life, and diftinguifhes a ftate of civilization, that is,
properly, a ftate of fubjection to juft government, from a ftate of favagenefs, that is a ftate
of fubjection to rude violence and brutal force. That thefe θεμιστες διος formed during the
Heroic ages the nature, the principle, the very effence of government is fully proved in

                                       the

Far nobler to declare how firſt ſhe bound 35
The ſacred ſheaves, and cut the corn around,
How firſt the grain beneath the ſteer ſhe laid,
And taught Triptolemus the rural trade.
Far nobler theme (that all his crime may ſhun)
To paint the woes of Triopas' proud ſon; 40
How meagre famine o'er his viſage ſpread,
When her fierce vengeance on his vitals fed.

Καλλιον, ὡς :αλαμην τε κ̀ ἱερα δραγματα ϖροτα 20
Ασαχυων απεκοψε, κ̀ ἐν βοος ἡκε ϖατησαι,
Ανικα Τριπτολεμος αγαθαν ἐδιδασκετο τεχναν·
Καλλιον, ὡς (ἱνα και τι: ὑπερβασιας αλεττ:ι)
Οηκατ. Ρεπεινα Τριοπεω γονον οικτρεν ιδεσθαι.

the Hiſtory of ancient Greece, Vol. 1. c. 2. It appears that Kings were nothing more than mere inſtruments in the hands of Jupiter, and that under the name of royalty, the government was really Theocratic. While they diſpenſed faithfully the θεμι, they were to i. reſpected and obeyed, but when they perverted or infringed theſe ſacred laws, they at the ſame moment diſgraced and depoſed themſelves; and the ſceptre, the external badge of their authority, dropped from their hands. See the Iliad and Odyſſey paſſim—particularly Odyſs. ii. 68— 69 Il. IX. 98, 99. Il. XII. 510, and ſeq. Kings were called θμιποχοι, the miniſters or ſervants of the θεω if which they were to defend, and as Ariſtotle tells us in his Politicks, the form of the oath conſiſted in ſtretching forth the ſcepter. Ariſtot. Polit. L. iii c. XIV. See alſo Dionyſ. Halicarn. Ant. Rom. L.ii. and L. v. p. 337. ex Edit. Sylburgii. The only perſonages in thoſe days who diſregarded the θμιγα; were the Cyclopes: they indeed were, each in his own family, arbitary princes, and made their will law—

τοισιν ατ' αγορει βουλτφορι, ατι θιμιστι;

.t

Not yet to Cnidia the Pelafgi came,
But rais'd at Dotium to bright Ceres' name
A facred wood, whofe branches interwove   45
So thick, an arrow fcarce could pierce the grove.
Here pines and elms luxuriant fummits rear;
Here fhone bright apples, there the verdant pear:
A chryftal fountain pour'd his ftreams around,
And fed the trees, and water'd all the ground.   50
With wonder Ceres faw the rifing wood,
The fpreading branches, and the filver flood,
Which, more than green Triopium, gain'd her love,
Than fair Eleufis, or bright Enna's grove.
But when, incens'd, his better genius fled   55
From Eryfichton, rafh defigns invade
His impious breaft: he rufh'd along the plain
With twenty ftrong attendants in his train,

Οὔπω ταν Κνιδιαν, ἐτι Δωτιον ἱρον ἐναιον,   25
Τιν δ' αυτα καλον ἀλσος ἐποιησαντο Πελασγοι
Δενδρεσιν ἀμφιλαφες· δια κεν μολις ἠλθεν ὀϊσος.
Εν πιτυς, ἐν μεγαλαι πτελεαι ἐσαν, ἐν δε κ̀ ὀχναι,
Εν δε καλα γλυκυμαλα· το δ' ὡς' ἀλεκτρινον ὑδωρ
Εξ ἀμαραν ἀνεθυε. Θεα δ' ἐπεμαινετο χωρω   30
Οσσον Ελευσινι, Τριοπω Θ' ὁσον, ὁκκοσον Εννα.
Αλλ' ἱκα Τριοπιδαισιν ὁ δεξιος ἀχθετο δαιμων,
Τυτακις ἁ χειρων Ερυσιχθονος ἀψατο βωλα.
Σευατ' ἐχων Θεραποντας ἐεικοσι, παντας ἐν ἀκμᾳ·

                    2

                                                      Of

Of more than mortal fize, and fuch their pow'r,
As could with eafe o'erturn the ftrongeft tow'r.   60
With faws and axes arm'd they madly ftood,
And forc'd a paffage thro' the facred flood.
A mighty poplar rais'd his head on high
Far o'er the reft, and feem'd to touch the fky
(The nymphs at mid-day fported in the fhade)   65
Here firft they ftruck: on earth the tree was laid,
And told the reft her fate in doleful moans;
Indignant Ceres heard the poplar's groans,

Παντας δ' ανδρογιγαντας (ὁλαν πολιν ἀρκιοι ἀραι)   35
Αμφοτερον πελεκεσσι κỳ ἀξιναισιν ὁπλισσας.
Ες δε το τας Δαματρος ἀναιδεες ἑδραμον ἀλσος.
Ἡς δε τις ἀιγειρος, μεγα δενδρεον, αιθερι κυρον·
Τῳ δ' ὑπο ται νυμφαι ποτι τῳνδιον ἑψιωντο.
Α πρατα πλαγεισα, κακον μελος ἰαχεν ἀλλαις.   40
Ἡσθετο Δαματηρ ὁτι οἱ ξυλον ἱερον ἀλγει·

V. 63 A mighty poplar raifed his head on high] Many Criticks confider this
grove of Ceres as a plain copy of the Garden of Eden; and think the μεγα δενδρεον
αιθερι κυρον exactly correfponds to the great tree in the midft of the Paradife of God.
Yet it is probable that Callimachus copied models of rural beauty lefs remote in time
and place, than the garden of Eden. The Kings and rulers of Egypt, Leffer
Afia, and the Eaft, formed in all ages of hiftorical antiquity, wherever they fixed their
refidence, thofe delightful gardens, fays Xenophon, called paradifes, filled with
flowers and fruit, and abounding in every thing beautiful or ufeful, that the earth
is capable of producing. Xenoph. de admin. domeft. l. v. p. 829. Edit. Leuncl.

A a   And

And thus with anger fpoke. What impious hand
Has cut my trees, and my bright grove profan'd ?   70
She faid, and inftant, like Nicippa rofe,
Her well-known prieftefs, whom the city chofe ;
Her holy hands the crowns and poppy bore ;
And from her fhoulder hung the key before.
She came where Eryfichton's rage began,   75
And mildly thus addrefs'd the wretched man.

    My Son, whoe'er thou art that wounds the trees,
My Son, defift, nor break high heav'ns decrees :
By thy dear Parent's love, recal thy train,
Retire, my Son, nor let me plead in vain :   80

Εἶπε δὲ χωσαμενα, τις μοι καλα δενδρεα κοπτει;
Αὐτικα Νικιππη (ταν οἱ πολις ἀρητειραν
Δαμοσιαν ἑξασαν) ἐισατο· γεντο δε χειρι
Στεμματα ιᵹ μακωνα· κατωμαδιαν δ' ἐχε κλαιδα.   45
Φα δε παραψυχοισα κακον ᵹ ἀναιδεα φωτα,
Τεκνον, ὁτις τα θεοισιν ἀνειμενα δενδρεα κοπτεις,
Τεκνον ἐλιννυσον, τεκνον πολυθεσε τοκευσι,
Παυεο, ᵹ θεραπεντας ἀποτρεπε· μη τι χαλεχθη

V. 73·74. Her holy hands the crowns and poppy bore
            And from her fhoulder hung the key before.]
    The crowns and poppy belonged to Ceres, the key to her prieftefs, whofe office it
was to lock and guard her temple. The poppy, vifibly abounding in feeds, is a natural emblem of fertility.

                                                        Left

Left Ceres' wrath come burfling from above,
In vengeance for her violated grove.

She faid: but fcornful Eryfichton burn'd
With fiercer rage, and fiercer frowns return'd,
Than the gaunt Lionefs (whofe eyes they fay   85
Flafh keener flames than all the beafts of prey)
Cafts on fome hunter, when, with anguifh torn,
On Tmarus' hills her favage young are born.
Hence, hence, he cried, left thy weak body feel
The fatal force of my refiftlefs fteel: 90
Above my dome the lofty trees fhall fhine,
Where my companions the full banquet join,
And fport and revel o'er the fparkling wine.

He faid. Fell Nemefis the fpeech records,
And vengeful Ceres heard th' infulting words;   95
Her anger burn'd: her pow'r fhe ftraight affum'd,
And all the Goddefs in full beauty bloom'd:

Ποτνια Δαματηρ, τας ιερον εκκεραιζεις.   50
Ταν δ' αρ' υποβλεψας χαλεπωτερον ηε κυναγον
Ωρεσιν εν Τμαριοισιν υποβλεπει ανδρα λεαινα
Ωμοτοκος, (τας φαντι πελειν βλοσυρωτατον εμμα)
Χαζευ, εφα· μη τοι πελεκυν μεγαν εν χροϊ παξω.
Ταυτα δ' εμον θασσει ςεγανον δομον, ω ενι δαιτας   55
Αιεν εμοις εταροισιν αδην θυμαρεας αξω.
Ειπεν ο παις, Νεμεσις δε κακαν εγραψατο φωναν.

A a 2   While

While to the ſkies her ſacred head aroſe,
She trod the ground, and ruſh'd amidſt her foes.
The Giant-woodmen, ſtruck with deadly fear,   160
That inſtant ſaw, that inſtant diſappear,
And left t'.eir axes in the groaning trees:
But unconcern'd their headlong flight ſhe ſees;
For theſe t' obey their Lord the fences broke,
To whom with dreadful voice the Goddeſs ſpoke.   105;

    Hence, hence, thou dog, and haſten to thy home;
Thᵉre ſhape the trees, and roof the lofty dome:
There thou ſhalt ſoon unceaſing banquets join,
And glut thy ſoul with feaſts and ſparkling wine.

Δαματηρ δ' αφατον τι κοτεσσατο· γεινατο δ' α θευς.
Ιθματα μεν χερσω, κεφαλα δε οι αιψατ' ολυμπω.
Οι μεν αρ' ημιθνητες, επει ταν ποτνιαν ειδον,   60
Εξαπινης απορυσαν, ενι δρυσι χαλκον αφεντες.
Λ δ' αλλυς μεν εασεν, (αναγκαια γαρ εποντο
Δεσποτικαν υπο χειρα) βαρυν δ' απαμειψατ' ανακτα,
Ναι ναι, τευχεο δωμα κυον, κυον, ω ενι δαιτας

*| While to the ſkies her ſacred head aroſe, ſhe trod the ground] Callimachus gives
a far nobler idea of Ceres than Ovid—capitiſque ſui pulcherrima motu concuſſit gra-
vidⁱs oneratos meſſibus agros.

    The reader may compare the whole ſtory as told in the VIIIth Book of the Me-
tamorphoſes, from v. 740 to the end. The Latin poet is never deficient in fancy, which
always flows with rapid vigour and rich exuberance. But in the ſublime, and eſpecially
in the pathetic, he is on this occaſion far ſurpaſſed by his Grecian model.

                              2

                                                                Her

Her fatal words inflam'd his impious breaſt;
He rag'd with hunger like a mountain-beaſt: 110
Voracious famine his ſhrunk entrails tore,
Devouring ſtill, and ſtill defiring more.
Unhappy wretch! full twenty ſlaves of thine
Muſt ſerve the feaſt, and twelve prepare the wine;   115
Bright Ceres' vengeance, and ſtern Bacchus' rage
Confum'd the man who durſt their pow'r engage:
For theſe combine againſt infulting foes,
And fill their hearts with anguiſh and with woes.
His pious parents ſtill excufes found   120
To keep their fon from banquets giv'n around.
And when th' Ormenides his prefence call
To Pallas' games, by facred Iton's wall,

Ποιησεις· θαμιναι γαρ ἐς ὑςερον ειλαπιναι τοι.   65
Α μεν τοσσ' ειποισ' Ερυσιχθονι τευχε πονηρα.
Αὐτικα οἱ χαλεπον τε κ͂, ἀγριον ἐμβαλε λιμον,
Αιθωνα, κρατερον· μεγαλη δ' ἐςρευγετο νεσῳ.
Σχετλιος, ὁσσα πασαιτο, τοσων ἐχεν ἱμερος αὐτις.
Εἰκατι δαιτα πενοντο, δυωδεκα δ' οινον ἀφυσσον.   70
Τοσσα Διωνυσον γαρ ἁ κ͂, Δαματρα χαλεπτει.
Και γαρ τᾳ Δαματρι συνῳςγισθη Διονυσος.
Οὐτε μιν εἰς ἐρανως ὗτε ξυνδειπνια πεμπον
Αἰδομενοι γονεες· προχανα δ' εὑρισκετο πασα.
Ημθον Ιτωνιαδος μιν Αθαναιας ἐπ' ἀεθλα   75
Th'

Th' impatient mother ſtill their ſuit deny'd.
The laſt revolving day ſhe ſwift reply'd,   125
To Cranon's town he went, and there receives
An annual tribute of a hundred beaves.
Polyxo comes, the ſon and ſire invites,
To grace her young Actorion's nuptial rites :
But ſoon the mournful mother thus replies,   130
With tears of ſorrow ſtreaming from her eyes :
    The royal Triopas will join thy feaſt ;
But Eryſichton lies with wounds oppreſt ;
Nine days are paſt, ſince with relentleſs tooth,
A boar on Pindus gor'd the unhappy youth.   135

Ορμενιδαι καλεοντες· απ' ουν ηρνησατο ματηρ·
Ουκ ενδοι. χθιζος γαρ επι Κρανωνα βεβηκε,
Τελθος απαιτησων εκατον βοας. ηνθε Πολυξω,
Ματηρ Ακτοριωνος, (επει γαμον αρτυε παιδι)   80
Αμφοτερον Τριοπαν τε κ̩ υιεα κικλησκ̈σα.
Ταν δε γυνα βαρυθυμος αμειβετο δακρυχε̈σα,
Νειται τοι Τριοπας· Ερυσιχθονα δ' ηλασε καπρος
Πινδον αν' ευαγκειαν, ο δ' εννεα φαεα κειται.
Δειλαια φιλοτεκνε, τι δ' ̈κ εψευσαο ματερ ;

V. 131. But ſoon the mournfull mother thus replies
            With tears of ſorrow ſtreaming from her eyes]
    Theſe and the verſes immediately following afford proofs of what we ſaid in the pre-
ceding note ; Ovid's artificial wit is leſs pleaſing then Callimachus' natural tenderneſs.

                                                                                        What

What fond excufes mark'd her tender care?
Did one the banquet, or the feaft prepare?
My fon is gone from home the mother cries:
Was he invited to the nuptial ties?
A Difcus ftruck him, from his fteed he fell,   140
Or numbers his white flocks in Othrys' dale.
Meanwhile the wretch, confin'd within the rooms,
In never-ending feafts his time confumes,
Which his infatiate maw devour'd as faft,
As down his throat the nourifhment he caft;   145
But unrecruited ftill with ftrength or blood,
As if in ocean's gulphs, had funk the food.

As fnows from Mima's hills diffolving run,
Or waxen puppets melt before the fun,

Δαινυεν ειλαπιναις τις; εν αλλοτριοις Ερυσιχθων.   85
Αγετο τις νυμφαν; Ερυσιχθονα δισκος ετυψεν·
Η επεσ' εξ ιππων, η εν Οθρυι ποιμνι αριθμει.
Ενδομυχος δ' ηπειτα πανημερες ειλαπινασας
Ησθιε μυρια παντα· κακα δ' εξαλλετο γαστηρ
Αιει μαλλον εδοντι. τα δ' ες βυσον οια θαλασσης   90
Αλεματως αχαρισα κατερρεεν ειδατα παντα.
Ως δε Μιμαντι χιων, ως αελιω ενι πλαγγων,
Και τητων ετι μειζον ετακετο· μεσφ' επι νευρας

Waxen puppets] Young Greek girls diverted themfelves with waxen puppets, which
when they grew up, they dedicated to Venus.

4   Ꞩo

So faft his flefh confum'd, his vigour gone,   150
And nervous fibres only cloath'd the bone.
His mother mourn'd; his fifters groans refum'd;
His nurfe and twenty handmaids wept around :
The frantic father rent his hoary hairs,
And vainly thus to Neptune pour'd his pray'rs :   155
 O Pow'r divine, believ'd my fire in vain ;
Since thou reliev'ft not thy defcendant's pain :
If I from beauteous Canace may claim
My facred birth, or Neptune's greater name ;
Behold a dire difeafe my fon deftroy :   160
Oh! look with pity on the wretched boy.

Δειλαιω ινες τε κϳ οϛεα μϰνον ελειφθεν.
Κλαιε μεν ά ματηρ, βαϱυ δ᾽ ἐ͂-ενον αἱ δὺ ἀϛελϕαι,   95
Χ ὠ μαϛος τον ἐπινε, κϳ αἱ δεκα ϖολλακι δωλαι.
Και δ᾽ αὐτος Τριοπας ϖολιαις ἐπι χειϛα; ἐϐαλλε,
Τοια τον ἐκ ἀΐοντα Ποϛειδαωνα κϰλιϛϱεων,
Ψευδοϖατωϱ, ἰδε τονδε τϰ τϱιτον· εἰϖεϱ ἐγω μεν
Σϰυ τε κϳ Αἰολιδος Κανϰκης γϰνος, αὐταϱ ἐμϰιϛ   100
Τϰτο τϲ δειλαιϲν γενετο βϱεφος. αἰθε γαϱ αὐτον

V. 153. His nurfe and twenty handmaids wept around] We fee, how much
nurfes were regarded by the Greeks, in the Tragic poets. The modern Greeks ftill
preferve this feature of their anceftors, calling nurfes by a word which denotes " fecond mothers". Guy's Voyage Litteraire en Greece.

Far

Far happier fate! had Phœbus' vengeful dart
Struck, with refiftlefs force, his youthful heart;
For then my hands had fun'ral honours paid,
And facred rights to his departed fhade.   165
But haggard famine, with pale afpect now,
Stares in his eyes, and fits upon his brow.
Avert, O gracious pow'r, the dire difeafe,
Or feed my wretched fon in yonder feas.
No more my hofpitable feafts prevail,   170
My folds are empty, and my cattle fail.
My menial train will fcarce the food provide;
The mules no more my rufhing chariot guide,
A fteer his mother fed within the ftall,
At Vefta's facred altar doom'd to fall;   175

Βλητον ὑπ' Απολλωνος ἐμαι χερες ἐκτερεϊζαν·
Νυν δε κακα βεβρωϛις ἐν ὀφθαλμοισι καθηται.
Η οἱ ἀποϛασον χαλεπαν νοσον, ἠε μιν αυτος
Βοσκε λαβων. ἀμαι γαρ ἀπειρηκαντι τραπεζαι.   185
Χηραι μεν μανδραι, κενεαι δε μοι αὐλιες ἠδη
Τετραπεδων. ἠδη γαρ ἀπηρνησαντο μαγειροι.
Αλλα κỳ ἑρχας μεγαλαν ὑπελυσαν ἀμαξαν,
Και ταν βων ἐφαγεν ταν Εϛια ἐτρεφε ματηρ,

V. 161. Phœbus vengeful dart] vengeful to the father only—for thofe who died
in early youth were fuppofed to be favourites of heaven; Apollo and Diana took the
boys and girls to themfelves.

This he devour'd, and next my warlike horfe,
So oft victorious in the dufty courfe.
Ev'n pufs efcap'd not, when his fury rofe,
Herfelf fo dreadful to domeftic foes.

Long as his father's houfe fupply'd the feaft   180
Th' attendants only knew the dreadful wafte.
But when pale famine fill'd th' imperial dome,
Th' infatiate glutton was expell'd from home,
And, tho' from kings defcended, rueful fate
In public ftreets, and begg'd at ev'ry gate: 185
Still, at the feaft, his fuppliant hands were fpread,
And ftill the wretch on fordid refufe fed.

Immortal Ceres! for thine impious foe
Ne'er let my breaft with facred friendfhip glow.
Beneath my roof the wretch fhall never prove   190
A neighbour's kindnefs, or a neighbour's love.

Και τον αεθλοφορον κỳ τον πολεμηϊον ιππον,   110
Και ταν αιλϗρον ταν ετρεμε θηρια μικρα.
Μεσφ' ιτε μεν Τριοπαο δομοις ενι χρηματα κειτο,
Μωνοι αρ' οικειοι θαλαμοι κακον ηπισαντο.
Αλλ' οτε τον βαθυν οικον ανεξηραινον οδοντες,
Και τοϑ' ο τω βασιληος ενι τριοδοισι καθησο,   115
Αιτιζων ακολϗς τε κỳ εκβολα λυματα δαιτος.
Δαματερ, μη τηνος εμιν φιλος ος τοι απεχθης
Ειη, μηδ' ομοτοιχος· εμοι κακογειτονες εχθροι.

Ye

Ye maids and matrons, thus with facred fong,
Salute the pageant as it comes along.
" Hail! Ceres, hail! by thee from fertile ground
Swift fprings the corn, and plenty flows around." 195
As four white courfers to thy hallow'd fhrine
The facred bafket bear; fo, Pow'r divine,
Let Spring and Summer, rob'd in white appear;
Let fruits in Autumn crown the golden year,
That we may ftill the fprightly juice confume, 200
To footh our cares in Winter's cheerlefs gloom.
As we, with feet unfhod, with hair unbound,
In long proceffion tread the hallow'd ground;
May thus our lives in fafety ftill be led,
O fhow'r thy bleffings on each favour'd head! 205
As matrons bear the bafkets fill'd with gold,
Let boundlefs wealth in every houfe be told.

Εἴπατε παρθενικαι, κ᾽ ἐπιφθεγξασθε τεκεσαι,
Δαματεο μεγα χαιρε, πολυτροφε, πουλυμεδιμνε. 120
Χ᾽ ὡς αἱ τον καλαθον λευκοτριχες ἱπποι ἀγοντι
Τεσσαρες· ὡς ἁμιν μεγαλα θεος ευρυαγατσα,
Λευκον εαρ, λευκον δε θερος κ᾽ χειμα φεροισα
Ηξει κ᾽ φθινοπωρον, ετος δ᾽ εἱς ἀλλο φυλαξει. 125
Ὡς δ᾽ ἀπεδιλωτοι κ᾽ ἀναμπυκες ἀςυ πατευμες,
Ὡς ποδας ὡς κεφαλας παναπηρεας ἑξομες αἰει.

V. 206. As matrons bear the bafket filled with gold] The bearers of bafkets

B b 2

" as

Far as the Prytaneum the pow'r invites
The women uninſtructed in the rites ;
Then dames of ſixty years (a ſacred throng)   210
Shall to the temple lead the pomp along.
Let thoſe who for Lucina's aid extend
Imploring arms, and thoſe in pain attend
Far as their ſtrength permits ; to them ſhall come
Abundant bliſs, as if they reach'd the dome.   215

Ὡς αἱ λικνοφοροι χρυσῳ πλεα λικνα φεροντι,
Ὡς ἀμμες τον χρυσον ἀφειδεα πασσαιμεσθα.
Μεσφα τα τας πολιος πρυτανηϊα τας ἀτελεσως,
Τας δε τελεσφοριας ποτι ταν θευν ἀχρις ὁμαρτειν,   130
Αἱτινες ἑξηκοντα κατωτεραι, αἱ τε βαρειαι·
Χ' ἁτις Ελειθυια τεινει χερα, χ' ἁτις ἐν ἀλγει,

" αι λικνοφοροι" women bearing ; λικνα, baſkets, or rather winnows, implements of the moſt ſacred importance in the ceremonies of Bacchus.

That God is himſelf called λυκνιτης, Orph. Hymn 45, by a natural metaphor from the winnow, becauſe he ſeparated the ſoul or active principle, from the ſenſitive, and all ter-reſtrial pollutions. The λυκνα were with great propriety introduced in the ceremonies of Ceres, from the cloſe connection between her and Bacchus—

> Vos, ô clariſſima mundi
> Lumina, labentem cœlo quæ ducitis annum
> Liber & alma Ceres : veſtro ſi munere tellus
> Chaoniam pingui glandem mutavit ariſta,
> Populaque inventis Acheloi miſcuit uvis.   Georg. I. 5. & ſeq.

Bacchus and Ceres, therefore, were the Sun and the Moon : the great material cauſes by which the generative and fertiliſing power of Deity, exerciſes its energy

                                                                Hail,

Hail, sacred Pow'r! preserve this happy town
In peace and safety, concord and renown :
Let rich increase o'erspread the yellow plain ;
Feed flocks and herds, and fill the rip'ning grain :
Let wreaths of olive still our brows adorn,   220
And those who plough'd the field shall reap the corn.
    Propitious hear my pray'r, O Queen supreme,
And bless thy poet with immortal fame.

Ὡς ἁλις ὡς αὐταν ἱκανον γουυ. ταιϲι δε Δηω
Δωϲει παντ᾿ επιμεϲα, κ᾿ ὡς ποτι νηον ἱκωνται.
Χαιρε θεα, κ᾿ τανδε ϲαω πολιν, ἐν θ᾿ ὁμονοιᾳ,   135
Εν τ᾿ εὐημεριᾳ· φερε δ᾿ ἀγροθι νοϲιμα παντα.
Φερϐε βοας, φερϐε μαλα· φερε ϲαχυν, οἰϲε θεριϲμον·
Φερϐε κ᾿ εἰραναν, ἱν᾿ ὁς ἀροϲε, κεινος ἁμαϲη.
Ιλαθι μοι τριλλιϲε μεγα κρειϲϲα θεαων.

v. 222. Propitious hear my prayer, O Queen supreme] Supreme may be applied
to Jupiter, or even to Juno, the Queen of Heaven ; but why is it applied to Ceres!
Those who read the ancient poets with any degree of attention, will be compelled often
to ask themselves such questions. They will find that the pagan divinities in general
have many names and many forms (πογυνυμα and πολυμοϱϕα : Orphic. Fragm.) and that
the epithets and attributes belonging to one God, are often transferred to another.
The difficulty can only be solved on the Pythagorean principle, that all these divinities
are emanations of the one eternal and infinite, (Vid. Proclum in Theologiam Platonicam
Boeth. de Confolat. Philofoph. and Cudworth's Intellectual Syftem) or rather
perfonified abſtractions of his attributes; and that though he himſelf be infinite, in-
comprehenſible, and indiviſible, yet laborious and frail mortality, mindful of its own
infirmity, has divided infinite Deity into parts, that each mortal might worſhip that
                                                                        attribute,

attribute, whose affiftance he immediately needed. Fragilis & laboriofa mortalitas in partes ifta digellet, infirmitatis fuæ memor, ut portionibus quifque coleret, quo maxime indig.ret. Plin. ii. 7. Among thofe attributes of Deity, the creative or amiable, and the deftructive or terrible, appear to have been very generally worfhipped among all the nations of antiquity both in the eaft and weft; becaufe the operation of thefe powers maintain and perpetuate the fyftem of the univerfe, according to thefe ancient and profound Greek verfes.

ε* αν γενοιτο χαρις ισθλα και κακα ;

αλλα εςι τις συγκρασις, ωστηχειν καλως·

This philofophy is expreffed, in more modern language, when it is faid " that the felf-begotten God had tied all things by the ponderous band of love," νοος αυτογενεθλος πασιν μιστηρι δεσμον περι,θη Ερωτος; which ponderous band of love is nothing elfe but attraction or gravitation, the great law of the material world. This power therefore was worfhipped under a variety of emblems (See d'Hankerville Recherches fur les Arts de la Greece,) fome of which fuggeft ideas, directly contrary to thofe which they were originally intended to excite; ideas, not holy and religious, but impure and impious. Plutarch de Ifid. & Ofir. cites Euripides to prove that the contention between two principles upheld the harmony of the univerfe; but Homer Il. 24. v. 527. makes Jupiter diftribute both good and evil; yet the preferving principle is in general perfonified by Jupiter, the deftroying by Hercules. The Sun ; Ζιυς Διονυσι, αιδης, πατεραης ; is the Lord of deftruction as well as of creation, the giver of life and the deftroyer. Orphic. Hymn. Edit Gefner. Since therefore all thofe attributes and epithets related to the fame Deity, and fince any one of them taken feparately, and perfonified, ferved as an index or fymbol of the whole, it is plain that any one of thefe perfonifications might arrogate to itfelf, in its figurative capacity, the title of fupreme. This feems to be the beft folution of the difficulty propofed in the beginning of this note; and will apply to cafes more difficult than the prefent, fince Ceres being the fertilifing or generative principle perfonified in a female, particularly deferves this epithet. We find therefore that v. 122 fhe is called, μεγαλη δια πρειαιαςος, the great Goddefs, of extenfive dominion. Which agrees with an infcription cf Gruter, ccix. i. ἡ συνοδος των μυςων της μεγαλης θεας Δημητρος : the fynod or affembly of the Priefts of the Great Goddefs Ceres.

END OF THE HYMNS OF CALLIMACHUS.

THE

LOCKS OF BERENICE.

TRANSLATED FROM THE LATIN OF CATULLUS.

T H E fage, who view'd the fhining heav'ns on high;
Explor'd the glories of th' expanded fky;

The locks of Berenice.] This poem is but the tranflation of a tranflation; the original Greek of Callimachus being long loft, and the Latin verfion, of which Voffius
fays, vix elegantius carmen Romano fermone fcriptum, being the work of the Roman
poet Catullus, a tender and elegant but licentious writer, who flourifhed in the age
of Cicero. The fubject of it is fuch, as nothing but the extravagance of court flattery, heightened by the credulity of fuperftition, could have made it a fit prefent
for Callimachus to offer, or for Ptolemy Euergetes to accept. That prince having un-
dertaken an expedition into Syria to punifh Antiochus Theus for the cruel treatment of
his Queen Berenice, who was Ptolemy's fifter, another Princefs of the fame name, who was
Ptolemy's wife, and the daughter of his uncle Magas, vowed that fhe would confecrate
her hair; (the finenefs of which formed no fmall ornament to her beauty,) provided
her hufband returned in fafety from the Syrian War. Ptolemy returned fafe and triumphant; the hair was lopped off, conveyed to the ifle of Cyprus, and folemnly dedicated in
the temple of Arfinoe, the Queen of Ptolemy Philadelphus, who was worfhipped on the
promontory Zephyrium under the name of the Zephyrian Venus. By the management

Whence rife the radiant orbs, where ftill they bend
Their wand'ring courfe, and where at length defcend,
Why dim eclipfe obfcures the blazing fun,   5
Why ftars at certain times to darknefs run,
How Trivia nightly ftole from realms above
To tafte, on Latmos' rocks the fweets of love,
Immortal Conon, bieft with fkill divine,
Amid the facred fkies behold me fhine,   10
Ev'n me, the beauteous hair, that lately fhed
Refulgent beams from Berenice's head ;
The lock fhe fondly vow'd with lifted arms,
Imploring all the pow'rs to fave from harms
Her dearer lord, when from his bride he flew,   15
To wreak ftern vengeance on th' Affyrian crew ;
While yet the monarch bore the pleafing fcars
Of fofter triumphs, and nocturnal wars.

O facred queen, do virgins ftill defpife
The joys of Venus, and the nuptial ties,   20

of the priefts, this confecrated hair fuddenly difappeared : Conon of Samos, a mathema-
tician and aftrologer refiding at Ptolemy's court, declared that the Queen's hair had
been fnatched to heaven ; and enforced his affertion by fhewing feven Stars, in the
form of a triangle near the tail of the Lion ; which had not as yet been taken within
any conftellation. The teftimony of a poet was only wanting to confirm the legend ; and this proof, the beautiful verfes of Callimachus fupplied. The Coma
Berenices, or Berenice's hair, was enrolled among the Stars, and continues to form a
conftellation to the prefent day.   2

When oft in bridal-rooms, their fighs and tears
Difturb the parent's heart with anxious fears ?
The tears defcend from friendly pow'rs above ;
The fighs, ye Gods ! are only fighs of love.
With tears like thefe fair Berenice mourn'd   25
When, for her virgin-fpoils, the monarch burn'd ;
With fighs like thefe fhe gave him all her charms,
And blefs'd the raptur'd bridegroom in her arms.
    But on the widow'd bed you wept alone,
And mourn'd the brother in the hufband gone.   30
What forrow then my penfive Queen oppreft,
What pangs of abfence tore her tender breaft ;
When, loft in woe, no trace remain'd behind
Of all her virgin-mirth, and ftrength of mind.
Hadft thou forgot the deed thy worth atchiev'd,   35
For which thy brows th' imperial crown receiv'd ;

V. 30. And mourned the brother in the hufband gone.] Hyginus in Poetica Aftro-
nomica, fuppofes that Berenice was really the fifter of Ptolemy, a fuppofition not altogether improbable, fince, we are told by Paufanias (in Attic) that by the Egyptian laws,
Brothers might marry their Sifters ; an inftitution, with which the Grecian Kings of
Egypt in feveral inftances complied. The commentators and tranflators of Callimachus
have implicity followed the opinion of Hyginus, which cannot, however, be founded
in truth, fince Ptolemy Euergetes married Berenice the daughter of his uncle Magas, and
his own Coufin German. Juftin. l. 26. c. 3. This circumftance of the near confan-
guinity of Ptolemy and Berenice may be indicated by the verfe in the text, and Berenice
is complimented for her delicacy of fentiment, in mourning with the tender affection
of a fifter rather than the ardent paffion of a lover.

V. 35. Hadft thou forgot, the deed thy worth atchiev'd,
    For which thy brows th' imperial crown received.]

Hyginus

The wond'rous deed, that plac'd thee far beyond
Thy fair compeers, and made a monarch fond.
But when for wars he left your tender arms,
What words you fpoke, with what endearing charms,   40
Still breath'd your foft complaints in mournful fighs,
And wip'd, with lifted hands, your ftreaming eyes.

Hyginus gives a romantic and incredible explanation of thefe verfes, in which he is
followed by modern commentators. But the poet certainly alludes to a great and memorable paffage in hiftory related by Plutarch in his life of Demetrius. Magas the brother uterine of Ptolemy Philadelphus, was by the influence of his mother, promoted to the
government of Cyrene and Libya. (Paufanias in Attic) He governed thofe provinces
many years with ability ; and having fortified his power by the affection of the natives
and by his marriage with Apamé, daughter of Antiochus Soter, king of Syria, he determined
to fecure to his own family, the dominion of countries which he had long ruled as a
viceroy. His revolt was fuccefsful ; but the fuppofed contingency which had firft infpired him with difaffection to his brother, failed to happen. He had reached the
extremity of old age, and his Queen Apamé had not brought him any male children
and only one daughter Berenice. Under this difappointment, Magas expreffed a defire
of compofing all differences with his Brother Ptolemy Philadelphus, by marrying his
only daughter with Ptolemy's eldeft fon, and giving, as her dower, the reflored alle-
giance of Cyrene and Libya. The treaty was accepted ; but Magas died before the con-
ditions of it were executed. The ambitious Apamé, unwilling that her hufband's in-
dependant kingdom fhould fink into a tributary province, invited to Cyrene Demetrius the
brother of Antigonus Gonatas, king of Macedon, promifing him her daughter in marriage. But the figure and accomplifhments of this young prince changed her refolution
and captivated her affections. Demetrius inftead of marrying the daughter, became the
paramour of the mother. But the flighted Berenice determined to revenge her wrongs.
A confpiracy was formed in the palace. Demetrius was flain in the embraces of
Apamé; the daughter conducting the affaffins to the chamber, and bed of her mother.
Apamé was fent into Syria, and Berenice repaired to Alexandria, and confummated
her marriage with young Ptolemy afterwards called Euergetes.

Didft

Didſt thou, fair nymph, lament by pow'r divine,
Or for an abſent lover only pine ?
Then to the Gods you vow'd with pious care,   45
A ſacred off'ring, your immortal hair,
With blood of ſlaughter'd bulls, would heav'n reſtore
Your Lord in triumph to his native ſhore ;
Should he, returning ſoon with high renown,
Add vanquiſh'd Aſia to th' Ægyptian crown :   50
And I fair lock, from orbs of radiance, now
Diffuſe new light to pay thy former vow.
But hear, O Queen, the ſacred oath I ſwear,   ⎫
But thy bright head, and yet remaining hair,   ⎬
I join'd unwilling this ætherial ſphere ;   ⎭   55
And well I know what woes the perjur'd feel :
But none can conquer unreſiſted ſteel.
Steel hew'd the mightieſt mountain to the ground,
That Sol beholds in his diurnal round,
Thro' Athos' rocky ſides a paſſage tore,   60
When firſt the Medes arriv'd at Phthia's ſhore :
Then winds and waves drove their ſwift ſhips along,
And through the new made gulph impell'd the throng,
It theſe withſtood not ſteel's all-conqu'ring blow,
What could thy hairs againſt ſo dire a foe ?   65
O mighty Jove ! may ſtill thy wrath divine   ⎫
Pour fierce deſtruction on their impious line,   ⎬
Who dug with hands accurſt the hollow mine ;   ⎭

Who firſt from earth could ſhining ore produce,
Firſt temper'd ſteel, and taught its various uſe.   70
   As thy bright locks bewail'd their ſiſter gone,.
Arſinoë's horſeman, Memnon's only ſon,
On flutt'ring wings deſcended from on high,
To bear the beauteous hairs above the ſky;
Then upward bent his flight, and ſoftly plac'd   75
Thy radiant lock in chaſte Arſinoë's breaſt,
Whom we Zephyritis and Venus name;
And on Canopus' ſhores her altars flame:
Where late the winged meſſenger came down
At her deſire, left Ariadne's crown   80
Should ſtill unrivall'd glitter in the ſkies;
And that thy precious hairs, a richer prize,
The ſpoils devoted to the pow'rs divine,
Might from the fields of light, as brightly ſhine.
Yet bath'd in tears I wing'd my rapid flight,   85
Swift from her ſhrine, to this ætherial height,
And plac'd amidſt the fair celeſtial ſigns
Thy lock, for ever with new glory ſhines,
Juſt by the Virgin in the ſtarry ſphere,
The ſavage Lion, and the Northern Bear;   90
Full to the Weſt, with ſparkling beams, I lead,
And bright Boötes in my courſe precede,
Who ſcarcely moves along the ætherial plain,
And late, and ſlowly, ſinks beneath the main.

                                                                Tho'

Tho' feet of Gods furround my throne by night,   95
And in the feas I fleep with morning light,
Yet, O Rhamnufian maid, propitious hear
The words of facred truth unaw'd by fear,
The words of truth I wifh not to conceal,
But ftill the dictates of my breaft reveal,   100
Tho' thefe refplendent orbs in wrath fhould rife,
And hurl me headlong from the flaming fkies,
Tho' plac'd on high, fad abfence I deplore,
Condemn'd to join my lovely queen no more,
On whofe fair head, while yet in virgin-bloom,   105
I drank unmeafur'd fweets, and rich perfume.

But now ye maids, and ev'ry beauteous dame,
For whom on nuptial nights the torches flame,
Tho' fondly wedded to fome lovely boy,
Your virgin-choice, and partner of your joy,   110
Forbear to tafte the pleafures of a bride,
Nor from the bofoms draw the veil afide,
Till oils in alabafter ye prepare,
And chaftely pour on Berenice's hair:
But I th' impure adultrefs ftill confound,   115
And dafh th' ungrateful off'ring to the ground.
From her no rich libation I demand,
And fcorn the gift of each unhallow'd hand.
But if the virtuous fair invoke my pow'r,
Unbounded blifs fhall crown the nuptial hour,   120

To

To her shall Concord from high heav'n descend,
And constant love her soft retreats attend.
　　And when, bright Queen, on solemn feasts, your eyes
Shall hail Arsinoë radiant in the skies ;
When she demands, bright-op'ning on your view,　　　　125
The sacred rights to heav'nly Venus due;
If thy lov'd lock appear resplendent there,
Let me with her an equal off'ring share.
But why should these surrounding stars detain
Thy golden hairs in this ætherial plain ?　　　　130
O could I join thy beauteous head once more,
The sacred head on which I grew before,
Tho' I should ever lose my light divine,
And moist Arcturus next the virgin shine.

END OF THE HYMNS.

THE

EPIGRAMS

OF

CALLIMACHUS.

EPIGRAM I.

A YOUTH, in hafte, to Mitylene came,
And anxious, thus reveal'd his am'rous flame

ΞΕΙΝΟΣ Αταρνειτης τις ανηρετο Πιττακον ετως
Τον Μιτυληναιον, παιδα τον Υρραδιυ.

Epigram I.] This excellent epigram has been much celebrated by ancient poets and philofophers; and likewife by modern commentators, particularly Salmafius, who calls it " Nobiliffimum epigramma." Diog: nes Laertius has tranfcribed it in his life of Pittacus, and the fame ftory is told, in profe, by the Scholiaft on the Prometheus of Æfchylus. Laertius tells us that Pittacus gave this ad ice to the young man, becaufe he himfelf had felt great inconvenience from an unequal marriage.   Martial carries this idea ftill farther, and fays that every man fhould chufe a wife not from an equal, but an inferior ftation, probably thinking that, unlefs this were the cafe, the hufband muft comply with the incli-

'   nations

To Pittacus the wife ; O facred Sire,
For two fair nymphs I burn with equal fire,
One lovely maid in rank and wealth like me,   5
But one fuperior, and of high degree.
Since both return my love, and each invites
To celebrate with her the nuptial rites,

Λττα γερον, ϴοιος με καλει γαμος· η μια μεν δη
   Νυμφη κỷ ϖλυτω κỷ γενεη κατ' εμε.
Ηδ' ετερη ϖροϐεϐηκε. τι λωϊον ; ει δ' αγε συν μοι   5
   Βυλευσον, ϖοτερην εις υμεναιον αγω.

nations of his wife in every circumftance, and have no will of his own *. It feems the
Ladies of ancient Greece and Rome had the fame paffion for governing their hufbands,
and probably the fame fuccefs as the fair fex in modern times; and when they were affifted by fuperiority of rank and fortune, the hufband muft, of neceffity, be reduced to a
cypher. I refer this Epigram to the ferious confideration of certain ingenious perfons,
commonly called *Fortune-Hunters*.

In Laertius the laft verfe but one begins in this manner; 'Ουτω και συ, Διων; as if Callimachus had addreffed his Epigram to a friend called Dion; but Huetius feems to have
reftored the true reading which the tranflator has followed. The thought in the two
laft lines has been copied by Bias †, Ovid ‡, and Erafmus. § And the epigram itfelf has
been attributed by fome to Alcaeus, though probably without foundation. Suidas indeed
has beftowed much commendation on it without naming the author § ; but fince
Laertius afcribes it to Callimachus, there can be little room for doubt. And it may be
obferved that this, and the following Epigrams, are not to be found in any feparate manufcript, having been collected by learned men, at different times, and at laft publifhed in
the Anthologia.

* Mart. Lib. VIII. Epigr. 12.   † Apud Gell. Lib V. cap. II.
‡ Herord. IX. 32.   § In Chil.   ¶ in verb. Αττα, Βιμϐ.ξ, Χρηματα

                                                                Perplex'd

Perplex'd with doubts, for fage advice I come :
Whom fhall I wed ? 'Tis you muft fix my doom.   10
So fpake th' impatient youth ; th' attentive fage
Rais'd the fupport of his declining age,
An ancient ftaff; and pointing to the ground
Where fportive ftriplings lafh'd their tops around
With eager ftrokes ; let yonder boys, he cry'd,   15
Solve the difpute, and your long doubts decide.
The youth drew nigh, and liften'd with furprize,
Whilft from the laughing croud thefe words arife,
" Let equal tops with equal tops contend."
The boys prevail'd, and foon the conteft end.   20
The youth departing fhun'd the wealthy dame,
And chofe th' inferior maid to quench his flame.
   Go thou, my friend, obey the fage, and lead
An equal beauty to thy nuptial bed.

Εἶπεν. ὁ δὲ σκιπῶνα, γεροντικον ὁπλον, ἀείρας,
  Ἡνίδε, κεινοι σοι πᾶν ἐρεουσιν ἔπος.
Οἱ δ' ἀρ' ὑπο πληγῆσι θοας ῥέμβικας ἔχοντες
  Ἐτρεφον εὑρείη παιδες ἐνι τριόδῳ.
Κεινων ἔρχεο, φησι, μετ' ἴχνια. Χὼ μεν ὑπέςη   10
  Πλησιον. οἱ δ' ἐλεγον, Τὴν κατα σαυτον ἐλα.
Ταυτ' ἀΐων ὁ ξεινος ἐρεισατο μείζονος οἴκᾳ
  Δραξασθαι, παιδων κληδονι συνθεμενος·
Τὴν δ' ὀλιγην, ὡς κεινος, ἐς οἴκον ἐπηγετο νυμφην,   15
  Οὕτω κ̀ συ γ' ἰων την κατα σαυτον ἐλα.

II.

I hear, O friend, the fatal news
  Of Heraclitus death.
A sudden tear my cheek bedews,
  And sighs suppress my breath.

For I must often call to mind,
  How from the croud we run ;
And how to jesting still inclin'd,
  We sported in the fun.

Εἶπε τις, Ηρακλειτε, τεον μορον· ἐς δε με δακρυ
  Ηγαγεν, ἐμνησθην δ' ἱσσακις ἀμφοτεροι
Ηλιον ἐν λεσχῃ κατεδυσαμεν. ἀλλα συ μεν πε
  Ξειν' Αλλικαρνησσευ τετράπαλαι σποδιη·

Epigram : II.] In this epigram Callimachus pays a most elegant compliment to the memory of his beloved friend and cotemporary Poet Heraclitus, who was a native of Halicarnassus, and, like our author, excelled in elegy. But his writings are long since destroyed by time, nothing remains except his name preserved in these beautiful lines ; and we have probably much reason to regret that the prophecy, contained in them, has not been fulfilled. His name is likewise mentioned by Läertius, who has given this epigram in the life of Heraclitus the philosopher, and by Strabo, who calls him the friend of Callimachus *,

V. 9. And sported in the sun.] Εν λεσχη κατεδυσαμιν. The word λισχη was used in different ages. Its original signification was a place exposed to the sun, where philosophers met for the sake of conversation, a custom, according to Arrian borrowed from the

* Strab. Lib. XᵢV.

Sophists

Alas! he's gone, and part we muſt,
And repartee's no more;
But, tho' my friend be ſunk in duſt,
His muſe ſhall ever ſoar.

The dart of death ſhall never fly
To ſtop her waving wings;
Like Philomel ſhe mounts on high
And ſtill, like her, ſhe ſings.

III.

I, Timon, hated human race;
Ye paſſengers be gone, .
Curſe as ye will, but leave the place,
And let me reſt alone.

Αἱ δε τεχι ζωϐσιν ἀηδονες, ἧσιν ὁ παντων
Αρπακτης ἀϊδης ἐκ ἐπι χειρα βαλει.

Τιμων μισανθρωπος ἐσοικεω· ἀλλα παρελθε,
Οἰμωζειν εἰπας πολλα, παρελθε μονον.

Sophiſts of India. Afterwards it came to mean any public place where the common people reſorted, ſuch as the ſhops of ſmiths in Greece, and of barbers in Rome, which were much frequented, particularly in winter. Some ancient authors inform us that theſe Leſche were conſecrated to Apollo. Vulcanius and Dacier.

Epigram; III.] Plutarch has inſerted this epitaph in his life of Anthony; and though

the

IV.

Say, Timon, funk in night, abhor'ſt thou now
The light above, or gloomy ſhades below!   ˙
" I hate the ſhades, ſince fill'd with human kind
" In greater numbers than I left behind."

Τιμων (ἐ γαρ ἐτ' ἐσσι) τι τοι, φαος ἡ σκοτος ἐχθρον;
Τ'ο σκοτος, ὑμεων γαρ πλειονες εἰν ἀϊδη.

the name of Timon the man-hater is, doubtleſs, familiar to every reader, yet as his ſtory
may not be ſo generally known, I ſhall give a ſhort abſtract of what Plutarch has ſaid
concerning him.

Timon was a citizen of Athens, and lived in the times of the Peloponneſian war.
He deſpiſed and avoided the converſation of mankind, but, when he met Alcibiades,
who was then very young, would ſalute him with great kindneſs. Apemantus, being
ſurpriſed at this preference, aſked Timon the reaſon of it, " I love him," he replied,
" becauſe I foreſee that he will one day ʾbe the cauſe of much miſchief to the Athenians."
His only friend was Apemantus, a man of the ſame moroſe humour, and his faithful
imitator. Every action of Timon's life, and every word that he ſpoke expreſſed his deteſt-
ation of mankind. And, after his death, he was buried at Halæ, a remote place on the
ſea coaſt, that his bones might reſt undiſturbed by their deteſted Society. An epitaph expreſſive of his predominant paſſion, and ſaid to be written by himſelf, was engraven on his tomb, though Plutarch tells us, that this by Callimachus was more generally known. Lucian has likewiſe introduced him in one of his dialogues, upon which
our immortal Shakeſpeare is ſaid to have founded his celebrated play, Timon of Athens.

Epigram: IV.] Timon finds himſelf more unhappy in the infernal ſhades than he
had been on earth, merely becauſe he is ſurrounded by greater numbers of mankind.
Auſonius relates that he was ſtoned to death by the Athenians; but I rather believe the
teſtimony of Plutarch and Suidas, that their curſes and maledictions put an end to his life.
Another Man-hater, called Cnemon, is mentioned by Ammonius and Ælian.   Brodæus.

V.

A facred fhell Zephyritis divine,
Fair Selenæa offers at thy fhrine,

Κογχος ἐγω, Ζεφυριτι, παλαιτερος· ἀλλα συ νυν με

Epigram: V.] Selenæa, the daughter of Clinias, a nobleman of Smyrna, dedicates a Nautilus (then a very great curiofity) to the famous Ægyptian princefs Arfinöe, who was worfhipped as a Goddefs under the names of Zephyritis, Venus and Chloris, as we find in the Coma Berinices.

This epigram is perhaps unequalled in any language, not on account of pointed wit, which feldom charafterizes the Greek Anthology, but for beauty of verfification, and becaufe it contains the whole natural hiftory of the Nautilus, in the compafs of a very few lines. Oppian's defcription of the fame animal, tho' he lived in the age of the Antonines, above three hundred years after Callimachus, and had therefore better opportunities of information, comes far fhort of this, being more verbofe, lefs poetical, and indeed feems little more than a verfification of Pliny, whofe account of this extraordinary fpecies of Polypus I fhall give in his own words.

" Among the greateft wonders of nature is that fifh called by fome Nautilus, and by others Pompilus. When he wifhes to come above water, he turns on his back, raifes himfelf up by little and little, and that he may fwim with greater facility, difcharges all the water within him from a pipe, which may be compared to a commonfewer. His body bei ; lightened, he turns up his two foremoft claws or arms, and ftretches out between them a membrance of wonderful finenefs. This ferves him for a fail above water, and with his remaining arms he works his way under it, directing his courfe with his tail in the midft, to fupply the place of a helm. Thus he makes way in the fea, like a fhip under fail; but, if he fhould happen to be frightened, immediately draws in water to encreafe his weight, and plunges to the bottom." *

The learned reader may compare this with Oppian's Halicutics, Book Ift. V. 338. and feq.

* Plin. Hift. Natur. Lib. I ', Cap. 47. Ed. Hardnin.

And

And thus thy Nautilus is doubly bleſs'd,
Since giv'n by her, and ſtill by thee poſſeſs'd.
Of late ſmall tackling from my body grew ;   5
Thin ſails I ſpread, when winds propitious blew,
But when the ſeas were calm, to gain the ſhores,
I ſtretch'd my little feet, like lab'ring oars,
And, from my buſy limbs and painted pride,
Was call'd a Polyp as I ſtem'd the tide ;   10
Till driv'n by winds, on Coan rocks I ſhone,
And now recline before Arſinoë's throne.
Depriv'd of life no more in ſeas I reſt,
Or draw young Halcyons from the wat'ry neſt ;

Κυπρι, Σεληναιης ἀιθεμα πρωτον ἐχεις
Ναυτιλον· ὁς πελαγεσσιν ἐπεπλεον· ἐι μεν ἀηται,
  Τεινας οἰκειων λαιφος ἀπο προτονων.
Ἐι δε γαληναιη, λιπαρη Θεος, ἐλος ἐρεσσων   5
  Ποσσιν, ἱν ὡσπερ κỳ τὔνομα συμφερεται.
Ἐς τ' ἐπεσον παρα Θινας Ιὔλιδος, ὀφρα γενωμαι
  Σοι το περισκεπτον παιγνιον Αρσινοης.
Μηδε μοι ἐν Θαλαμησιν ἐθ' ὡς παρος, ἐιμι γαρ ἀπνους,

V. 12. Till driv'n by winds on Coan rocks I ſhone.] The original is Ἐς τ' ἐπεσον παρα
Θιας Ιὔλιδος ; and Vulcanius imagines that Julis was the ſame with Julis polis, a city in
the neighbourhood of Alexandria. But this conjecture is certainly without foundation,
the city of Julipolis not being in exiſtence when Callimachus wrote. Madame Dacier
has rectified the miſtake : Julis was ſituated in the iſle of Cos, and a Nautilus brought
from thence would no doubt be more acceptable to the queen of Ægypt, becauſe her
huſband Ptolemy Philadelphus was born in that iſland.

But

But be this boon to Clinia's daughter giv'n,   15
A virtuous maid and fav'rite of high heav'n ;
The precious boon let Selenæa gain,
When she from Smyrna ploughs the foaming main.

Τικτει τ' αινοτερης ωεον Αλκυονης.   10
Κλεινιε αλλα θυγατρι διδοι χαριν. οιδε γαρ εσθρα
Ρεζειν, κ̃ Σμυρνης εςιν απ' Αιολιδος.

V. 15. But be this boon to Clinias' daughter giv'n.] It is not to be suppofed, from thefe words, that Selenæ wifhes to plunder the neft of the poor timorous Halcyon, and to feed like a Nautilus upon her eggs. She begs the Goddefs to grant a profperous voyage from Smyrna, and hopes to fee thefe nefts floating on the ocean, as a fign that her prayers are heard. For the ancients imagined, as we learn from the fable of Ceyx and Halcyone, that this bird was particularly favoured by the Gods, who decreed that there fhould be no ftorm, while fhe continues to fit on her neft, which floats on the furface of the Sea *. This is confirmed by the following lines of Theocritus.

X' αλκυοιις ςορισιωιτι τα κυματα, ταν τι θαλασσαν,
Τον τι ιοτον, τον τ'ευρον, ὁς εχατα φυκια κινιι.
'Αλκυοιις, γλαυκαις Νηρϊσι ται τι μαλιςα
'Ορνιχων ιφιλαθη †.

May Halcyons fmooth the waves, and calm the feas,
And the rough fouth-caft fink into a breeze ;
Halcyons, of all the birds that haunt the main,
Moft lov'd and honour'd by the Nereid train.   FAWKES.

But it feems that neither the love of the Nereids, nor the favour of Jupiter himfelf were fufficient to defend them from the ravages of the Nautilus, fmall and inconfiderable as it is ; an inftance, among many others, of the monftrous abfurdities contained in the Pagan Mythology. From thefe fables in all probability, the phrafe, Halcyon days, was applied to fignify any uncommon piece of good fortune.

* Ovid. Metamorphos. Lib XI.   † Theocr. Idyll. VII. and. 57.

A

VI.

A Samian gave me birth, the facred bard
Whofe hofpitable feaft great Homer fhar'd;
For beauteous Iole my forrows flow,
And royal Eurytus opprefs'd with woe:
But mightier names my lafting fame fhall crown,
And Homer give Creophilus renown.

Τȣ Σαμιȣ ϖονος ειμι, δομῳ ϖοτε θειον Ομηρον
Δεξαμενȣ· κλαιω δ' Ευρυτον, ἱσσ' επαθεν,
Και ξανθην Ιολειαν. Ομηρȣ νυν δε καλευμαι
Γραμμα· Κρεωφυλῳ, Ζευ φιλε, τȣτο μεγα;

Epigram: VI.] We may fuppofe this epigram to have been wrote on fome blank page of a poem entitled the deftruction of Oechalia, afcribed by fome to Homer, but by Callimachus to Crefphylus. And hence he tells us that the name of Homer will immortalize the poem of Creophylus, a Samian who entertained this renowed bard of antiquity for fome time in his houfe, and, if we may believe Plutarch, his grand children preferved the writings of Homer*. The fubject of this poem, according to Euftathius, was the ravaging of Oechalia by Hercules, becaufe Eurytus king of the country refufed him his daughter Jole†. Euftathius gives this epigram, and agrees in opinion with our author, but Strabo tells us, that Homer left his manufcript with Crefphylus, who was afterwards fuppofed to have been the writer‡. Let the learned decide.

     * Plutarch. in vit. Lycurg.   † Euftath in Il. II.   ‡ Strab. Lib. XIV.

A

VII.

A pious youth approaching where
  His ftepdame's body lay,
Officious crown'd her ftatue there
  With flow'rets frefh and gay.

Nor thought his father's wife, when dead,
  Her malice could retain;
The ftatue thunder'd on his head
  And fix'd him to the plain.

Ye fofter-fons avoid his doom
  Nor hang a flow'ry wreath
Around an envious ftepdame's tomb,
  Left ye too fink in death.

Στηλην μητρυιης, μικραν λιθον, ἐϛεφε κꭒρος,
  Ως βιον, ἠλλαχθαι κ̓ τροπον οἰομενος.
Η δε ταφω κλινθεισα κατεκτανε ϖαιδα ϖεσꭒσα·
  Φευγετε μητρυιης κ̓ ταφον οἱ ϖρογονοι.

Epigram VII.] This is one of the few Greek epigrams that may be termed humor-ous though the fubject is fufficiently tragical, the boy having paid dear for his rafhnefs. Bentley propofes an alteration in the phrafe μικραν λιθον, becaufe fays he, how could fo fmall a ftatue kill a great boy. But in this inftance Madame Dacier has beat our learned Grammarian at his own weapons, by giving the true fignification, namely that this ex-preffion fignifies *felitum marmor, lapis politus,* when the word μικρꭒς is in the feminine.

The

VIII.

No wreaths of ivy Theætetus crown,
Who chofe the certain path to high renown
Unfkilful judges his great worth defpife,
And undeferving bards obtain the prize:
Yet envy not, my friend, their fhort-liv'd fame;
Admiring Greece fhall ftill refound thy name.

Ηλθε Θεχιτητος καθαρην οδον. ει δ' επι κισσον
    Τον τεον ὐχ αὐτη, Βακχε, κελευθος ἀγει.
Αλλων μεν κηρυκες ἐπι βραχυν ὐνομα καιρου
    Φθεγξονται, κεινυ δ' Ελλας ἀει σοφιαν.

The ftatues and pillars raifed over dead bodies among the ancients, were crowned with Parfley; and hence people labouring under a mortal difeafe were faid τυ σιλνυ δυθυι, "to ftand in need of Parfley." Servius gives the origin of thefe pillars in the following words, "In the times of our anceftors, noblemen were buried at the foot of fome diftant hill, and huge pillars or pyramids were placed over their graves in token of their great quality." But thefe pyramids were always erected over the bodies of kings and rich men only. Brodæus.

Epigram VIII.] There was an annual competition among the Grecian poets at the feftival of Bacchus, when the victorious bard was rewarded with a crown of Ivy. And the fi.ft Ptolemy's, fond of adopting the cuftoms of a country where their anceftors had lived, introduced this at Alexandria, as we may learn from the following lines of Theocritue.

'Ουδε Διωιυσε τις αιηρ ιερης κατ' αγωνας
'ἱκιτ' ἱσιτυμιιος λιγυραν ἀναμελψαι ἀυιδαν,.
Ω, ἁ ὑστιται ἀνταξιοι ὡπασι τιχνας *.

                * Theocr. Idyll. v. 112.

IX.

The feweſt words are ſtill expreſt
By him who gain'd at Bacchus feaſt,
He ſays in ſimple phraſe, " I've won.''
But Phœbus more unlucky ſon,

Μικρη τις, Διονυσε, καλα πρησσοντι ποιητη
Ρησις. ὁ μεν, νικω, φησι το μικροτατον.

" Nor does any ſkilful bard attend the ſacred competition of Bacchus, without receiving a reward equal to his merit from thee."

Theætitus was an unſucceſsful competitor for this prize, and a friend of Callimachus,
who conſoles him for his misfortune. The Greek Scholiaſt mentions one of the ſame
name a ſcholar of Plato, but certainly not the perſon addreſſed by our poet, who ſeems
to have been his contemporary——Horace alludes to the above mentioned cuſtom in his
firſt ode,

> Me doctarum hederæ proemia frontium
>
> Diis miſcent ſuperis:

And Mr. Francis, not adverting to this poetical competition, and being miſled by
Ruigerſius, has evidently perverted the ſenſe of this paſſage by exchanging the pronoun
me for *te*, and thus transfering the crown of Ivy from the poet to the patron.

> An Ivy wreath, fair learning's prize,
>
> Raiſes Mecænas to the ſkies.   FRANCIS.

Epigram IX.] This epigram may be called a continuation of the laſt; and though
the humour of it plainly turns upon one word νικω, it is not a little ſurpriſing that the five
Annotators who have commented on it, ſhould diſagree ſo much among themſelves, and
find three or four difficulties in every line. The ſignification ſeems to be this: the poet
who gains the prize, at the feaſt of Bacchus, ſatisfied with his victory, makes no long
ſpeech, but ſimply tells his friend " I have won." The unfortunate competitor, on the
other hand diſguſted with his loſs, makes a long harrangue to the multitude; in order to

Whose prize is gone, whose hopes are croft,
Should any afk how he had loft,
On fickle fortune throws the blame,
And tells in long harangues his claim:
No judges hence the prize affign;
O may the fhorteft phrafe be mine.

X.

Beneath this tomb, in facred fleep,
   The virtuous Saon lies;
Ye paffengers forbear to weep,
   A good man never dies.

Ω δε συ μη πνευσης ενδεξιος, ην τις ερηται
   Πως εβαλες; φησι, σκληρα τα γιγνομενα.
Τω μερμηριξαντι τα μηνδικα, τυτο γενοιτο
   Τεπος, εμοι δ' ω 'ναξ η βραχυσυλλαβιη.

Τηδε Σαων ο Δικωνος Ακανθιος ιερον υπνον
   Κοιμαται. Θνησκειν μη λεγε τυς αγαθυς.

regain his reputation, and, like many people now a days, calls his mifconduct a misfortune. But, all this eloquence being loft on the judges, Callimachus wifhes, that when he
contends for the prize, he may need only to fpeak the word expreffive of victory.

  Epigram X.] It is uncertain whether Saon was a Thracian or Egyptian. Callimachus calls him a native of Acanthus, and Stevens writes that there were two cities of
that name, the one in Thrace and the other in Egypt.—Obfopæus.—Were it worth
                               while.

XI.

Say, doſt thou ſeek Timarchus now,
To talk with him in ſhades below,
Of truths before unknown to thee,
As, where th' immortal mind muſt be ?
Go ſearch the fam'd Elyſian plain,
For ancient Ptolemæus train,
You'll find him there (his body's duſt)
Amid th' aſſemblies of the juſt.

Ην διζη Τιμαρχον εν αιδος, οφρα πυθηαι
Η τι περι ψυχης η παλι πως εσεται.
Διζεσθαι, φυλης Πτολεμαιδος, υιεα πατρος
Παυσανιυ· δηεις δ' αυτον εν ευσεβεων.

while to ſettle the diſpute, the preference would certainly be given to the latter opinion, as it is much more probable that our Poet ſhould write an epitaph on a countryman of his own than on a ſtranger.

Short and ſimple as this epigram is, the Commentators have not failed to differ about it, and to perplex the ſenſe, as uſual. Vulcanius ſuppoſes, without the leaſt ſhadow of reaſon, that the word ύπνος ſhould be tranſlated perpetual; Madam Dacier quotes Virgil and Horace, and Grævius Æſchylus and Lycophron, to give the reader a piece of information, which a child would have told him, namely, that the word *Sleep* is ſometimes uſed to ſignify *Death*: one inſtance of the trifles to which theſe learned Scholiaſts will deſcend, when they can find nothing in an Author to diſpute about.

Epigram XI.] Obſopæus tells us that Timarchus was an Athenian, a diſciple of Epicurus, and that he had long diſputed concerning the nature of the ſoul. But Madam Dacier calls him a Pythagorean, and ſays that Callimachus did not believe in the immortality of the ſoul; though certainly the words in the text contain no proof of this laſt opinion.

XII.

Here Theris lies in endleſs reſt ;
A little ſpot contains the gueſt,
Once victor in th' Equeſtrian ſtrife,
And now has reach'd the goal of life,
His body ſhort, his tomb not long,
And ſhort, like them, ſhall be my ſong.

Συντομος ἦν ὁ ξεινος, ὁ κ̣ ταφος. ἐ μακ̣α λεξω,
Θηρις Αρι;αιε, Κρης, ὑπ' ἐμοι, δολιχον.

opinion. At the ſame time, if I were inclined to heſitate about the authenticity of any part of our author, this and the preceding epigram afford moſt room for doubt, the ſtile bearing a greater reſemblance to the enlightened times of Chriſtianity, than the dark ages of Heatheniſm. And we are informed by the Scholiaſt on Ariſtophanes that the Ptolemaic tribe in Egypt were ſuſpected of having apoſtolized from the ancient religion *. To which it may be added that the laſt line ends in the ſame manner with the fifth verſe of the firſt Pſalm, ἐν ἐυσεβιων in " piis coetibus" ἐν βαλη δικαιων, which has exactly the ſame ſignification †.

Epigram XII.]   The force of this epigram ſeems to have been miſunderſtood both by Stephens, in his Latin tranſlation, and by ſome other commentators in their annotations. It conſiſts chiefly in a Pun in the word Δολιχος, which may be tranſlated both by the adjective long, and by a place for Horſeracing, ſaid to have been 20 or 25 Stadia in length. Theris, though a little man, had once obtained the prize in this conteſt, and the Poet expreſſes his victory in the race, and his victory over life (if I may be allowed the expreſſion) by a ſingle word. The reader may obſerve that the tranſlator has attempted to preſerve the double meaning in Engliſh ; but a complete transfuſion of ſuch

* In ολαις.   † Septuag. Ψυχα. I.

expreſſions.

XIII.

When you, my friend, to Cyzicus repair,
Good Hippacus and Didyme the fair
Are found with eafe, amid th' extended town,
Since both defcend from fires of great renown :
Then fadly tell their fon's untimely doom,
For youthful Critias lies beneath this tomb.

Κυζικον ην ελθης, ολιγος πονος Ιππακον ευρειν
Και Διδυμην. αφανης ετι γαρ ή γενεη.
Και σφιν ανιηρον μεν εφεις επος, εμπα δε λεξον
Τευθ', οτι τον κεινων υιον εχω Κριτιαν.

expreffions into any modern language muſt, neceſſarily, be impoſſible. Suidas would make us believe, though Kuſter differs from him, that a grave accent was placed over the penult of the word Δολιχος fignifying *long*; but an acute accent over the laſt fyllable but one, when the meaning was a *Horſe race* *. And if we may give credit to what fome Grammarians affirm, namely that the fole ufe of the Greek accents was to modulate the tone of the voice in reading, probably Suidas may be in the right.

Epigram XIII.] This epigram, or epitaph, if I may fo call it, is a proper contraſt to the preceding. being wrote in the fimple ſtile of ancient Greek Anthology. Indeed the fubject feems too pathetic to admit of any play upon words. or quaintnefs of expreſſion; but we know nothing of either Critias or his parents. The city of Cyzicus was fituated on the Propontis.

* Suid. in verb. Δολιχ.

XIV.

Stranger. Where's Charidas buried? I fpeak without fear.
Monument. The fon of Arimnas lies mouldering here.
Stranger. O tell me, good Charidas, what's in thy tomb?
Charidas. Inquifitive mortal, there's nothing but gloom.
Str. Say wilt thou return?—*Char.* Wicked trifler begone.
Str. What's Pluto?—*Char.* A fable, and we are undone.
If there's pleafure in death, and fure I fpeak true,
Pellæus' fat ox will be happy as you.

Η ρ' ύπο σοι Χαριδα; αναπαυεται; ει τον Αριμνα
  Τ8 Κυρηναι8 παιδα λεγεις, ύπ' εμοι.
Ω Χαριδα, τι τα νερθε; πολυ σκοτος. αι δ' ανοδοι τι;
  Ψευδος. ό δε Πλ8των; μυθος. απωλομεθα.
Ούτος εμος λογος ύμμιν αληθινος. ει δε τον ήδυν
  Β8λει, Πελλαι8 β8; μεγας εις αιδην.

Epigram XIV.] A ftranger comes towards a fepulchral Monument to inquire after the welfare of his dead friend Charidas. The monument anfwers his firft queftion, and Charidas the reft. And we may obferve that Callimachus, like Homer, gives life and vigour to the moft inanimate parts of the creation. His genius, like the lyre of Orpheus, infpires trees, ftones, iflands and mountains with fpeech, motion and activity. This is the true fpirit of Poetry. It muft, however, be confeffed, that the prefent epigram is the moft ludicrous in the whole collection, and, at firft view, feems to favour a little of that Atheifm with which our author has been taxed. But let us not decide too haftily : many of the Greek Poets and Philofophers imagined that departed fpirits exifted, if not in mifery, at leaft in a ftate of infipid indolence, and diffatisfaction. Nobody ever denied
                                                                        that

XV.

Who knows if any pow'r will give
Another day for him to live ?

Δαιμονα τις δ᾽ εὐ οἰδε τον ἀυριον ; ἠνικα και σε

that Homer believed in a future ftate, and yet we find Achilles as unhappy in the infernal fhades as Charidas is reprefented in this epigram.

Μη δη μοι θανατον γε παραυδα, φαιδιμ᾽ 'Οδυσσιν *.
Βυλοιμην κ᾽ επαρυρος εων θητευμιν ἀλλω
'Ανδρι παρ᾽ ἀκληρω ᾡ μη βιοτος πολυς ειη
'Η πασιν νικυσσι κατα φθιμινοισιν ἀνασσιν.
Talk not of ruling in this dol'rous gloom,
Nor think vain words (he cry'd) can eafe my doom :
Rather I chufe laborioufly to bear
A weight of woes, and breathe the vital air,
A flave to fome poor hind that toils for bread ;
Than reign the fcepter'd monarch of the dead. POPE.

V. 8. Pellæus' fat Ox will be happy as you.] Some of the Commentors, and particularly Stephens, have, with wonderful ingenuity, transformed the ox of Pellæus into
the Bucephalus of Alexander. And others, with equal reafon, fuppofe that Pellæus himfelf is meant, and not his Ox, becaufe a famous boafter of antiquity was called Philippus
Pellæus. The word Philippus probably occafioned the firft miftake ; for, with thefe gen-
tlemen, a word to the wife is commonly fufficient. Madame Dacier alone has ftuck clofe
to the original ; and, for the honour of the fex, I fhall give her tranflation of the laft part
of this epigram in her own words. " Mais le bon eft, que le gros boeuf de Pelleus
y eft auffi-bien avec fon immortalite, que les autres."

Epigram XV.] This epigram contains little interefting : for we know nothing of
either Charmis, or his father. Brodæus afcribes it to Simonides ; but whoever was the

---

* Hom. Odyff. XI. v. 487.

writer.

Methymne too, the city's name,
  Engraven on her tomb
With old Timotheus, gives to fame
  Her much-lamented doom.

Tho' time will fome relief impart
  To foothe a father's woe,
Deep forrow rends her hufband's heart,
  His tears for ever flow.

XVII.

The Samian virgins us'd often to play
With Crethis the witty, the pleafant and gay,

Στηλη, ϗ Μηθυμνα τεη ϖολις· η μεγα φημι
  Χηρον ανιασθαι σον ϖοσιν Ευθυμενη.

Κρηθιδα την ϖολυμυθον, επιςαμενην καλα ϖαιζειν,

but the name of the father, grandfather, the place of nativity, refidence, &c. And in
every Church-yard we fee monuments erected to the memory of obfcure perfons, remarkable for nothing, but that they were born, and that they died; a proof of Dr. Young's
celebrated pofition, that the love of fame is the univerfal paffion.

V. 5. Methymne too, the city's name] Methymne was a city of Lefbos the inhabitants of which were celebrated for making wine, which Galen calls fweet and fragrant.
This place is fometimes named Methone. Brodæus.

Epigram XVII.] There is nothing remarkable here except the word ἀποβριζω. Athenæus remarks that ἀπζω had the fame fignification with καθευδω; and a Goddefs called

But now, when they feek her, fhe cannot be found,
Their fportive companion fleeps here under ground,
Difcharging the debt which to nature we owe;
For all muft defcend to the regions below.

XVIII.

Had never veffel crofs'd the main,
Our prefent grief had been in vain ;
But we for Sopolis muft weep,
Now plung'd beneath the whelming deep :
The furges tofs his breathlefs frame ;
An empty tomb preferves his name.

Διζονται Σαμιων πολλακι θυγατερες,
Ηδιςαν συνεριθον, αει λαλον· η δ' αποϐριζει
Ενθαδε τον πασαις ὑπνον οφειλομενον.

Ωφελε μηδ' εγενοντο θοαι νεες. ὀ γαρ ἀν ἡμεις
Παιδα Διοκλειδῳ Σωπολιν εςενομεν.
Νυν δ' ὁ μεν εὶν ἁλι πυ φερεται νεκυς, αυτι δ' εκεινε
Οὐνομα κὴ κενεον σαμα παρερχομεθα.

Brizo was fuppofed to prefide over divination by dreams. Sacred rites were paid to this Deity in the Ifland of Delos; and thofe perfons who pretended to foretel future events by dreams were called Brizomantes. Vulcanius.

Epigram XVIII.] It was ufual among the ancients to raife a Cenotaph or empty monument, to the memory of thofe who fuffered death by fhipwreck, or any other extra-

I   traordinary

XIX.

Not on the land could Lycus die,
Nor in his native Naxos lie,
But on the main by tempefts toft,
His life and fhip together loft,
When firft he left Ægina's fhore,
And o'er him now the furges roar :
An empty marble only keeps
His name from the devouring deeps.
Obey my words and fhun the feas,
Ye mariners, in times like thefe,
When to the main the goat declines,
Nor in the fky with Phœbus fhines.

Ναξιος ἐκ ἐπι γης ἐθανεν Λυκος, ἀλλ' ἐνι ποντω
  Ναυν ἁμα κỳ ψυχην ειδεν ἀπολυμενην,
Εμποϱος Αἰγινϑεν ὁτ' ἐπλεε. χὼ μεν ἐν ὑγϱη
  Νεκϱος. ἐγω δ' ἀλλως ἔνομα τυμϐος ἐχων,
Κηϱυσσω παναληθες ἐπος τοδε. φευγε θαλαττη
  Συμμισγειν ἐριφων ναυτιλε δυομϽνων.

traordinary accident; and fuch monuments are fometimes built in our own times, in honour of illuftrious perfons. Dacier.

Epigram XIX.] Lycus, a merchant of Naxos, one of the Cyclades, having been loft in a ftorm, while he was on a voyage from the ifland of Ægina fituated in the Saronic Gulph, the poet laments his fate, and warns mariners againft going to fea, when Capricorn fets at fun-rife. For the ancients imagined that the rifing and fetting of this con-

XX.

Nicoteles lies buried here,
Philippus o'er him drops a tear,
And mourns his twelfth and only boy,
The father's hope, his pride and joy.

XXI.

This morning we beheld with ſtreaming eyes
The flames from Melanippus' body riſe ;
At eve, fair Baſile reſign'd her breath,
Diſdaining to ſurvive a brother's death ;

Δωδεκετη τον παιδα πατηρ απεθηκε Φιλιππος
Ενθαδε, την πολλην ελπιδα, Νικοτελην.

Ηωοι Μελανιππον εθαπτομεν, ηελιυ δε
Δυσμενυ Βασιλω κατθανε παρθενικη,
Αυτοχερι. ζωειν γαρ, αδελφεον εν πυρι θεισα,

ſtellation either with, or in oppoſition to the ſun, were always attended with uncommonly
high winds.

Epigram XX.] This little epitaph is rendered intereſting by the uncommon circumſtance of a father lamenting the death of his twelfth ſon. Stephens, for I know not what
reaſon, has tranſlated the word Δωδεκετη, quartam trieterida.

Epigram XXI.] The particulars of this tragical ſtory are not known. The epigram
itſelf was firſt publiſhed in the Anthologia, lib. III. cap. 23.

With

With frantic hands fhe gave the deadly blow
That fent her foul to gloomy fhades below.
Two mighty ills the wretched fire muft mourn,
And weep around a fon and daughter's urn;
Old Ariftippus funk in grief appears,
And all Cyrene melts in briny tears.

XXII.

Whoe'er with hallow'd feet approaches near,
Behold, Callimachus lies buried here,
I drew my breath from fam'd Cyrene's fhore,
And the fame name my fon and father bore.

Οὐκ ἐτλη. διδυμον δ᾽ οἰκος ἐσειδε κακον
Πατρος Αριςιπποιο. κατηγρησεν δε Κυρηνη
Πασα, τον εὐτεκνων χηρον ἰδυσα δομον.

Οςις ἐμον παρα σημα φερεις ποδα, Καλλιμακυ με
Ισθι Κυρεναιυ παιδα τε κỳ γενετην.

Epigram XXII.]   Doctor Kennet obferves very juftly that from thefe beautiful verfes alone, Martial had fufficient reafon to affign the palm to Callimachus as the firft Greek writer of Epigram.   Both Doctor Kennet and Doctor Dodd have given them in Englifh, and both feem to have mifunderftood the meaning of the author, by fuppofing that this epitaph was intended for his father, and not for himfelf.   They have likewife omitted the material circumftance of his being a native of Cyrene.   The Poetry in each is below criticifm.

My

My warlike fire in arms much glory won,
But brighter trophies grac'd his favour'd fon ;
Lov'd by the tuneful nine he fweetly fung,
And ftopt the venom of th' invidious tongue :
For whom the mufe beholds with fav'ring eyes,
In early youth, fhe'll ne'er in age defpife.

XXIII.

O'er Cretan hills a virgin chanc'd to ftray,
And bore the fwain Aftacides away,
To Dicte's wood his inftant flight compells, ·
Where under ruftling oaks a prieft he dwells :

Εἰδειης δ' αμφω κεν. ὁ μεν ποτε πατριδος ὁπλων
Ηρξεν, ὁ δ' ἡεισεν κρεισσονα βασκανιης.
Οὐ νεμεσκ· Μυσαι γαρ ὁσους ἐδον 'ομματι παιδας
Αχρι βιυ πολιους ἐκ ἀπεθεντο φιλυς.

Αςακιδην τον Κρητα, τον αἰπολον ἡρπασε νυμφη
Ἐξ ὁρεος. κ̃ νυν ἱερος Αςακιδης

Epigram XXIII.] All the Commentators have paffed over this epigram in filence;
but the meaning f ems pretty plain : A young fhepherd retires with his miftrefs to the
mountain of Dicte. They live in a wood ; he becomes a Prophet, utters predictions,
which, according to the fuperftition of the times, are fuppofed to be communicated to him
by the neighbouring trees : and they would no doubt make a tolerable livelihood by prefents received from their credulous countrymen, who came to have their fortunes told.

Yc

u
Ye shepherds, ceafe to fing in Daphne's praife;
To fam'd Aftacides your voices raife.

XXIV.

Cleombrotus, high on a rock,
  Above Ambracia ftood,
Bade Sol adieu, and, as he fpoke,
  Plung'd headlong in the flood.

From no mifchance the leap he took,
  But fought the realms beneath,
Becaufe he read in Plato's book,
  That fouls live after death.

Οἴκει Δικταιησιν ὑπο δρυσιν. ἐκ ἐτι Δαφνιν
  Ποιμενες, Ασακιδην δ' αἰεν ἀεισομεθα.

Εἰπας, Ηλιε χαιρε, Κλεομβροτος ὡ 'μβρακιωτης
  Ηλατ' ἀπ' ὑψηλε τειχεος εἰς ἀϊδην.
Αξιον ἐδεν ἰδων θανατε κακον, ἀλλα Πλατωνος
  Εν το περι ψυχης γραμμ' ἀναλεξαμενος.

Epigram XXIV.] This epigram is one of the moft celebrated little Poems of anti-
quity, and fhews the great value that was put even upon the fmalleft productions of our
Author. It has been copied by Ammonius, and tranflated verbatim into Latin profe by
Cicero *.

  * Cicer. Tufculan. quæft. Lib I.

G g

St.

XXV.

Small is my fize, and I muft grace
Eetion's porch, a little place;
A hero's likenefs I appear,
And round my fword a ferpent bear.

Ηρως Πετιωνος επι ϛαθμον Αμφιπολιτεω
Ιδρυμαι, μικρω μικρος επι προθυρω.

St. Auguftine likewife mentions the fate of the unfortunate Cleombrotus, and Hieronymus calls him a martyr to the Philofophy of a fool. It is faid by Callimachus that he leapt ἐις ἀδην, into Tartarus, but Cicero, " fe in mare abjeciffe," that he threw himfelf into the fea; and the learned commentators have been much puzzled in what manner to reconcile the difference betwixt the Poet and the Philofopher. There feems to me but one method of fettling the difpute, and that natural and eafy, fuppofing what is much in the fpirit of thefe epigrams, namely that the word ἀδην is capable of two fignifications: and that phrafe ᾮλατο ἐις ἀδην expreffes both the death of Cleombrotus and the manner of it, as if we were to fay in Englifh he leapt into the *Gulph*, which may fignify either a Gulph of the ocean, or the Guph of Tartarus.

The bay or Gulph of Ambracia, fo called from a city of that name, is fituated on the coaft of Epirus, and now called Golfo di l'arta *. Cleombrotus is faid, in the original, to have leapt from the wall of Ambracia: but as that city flood at the diftance of 80 ftadia from the fea, it is commonly fuppofed that he threw himfelf headlong from a rock, and in that fenfe I have tranflated the paffage, as Stephens had done before me.

Epigram XXV.] Eetion of Amphipolis was a fkilful ftatuary of that age, who is fomewhere commended by Theocritus. And we learn from Virgil that ferpents were engraved on the tombs of Heroes. Dacier.

A Warrior of a fhort ftature having loft his life by a fall from a mettlefome horfe,

* Cellar. Georgr. p. 57.

Eetion

But fince Eetion views, with hate,
The prancing fteed that caus'd my fate,
Refolv'd that we no more fhould meet,
He plac'd me here upon my feet.

Λοξὸν ὄφιν κỳ μῦνον ἔχων ξίφος. ἀνδρι δὲ ἵππει
Θυμωθεὶς, πεζὸν κάμε παρωκίσατο.

Eetion erected a pedeftrian ftatue to the memory of this little Hero, in his own porch or
Veftibule, according to the cuftom of the times; and fuppreffed the fteed, that the likenefs of this unruly animal might never be known to pofterity. And perhaps he thought
that a man, who had been killed by a fall of this nature was not fit to appear on Horfe-
back.

V. 4. And, round my fword a ferpent bear.] Artemidorus tells us, that a dragon or
ferpent was facred to Jupiter, Apollo, Ceres, Proferpine and Æfculapius, as well as to
Heroes and Demigods. Befides the Phoenicians and Egyptians imagined that ferpents
partook of the divine nature; becaufe they moved along with incredible fwiftnefs, and
nimbly twifted their bodies into different forms, without the affiftance of limbs or
members like other animals. Alfo becaufe they were thought capable of renewing their
youth, by cafting their fkins at a certain age. And hence Eufebius writes that the Egyptians reprefented the univerfe by two circles, one within the other, and a ferpent, with the
head of a hawk, twining his folds around them. The circles reprefented the magnitude
and fhape of the world, and the ferpent the good genius or univerfal Preferver; that is,
the fpirit which pervades all, and from whom all receive life, nourifhment, and vigour.
Vulcanius.

This is a confirmation of what was obferved in the beginning of thefe notes, that the
idea of one fupreme being was never totally loft in the ancient world.

Fond

XXVI.

Fond Callignotus figh'd and fwore,
'Tis Violante I adore,   .
The brighteft beauty on the plain,
And fhe alone my heart fhall gain,
He fwore ; but lover's vows, they fay,
To heav'n could never make their way,
Nor penetrate the blefs'd abode,
Nor reach the ears of any God.
While for another maid he burns,
Forfaken Violante mourns
Her blafted hopes, her honour gone ;.
As Megra's race were once undone.

Ὡμοσε Καλλιγνωτος Ἰωνιδι, μηποτ᾽ ἐκεινης

    Εξειν μητε φιλον κρεισσονα, μητε φιλην.

Ὡμοσεν. ἀλλα λεγυσιν ἀληθεα, τους ἐν ἐρωτι,

    Ορκυς μη δυνειν ὐατ᾽ ἐς ἀθανατων.

Νυν δ᾽ ὁ μεν ἀλλης δη ϑερεται πυρι, της δε ταλαινης

    Νυμφης (ὡς Μεγαρεων) ὐ λογος, ὐτ᾽ ἀριθμος,.

Epigram XXVI.] The Heroine of this little Poem is called in the original Ἰωνς, in Latin *Violantilla*, the Greek word fignifying a bed of violets : a pretty name. Dacier.

   V. 12. As Megra's race were once undone.] It is faid that the inhabitants of Megara, the capital of a fmall ftate betwixt Boeotia and Attica, lying to the north of the Saronic Gulph, once entertained a vain conceit that they were the braveft of the Greeks. But upon confulting the oracle of Delphi, the Pythonefs to their utter confufion anfwered,

XXVII.

Short was my life, and Micylus my rame;
I gain'd with little wealth a poet's fame,
And wifely pafs'd without offence my time,
Friend to the good, unconfcious of a crime.
If e'er I prais'd the bad, revenge it now,
Thou mother Earth, and all ye pow'rs below:
Lie not, O Goddefs, lightly on my breaft,
Nor let th' infernal furies grant me reft.

Εἶχον ἀπο σμικρὸν ὀλιγον βιον, ὔτε τι δεινον
Ρᵃξων, ὔτ᾽ ἀδικων ὔδενα, γαια φιλη,
Μικυλος. εἰ τι πονηρον ἐπηνεσα, μητε συ κυρη
Γιγνεο, μη τ᾽ ἀλλοι δαιμονες ὁι μ᾽ ἐχετε.

fwered, that fo far from excelling their neighbours in valour, they did not deferve to be admitted into the Grecian army. This refponfe of the oracle expofed them to the derifion of the furrounding ftates, and foon become a proverb *. The Lady mentioned in the text feems to have poffeffed an abundant fhare of this vain-glorious difpofition, foolifhly imagining, what has induced many frail fifters to go aftray, that the force of her charms would be fufficient to retain her lover after fhe had yielded to his defires. And we may obferve that the young men of ancient Greece were not more faithful to their Miftreffes than thofe of our times; fince the common faying, " Jupiter Laughs at Lovers' oaths," was become a proverb even in the days of Callimachus. Tibullus ufes the fame expreffion:

———— perjuria r'det amantum
Jupiter, et ventos irrita ferre jubet.

Epigram XXVII.] Micylus, a certain Poet whofe hiftory is not known, fpeaks his own epitaph. Dacier.

      * Suid. in Ὑμης ω Μιy; & Theocr. Idyll. xiv. 48.

XXVIII.

This book is fure exactly wrote
In Hefiod' manner, ftyle, and thought,
Of Grecian poet's not the leaft.
And here his pow'rs are all expreft.
I fear, my friend, you fay too much,
His verfe is foft, his genius fuch,

Ησιοδυ τοδ᾽ αεισμα κȣ ὁ τροπος ȣ τον αοιδον
Εσχατον, αλλ᾽ ὁ καισωμητο μελιχροτατον,

V. 7. Lie not, O Goddefs, lightly on my breaft.] μητι συ κυφη γιγνȣ; " neque tu mihi terra efto levis." Here we have the original of that celebrated phrafe ; fo often repeated among modern poets and Novel-writers; as in Mr. Pope's elegy on the death of an unfortunate Lady :

> Yet fhall thy grave with rifing flow'rs be dreft,
> And the green turf lie *lightly* on thy breaft.

And in Mr. M'Kenzie's Man of Feeling;

" Light be the Earth on Billy's breaft, and green the fod that wraps his grave."

On account of the change in religion, this expreflion has now loft much of its original forre : But it was particularly proper in ancient times, when the earth was ranked among the moft powerful Deities. The meaning feems plainly to have been this; " O Goddefs earth be merciful to the deceafed:" and Madame Dacier informs us that it was cuftomary both among the Greeks and Romans, (probably at funerals) to utter the following fhort ejaculation; in Greece, Κυφη γη τȣτον ἡ ταυτην καλυπτοι; and at Rome, *fit tibi terra levis*.

What is commonly reckoned the twenty feventh epigram has not been tranflated, being only a fragment. The meaning is, that the inhabitants of Cyrene, the native country of Callimachus, came originally from an ifland called Callifte, and afterwards Thera. For the particulars of this expedition fee Hymn fecond.

Epigram XXVIII.] Aratus was a celebrated poet, born at Soli a city of Cilicia, co-

3

That Soli's fon will find it hard
To emulate fo fweet a bard.
Farewel Aratus' empty themes,
His idle thoughts, and heavy dreams.

\

Των επεων ο Σολευς απεμαζατο. χαιρετε λεπται

Ρησεις Αρητε συγγονοι αγρυπνιης.

temporary with Callimachus, and wrote under the patronage of Antigonus Gonatas King Macedon. There is a great difagreement among ancient authors concerning his Poems; Cicero praifes, and Quintilian cenfures them. As thefe were divided in their opinions about the genius of Aratus, fo modern Commentators have been as much at a lofs ro find out the meaning of this epigram : fome affirming that it contains an encomium, and others a fatire, on his works. Erneftus adopts the former opinion, and endeavours to prove, contrary to the judgment of Salmafius, Voffius and Fabricius, that thefe verfes were wrote in praife of the poet. He has made great alterations in the original not upon the authority of any claffic author, or ancient manufcript, but merely with a view to make it coincide with his own ideas; and for the farther fupport of his hypothefis, he has wrote an immenfe commentary on this fingle epigram, which the reader will find in his edition of Callimachus. But whoever confiders the doubtful charafter of Aratus as a poet, the fatyrical difpofition of our author, and above all, the words of the text, will be at no lofs to perceive that he intended to ridicule his cotemporary. The verfes themfelves feem to be wrote, in the ftyle called by Rhetoricians Dialogifmus ; that is, when a propofition is advanced, and immediately overturned, either by the fpeaker himfelf or fome other perfon.

I hate

XXIX.

I hate the bard who ſtrolls along,
And ſells in ſtreets his borrow'd ſong;
I ſeldom walk the public way,
Where here and there the vulgar ſtray;
Inconſtant friends I never court,
Nor to the common ſpring reſort.
I ſtill deſpiſe the rabble's rage,
Nor with the noiſy croud engage;

Εχθαιρω το ποιημα το κυκλικον, ὐδε κελευθω
    Χαιρω τις πολλὺς ὡδε κ̀ ὡδε φερει.
·Μιϲω κ̀ περιφοιτον ἐρωμενον, ὐτ' ἀπο κρηνης
    Πινω. συγχαινω παντα τα δημοσια

Epigram XXIX.] This epigram ſeems addreſſed to the Strollers of Antiquity who
went about the ſtreets, and ſold Ballads extracted from the writings of more eminent Poets.
At the ſame time Authors are not agreed about the meaning of the Phraſe ἰχθαιρω το ποιημα
το κυκλικον " I hate a Cyclic Poem." We are told by the ſcholiaſt on Ariſtophenes that
the fiſh market of Athens was called Κυκλος, a very proper place for vending ſuch Ballads,
and by Suidas, that the ſame name was given to places appropriated to the ſelling of
ſlaves; becauſe the perſons expoſed to ſale ſtood in a circle *. But others and particularly
Salmaſius make this expreſſion allude to poets, who expreſs every circumſtance too mi-
nutely †. I have chozen the firſt ſignification, as being moſt agreeable to the ſpirit of the
epigram.

V. 7. I ſtill deſpiſe the rabble's rage.] Συγχαινω παντα τα δημοσια; Horace has copied
this expreſſion.

* Suidas in verb. κυκλοι.   † Salm. Plin exercitat. cap XL.

                                                                    Odi

'Tis fine, 'tis fine, a reader cries;
Indignant Echo thus replies,
Tho' ne'er fo good, perhaps divine,
Another bard wrote ev'ry line.

Λυσανιη, συ δε ναιχι καλος καλος αλλα πριν ειπειν
    Τοδε μαφως ηχω φησι τις αλλος εχει.

Odi profanum vulgus, et arceo, which is in every body's mouth, while the more elegant
original has hitherto remained in obfcurity.

V. 9. 'Tis fine, 'tis fine, a reader cries.] The reader in the Greek fays ναιχι καλος, to
which echo anfwers εχω αλλος; from which Bentley imagines that " αι" and " ι" had the
fame found in the time of Callimachus: an argument of much the fame force as if a
foreigner were to fuppofe the letter g quiefcent in the Englifh word Pudding, becaufe the
two following lines are to be found in the Echo of Hudibrafs.

> For who would grutch to fpend his blood in
> His honour's caufe? quoth fhe a pudding.

V. 12. Another bard wrote every line] In that Auguftan age of Egypt, when the
great encourager of learning, Ptolemy Philadelphus, invited all the wits of his time to re-
fide at his court, every poet boafted of originality, no doubt with a view to recommend
himfelf to his illuftrious patron. And it muft be owned that both Callimachus and Theocritus deferve the fame praife, on that account, from fucceeding ages, as they received
from their cotemporaries. Theocritus had not faiied to mention himfelf as being poffeffed of this invaluable quality.

> A Syracufian born, no right I claim
> To Chios, and Theocritus my name:
> Praxagoras' and fam'd Philina's fon;
> My Laurels from unborrow'd verfe are won.   FAWKES.

But fome critics feem to have carried this idea too far, by affirming that no writer of
verfe can lay claim to the character of a Poet, unlefs every thought in his poems be altogether his own, without the mixture of a fingle expreflion from any brother-bard. But
no criticifms can deftroy the practife of above twenty centuries; and in all that time poets

XXX.

Pour the wine, and drink it up,
But mix no water in the cup;
The facred cup we fill with joy
To thee, Diocles, beauteous boy:

Εγχει κỳ παλιν ειπε Διοκλεες, ᾶδ' Αχελωιος
Κεινᾶ των ιερων αισθανεται κυαθων.

have conftantly had an exclufive privilege of borrowing from one another. Every reader muft know that the Æneid is a compound of the Iliad and Odyffey; the Jerufalem Delivered, of Taffo, has been formed upon thefe three: and a certain learned man obferves that the Devils of Milton are only Homer's Heroes in difguife. To go through the poets of inferior rank would be endlefs, every one having borrowed, with impunity, from thofe great Model, as much as he judged fuitable to his purpofe. And there are certain expreffions, fuch as "lofty towers, watery Go's, purling ftreams, fhady groves, gentle breezes," &c. that have been bandied about among all poets time out of mind. There are others, fuch as "golden Sun, filver moon, veffels of gold, fringes of filver," &c. that cannot be too often repeated: for fuch has been the attachment of mankind, in all ages, to thefe two precious metals, that the bare mention of the names, though but in a page of a vifionary poet, conveys agreeable founds to the ear, and delightful imaginations to the heart. Therefore as Ariftotle is faid to have drawn his rules of Epic Poetry from the writings of Homer, fo, I think, I may be allowed to bring one maxim from the practice of all poets ancient and modern; namely, that every bard may take a word, a thought, a line, and perhaps part of his plan from his predeceffor or even his cotemporary, providing he borrows confiftently; that is to fay, if the gold of the poet, that he borrows from, does not fhine through his own duft, like a Diamond fet in a Dunghill. To which it may be added that borrowing implies lending, and therefore he who borrows fhould be ready to lend when occafion ferves.

Epigram XXX.] The word Αχελωος, in the firft verfe, fignifies any kind of water, according

O more than beauteous, youth divine,
Should all refuse to drink the wine,
Should all refuse thy charms to fee,
Then would the boy be left with me.

XXXI.

Cleonicus, unhappy man,
Say whence thy forrows firſt began?

Καλος ὁ παις, Αχελωε, λιην καλος. ουδε τις ουχι
Φησιν, επιςαιμην μουνος εγω τα καλα.

Θεσσαλικε Κλεονικε ταλαν, ταλαν, ου μα τον οξυν

according to Hefychius; and therefore the meaning muſt be " mix no water with the
wine drank to the health of Diocles." The laſt verſe, and part of that immediately preceding may be tranſlated thus: Si quis negat Dioclem eſſe pulchrum; abſtineat; et ego
folus eum habeam fine rivali. Bentley.

The concluſion of this Epigram is beautifully imitated by Tibullus.

> Atque utinam poſſis uni mihi bella videri!

> Diſpliceas aliis! fic ego tutus ero *.

Epigram XXXI.] Two poets are in love with the fame Lady, who feems to have
rejeĉted the one, and accepted the other. The happy Lover addreſſes his brother-bard,
who is reduced to a ſkeleton by unfucceſsful paſſion, but gives him no confolation; and it
muſt be owned that this is one of the leaſt valuable epigrams in the whole collecŧion.

The tranſlator has fometimes been obliged to change the fexes in thefe poems, for reafons obvious to the learned reader.

For, by yon' blazing orb of light,
I ne'er beheld fo fad a fight.
Where haft thou been? thy flefh is gone,
And nothing left but fkin and bone.
My dæmon fure and haplefs fate,
Reduc'd thee to this wretched ftate;
Eufithea ftol: thy heart, like mine;
When firft you faw the nymph divine,
You gaz'd on her with wifhful eyes,
And hence, I fear, your woes arife.

Ηλιον ἐκ ἐγνων, σχετλιε, ππε γεγονας,
Οςεα σοι κἠ μουνον ἐτι τριχες, ἡ ῥα σε δαιμων
Οὑμος ἐχει, χαλεπη δ' ἡντεο θευμοριη;
Εγνων, Εὐξιθεος σε συνηρπασε. κἠ συ γαρ ἐλθων
Τον καλον ὡ μοχθηρ' ἐβλεπες αμφοτεροις.

V. 7. My Dæmon fure and haplefs fate.] Madam Dacier propofes to make an alteration in the original of this verfe by changing τὸ μες into ὥμος, but I think without reafon.
For the moft cruel fair can hardly be thought deferving of fo terrible an epithet: befides
it is not agreeable to the general meaning of this epigram.

The

XXXII.

The huntfman o'er the hills purfues
The timid hare, and keenly views
The tracks of hinds amid the fnow,
Nor heeds the wint'ry winds that blow.
But fhould a ftranger mildly fay,
Accept the game I kill'd to day;
The proffer'd gift he quickly fcorns,
And to th' uncertain chace returns:
Such is my love; I never prize
An eafy fair, but her who flies.

Ωγρευτης, Επικυδες, εν ευρεσι παντα λαγωον
Διφα, κ̓ πασης ιχνια δορκαλιδος,
Στιβη κ̓ νιφετω κεχρημενος, ην δε τις ειπη
Τη, τοδε βεβληται θηριον, ουκ ελαβεν.
Χ' ουμος ερως τοιος δε, τα μεν φευγοντα διωκειν
Οιδε, ταδ' εν μεσσω κειμενα παρπεταται.

Epigram XXXII.] Horace alludes to this epigram in one place, and has given almoft
a compleat tranflation of it in another: but attempting to comprefs the thought he has
deftroyed much of its original perfpicuity. And Mr. Francis very well obferves, that the
following paffage of Horace would have been almoft inexplicable, had it not been for
this little fong of Callimachus. The fimilarity betwixt them was firft obferved by Scaliger
and Heinfius.

——————————Leporem venator, ut altâ
In nive fectatur, pofitum fic tangere nolit:
3   Cantat

XXXIII.

That I am poor is known to me,
My good Menippus, as to thee;

Οἶδ᾽ ὅτι μοι πλᾶτᾶ κενεαι χερες, ἀλλα Μενιππε

> Cantat et apponit : meus eſt amor huic ſimilis ; nam
> Tranſvolat in medio poſita, et fugientia captat *.
> As when a ſportſman, through the ſnowy waſte,
> Purſues a hare, which he diſdains to taſte,
> So (ſings the rake) my paſſion can deſpiſe
> An eaſy prey, but follows when it flies.   Francis.

    The paſſage, where the fame author alludes to the preſent epigram, is in the firſt Ode of the firſt Book.

> ————Manet ſub Jove frigido
> Venator, teneræ conjugis immemor ;
> Seu viſa eſt catulis cerva fidelibus,
> Seu rupit teretes Marſus aper plagas.
> The ſportſman, chill'd by midnight Jove,
> Forgets his tender, wedded Love,
> Whether his faithful hounds purſue,
> And hold the bounding Hind in view ;
> Whether the boar, fierce foaming, foils
> The chace, and breaks the ſpreading toils :   Francis.

    Epigram XXXIII] This may be called a moral ſentence, rather than an epigram, and affords a uſeful leſſon to thoſe perſons who look on their friends with contempt, merely becauſe they happen to poſſeſs ſmaller fortunes than themſelves : and who think that learning, honour, honeſty, and the practice of every moral virtue ſhould be ſacrificed

---

* Hor. Sat. Lib. I. Sat. 2. v. 105.

Then, by our love, infift no more
On what I knew too well before:
Such truths offend a ftranger's ear,
But to a friend are moft fevere.

XXXIV.

Plac'd here by Phileratis' hands,
This image of Diana ftands;
Accept the gift, attend her pray'r,
And ftill, O Goddefs, guard the fair.

Μη λεγε προς χαριτων τ' εμον ονειρον εμοι,
Αλγεω την δια παντος, επος τοδε πικρον ακεων
Ναι φιλε ταν παρα σε τετ' ανεραςτατον.

Αρτεμι, τιν τοδ' αγαλμα φιληρατις εισατο τηδε,
Αλλα συ μεν δεξαι ποθνια, την δε σαε.

to the acquifition of a little money. Such characters are but too common in every country, particula.ly among the mercantile clafs of mankind.

V. 4. On what I knew too well before.] The original words are μη λεγε —— τ' εμον ἱπερ ἰοη, " ne mihi meum fomnium dicito," a proverb commonly repeated by thofe wh were informed of a piece of news which they had often heard before. Dacier.

Ep'gram XXXIV.] Thefe infcriptions for ftatues, and other offerings to the Deities, which occur fo frequently in the Greek Anthology, contain little interefting to a modern reader, having only fimplicity of thought and eafe of verfification to recommend them; and thefe it is often very difficult for a tranflator to copy. When that can be done with
tolerable

XXXV.

Club. A ftranger cut me from a tree,
A beechen club, a gift to thee,
Who ftopt the roaring lion's breath,
And laid the foaming boar in death.
Herc. Declare his country, and his name.
Club. Archinus he; from Crete he came.
Herc. And, for the pious giver's fake,
The proffer'd gift I freely take.

Τιν με λεονταγχανε, συοκτονε, φηγινον οζον
Θηκε. τις ; αρχινος. ποιος ; ο Κρης. δεχομαι.

tolerable fuccefs, the verfes are many times not unpleafant; and from the prefent lines,
fhort as they are, we naturally intereft ourfelves in behalf of the young Lady, who erects
a ftatue, with her own hands, to the guardian of female chaftity.

Epigram XXXV.] Archinus, a native of Crete, dedicates a beechen club to Hercules. The Club fpeaks, and Hercules anfwers.

V. 4. Who ftopt the roaring Lion's breath.] Hercules killed the Nemœan Lion, neither by the fword, nor by arrows; but feizing him by the throat, ftrangled him with his
hands. A particular account of this exploit is given by Apollodorus, lib. II. Dacier.
The original of the above line confifts of only one word λεονταγχων "Lion ftrangler,"
which according to Madam Dacier is an elegant expreffion; but Erneftus calls it a monfter
of a word ; and, upon the authority of Walkenar, propofes to fubftitute γεντανχ' ωδε in its
place. This obfcures the fenfe, but takes nothing from the monftrofity.

Approach

XXXVI.

Approach this tomb with filent feet,
The dead Battiades to greet;
Alive, renown'd for facred fong,
And mirth to charm the feftive throng.

XXXVII.

Twice Erafixen fill'd his cup,
And twice he drank the liquor up;
He drank his wine, but much too deep,
And clos'd his eyes in endlefs fleep.

Βαττιαδεω παρα σημα φερεις ποδας εὐ μεν ἀοιδην·
Εἰδοτος, εὐ δί οἰνῳ καιρια συγγελασαι.

Εἰς Ερασιξενον τον ποτην.
Τον βαθυν οινοποτην Ερασιξενον, ἡ δις ἐφεξης
Ακριτυ προποθεισ ὠχετ ἐχουσα κυληξ.

Epigram XXXVI.] The following title is wrote above thefe lines in the Manufcript : Καλλιμαχυ ἱς τυα Βαττυ ὑια ἡ Βαττιαδην συκτην, as if Callimachus had been a Boxer inftead of a poet. Read ποιητην; υ occurs frequently for οι in the Greek manufcripts. The writer of this epitaph is not known. Bentley.

Epigram XXXVII.] The original words, with fome variation, are to be found in Athenæus. X. p. 436, from whom Caufaubon endeavours to prove that Erafixen fell a victim to moderation rather than excefs, having been a man of fobriety, who died from

i   being

XXXVIII.

Menœtas, tir'd with wars alarms,
Gave to the Gods his fhining arms,
And faid, this quiver and this bow
On thee, Serapis, I beſtow;
This empty quiver; for my darts
Are all infix'd in hoſtile hearts.

Ὁ Λυκτιος Μενοιτας τα τοξα ταυτ᾽ επειπων
Εθηκε· τη κεραστοι, διδωμι ᾳ φαρετρην
Σαραπι, τᵹς δ᾽ οἰστους εχᵹσιν εσπεριται.

being accidentally overtaken with liquor. Madam Dacier contradicts him; and I leave the Lady and the Gentleman to decide the quarrel by themſelves.

Epigram XXXVIII.] The word κεραστοι, in the ſecond verſe of the original has puzzled all the commentators. Madam Dacier quotes Herodotus to ſhew that the Goddeſs Iſis, the Egyptian Diana, was called βᵹκερως, " Cornigera;" and therefore ſuppoſes the true reading to be κεραστη, as if Menœtas had dedicated his bow to that Goddeſs, and his quiver to Serapis. But the explication given by Bentley ſeems preferable, being ſupported by the authority of the Leipſic Manuſcript; namely that the reading in the common editions is right : but that, by the careleſſneſs of ſome tranſcriber, two words have been joined in one, and therefore the paſſage ſhould ſtand thus τη κερας τοι διδωμι και φαριτρη, Σαραπι, " O Sera-pis, accept the bow and quiver, which I dedicate to thee ;" the word κερας often ſignifying a bow, becauſe the bows of the ancients were frequently made of horn, as we learn from Homer's deſcription of the bow of Pandarus *.

V. 6. Are all infix'd in hoſtile hearts.] Theſe enemies are called in the Greek Ἑς-ιπεριπαι; and Madam Dacier with all her learning, confeſſes that ſhe can give no informa-

---

* Hom. Il. IV. v. 105. & ſeq.

tion

XXXIX.

Silena, changeful as the fea,
Bright Venus, dedicates to thee,
Her image, and the zone that bound
Her fwelling breaft with beauty crown'd.

Τα δωρα τη Αφροδιτη
Σειληνη περιφοιτος εικον' αυτης
Ε'ηκεν, την τε μιτρην
Ημας τας εφιλησε τον τε Πανα.

tion concerning them. But Stephens tells us, on the authority of Ptolemy that Helperis was a city of ancient Libya; and, on his own, that it ftill exifts under the name of Beronice.

Epigram XXXIX.] Thefe verfes are imperfeft in the original, and feem to have been the beginning of a longer poem. Bentley has fupplied the name Silena from his own conjecture, affifted by the fyllable Σα which he found in an old manufcript. The reft of his emendations, and thofe of other commentators, being unfatisfactory to themfelves, would probably be more fo to the reader.

It was ufual for the girls of antiquity to wear a zone or belt girded faft round their bofoms, probably in place of the modern ftays or boddice; as we learn from the twentieth Ode of Anacreon; and Madam Dacier, for the good of her fex, has illuftrated this interefting fubject yet farther, by the following paffage of Terence: Haud fimilis virgo eft virginum noftrarum, quas matres ftudent demiffis humeris effe, vincto pectore, ut graciles fient. "This girl bears no refemblance to the young Ladies of our country who are inftructed by their mothers to keep down the fhoulders, and gird the breaft very tight, in order to make them appear flender;" give them a fine fhape.

Acrifius

XL.

Acrifius of Pelafgian race
To Ceres rais'd this holy place,
Where Timodemus pays his vow
To her, and Proferpine below :
Triumphant from his naval toil,
He gives the tenth of ev'ry fpoil.

Δημητρι τη ωυλαιη τυτον υκ Πελασγων
Ακρισιος ηον νηον εδειματο ταυθ' ο Ναυκρατιδης
Και τη τατω θυγατρι τα δωρα Τιμοδημος
Εισατο των κερδεων δεκατευματα, κ̀ γαρ ευξαθ' υτως.

Epigram XL.] The Pelafgi were the firft inhabitants of Theffaly ; and hence the fame
name is often given, by the poets, to the whole inhabitants of Greece.

V. 5. Triumphant from his naval toil.] Timodemus is called in the Greek, Nau-
cratites; and Bentley tells us, but without giving his authority, that he was a citizen of
Naucratis, in Egypt. I rather incline to the opinion of Madam Dacier that Ναυκρατιτης,
is the fame with Ναυκρατης, navium victor; becaufe it was cuftomary among the ancients
to promife an offering to fome Deity before going upon a dangerous expedition ; and they
feldom failed to perform their vow, efpecially when the enterprize terminated prof-
peroufly.

Whoe'er

XLI.

Whoe'er fhall to this tomb draw nigh,
Behold, in death, a prieftefs lie ;
I facred Ceres firft implor'd,
The great Cabiri next ador'd.

Εἰς ἱερειαν τινα Δημητρος γραυν αἰσιως τελευτησασαν, ἐπι τετραμετρῳ
ἑνδεκασυλλαβῳ.

Ἱερεη Δημητρος ἐγω ποτε κỵ παλιν Καβειρων
Ωνερ κỵ μετεπειτα Δινδυμενης

Epigram XLI.] This may be ranked among the moft elegant as well as pleafant of
our authors epitaphs. The verfification is flowing and the fentiment agreeable. The
venerable matron lived and died happily, and feems to have enjoyed all the fatisfaction that
her ftation in life could afford. The third Greek verfe wants part of the laft word, which
Bentley has very properly fupplied by ἀρχηγος ; for it is eafy to perceive that this compleats
the fenfe.

V. 3. The great Cabiri next ador'd.] The Gods called Cabiri, that is, great and
powerful, from the Phoenician or Hebrew word Cabir, make a great figure in ancient
mythology. They were worfhipped with many myfterious rites, in Samothracia an Ifland
on the coaft of Thrace ; but authors difagree with regard to their number, fome making
them only two *Coelus & Terra** ; fome three, Jupiter, Juno, Minerva †; and others four,
Ceres, Proferpine, Pluto, Mercury ‡. The nature and properties of thefe Cabiri is yet more
uncertain than their number, which has commonly been reduced to the three mentioned
by Macrobius ; and as fome Philofophers imagine that Plato drew his ideas of a Triad from
that paffage in the fifteenth Iliad, where Homer reprefents the univerfe to have been di-

---

* Varro lib. IV.   † Macrob. Saturnal. lib. IV.   ‡ Schol. in Apoll.
Argonaut.

Grew old on Dindymene's plains,
And now my duſt alone remains.

Alive, I ſeldom fail'd to lead
The ſprightly dance along the mead;
I bore two ſons, I ran my race,
And dy'd with joy, in their embrace.
Go friend; prepare for life's decline;
And may thy death be bleſt as mine.

Η γρηυς γενομην η νυν κονις ηγο * * * * * *
Πολλων προςαςιη νεων γυναικων.
Και μοι τεκν' εγενοντο δυ' αρςενα, κηπεμυσ' εκεινων
Ευ γηρως ενι χερσιν, ερπε χαιρων.

vided among three brothers, Jupiter, Neptune, and Pluto * ; in like manner, from the
prevailing opinion that the Samothracian Deities were in number three, Voſſius and other
mythologiſts will have it, that there muſt have been an obſcure tradition of the ſacred
Trinity remaining among the ancients †. But though this conjecture were not refuted by
its own abſurdity, an ancient Greek inſcription preſerved by Gruter, informs us that the
ſame appellation was given to Caſtor and Pollux ‡. Wherefore, we may ſuppoſe the word
Cabir to have been a general name for deities of ſuperior rank : but if their number
ſhould ſtill be reſtricted to three, we muſt have recourſe to Macrobius for a Mythological
explication; and he tells us that Jupiter ſignifies the middle region of the air, Juno the
clouds together with the earth, and Minerva the upper region or æther §. to which if
we may add Pluto. or the infernal regions, the Cabiri will comprehend the whole ſyſtem
of the univerſe.

V. 9. I bore two ſons, I ran my race.] Madam Dacier declares that a corruption of

* Hom. Il. XV. v 187.　　　　† Voſſ. de Theol. Gentil. lib. VIII. cap. 12.
‡ Theſaur. p. 319.　　　　§ Macrob. lib. III.

the

XLII.

I breathe in fighs; for half my foul
By love or death was lately ftole :
Perhaps the fool, too furely gone,
Is now poffefs'd by love alone,
And to fome beauteous boy draws nigh,
From whom I warn'd him oft to fly.
Retire, my foul, left thou fhould'ft prove
The pangs of unfuccefsful love ;
For well I know thou'lt foon return
In anguifh, and difmifs'd with fcorn.

Ημισυ μευ ψυχης ετι το πνεον, ἡμισυ δ' ἐκ' ειδ'
  Ειτ' ερος, ειτ' Αϊδης ἡρπασε, πλην αφανες.
Η ρα τιν' ἐς παιδων παλιν ὠχετο κỳ μεν απειπων
  Πολλακι την δρησιν μη ὑπεχεσθε νεοι.
Ουκ ισον εφη σον, ἐκεισε γαρ ὁ λιθολευσος
  Κεινη κỳ δυσερως, οιδ' ότι πε τρεφεται.

the text has rendered the concluding verfes unintelligible; but the meaning is obvious,
and the learned Lady has not behaved with her ufual candour, probably wifhing to conceal the fruitfulnefs of this venerable Prieftefs from the profane eyes of modern readers.

Epigram XLII] We may fuppofe this epigram to be fpoke by a love-fick Lady, who
feems to be loft while fhe deliberates, and wifhes to regain her heart only becaufe fhe fears
that her paffion will prove unfuccefsful. The learned Scaliger fhews that thefe verfes
were tranflated by an old Latin Poet, Quintus Catullus ; and I make no apology for pre-
fenting the reader with his tranflation, which is not only elegant, but an improvement on
the original. 3

XLIII.

If fober, and inclin'd to fport,
To you, my fair one, I refort;
The ftill-forbidden blifs to prove,
Accufe me then, and blame my love.
But if to rafhnefs I incline,
Accufe me not, but blame the wine :
When Love and Wine at once infpire,
What mortal can controul his fire.
Of late I came, I know not how,
Embrac'd my fair, and kifs'd her too;
It might be wrong; I feel no fhame,
And, for the blifs, will bear the blame.

Εἰ μεν ἑκων ἀρχειν ἐπεκωμασα, μυρια μεμψυ.
 Εἰ δ᾽ ἀκων ἡκω την προπετειαν ἐχων
Ακρητος ᾳ ἐρως με ἀναγκασεν, ὡν ὁ μεν αὑτων
 Εἱλκεν, ὁδ᾽ ἐκ εἰα σωφρονα θυμον ἐχειν.
Ελθων δ᾽ ἐκ ἐβοησα τις ἡ τινος. ἀλλ᾽ ἐφιλησα
 Την ἰαρην. εἰ τυτ᾽ ἐς᾽ ἀδικημα ἀδικω.

Aufugit mi animus, credo, ut folet, ad Theotimum
 Devonit. fic eft : Perfugium illud habet.
Quid fi non interdixem ne illum fugitivum
 Mitteret ad fe intro : fed magis ejiceret ?
Ibimu' quæfitum. Verum ne ipfi teneamur
 Formido. Quid ago ? Da Venu' confilium.

Epigram XLIII.] Madam Dacier is much out of humour with thefe elegant verfes;

and

XLIV.

Behold our hoſt by Love depriv'd of reſt,
A ſecret wound deep-rankling in his breaſt;
He breathes in ſighs, opprefs'd by pow'r divine,
And thrice the thirſty earth has drank the wine.

Ελκος εχων ὁ ξεινος ελανθανεν ὡς ανιηρον
Πνευμα δια ϛηθεων ειδες ανηγαγετο.
Το τριτον ἡ γη επινε, τα δε ῥοδα φυλλοϲολευντα

and begins by telling us, that unlefs we can procure more correct manuſcripts, the very
firſt line of the Text muſt remain unintelligible; no doubt with a view to deter every
reader from examining the reſt. But, as Bentley obferves, the firſt verfe may be rendered
quite plain by fubſtituting the proper name "Αϸχ̔" inſtead of the verb εϸχ̔ι, and thus making an alteration of only one letter. The tranſlator has omitted the name for obvious
reaſons.

V. 7. When love and wine at once infpire.] A parallel paſſage occurs in the Adel-
phi of Terence:

> Perfuafit nox, amor, vinum, adolefcentia.

Epigram XLIV] Though the Hero of this little fonnet belong to a different fex,
he is reprefented by our author in the fame condition with Dido and Sappho; the one
beautifully defcribed by Virgil in the beginning of the fourth Æneiad, and the other by
Ovid, in the celebrated epiſtle to Phaon.

> At Regina, gravi jamdudum faucia cura,
> Vulnus alit venis, et coeco carpitur igni:
> But anxious cares already fiez'd the Queen;
> She fed, within her veins, a flame unfeen. Dryden.
> Uror, ut, indomitis ignem exercentibus Euris,
> Fertilis accenfis meſſibus ardet ager.

I burn,

Lo! from his neck, the rofy garlands fade,
And, on the ground, the with'ring leaves are fpread;
He burns, he burns; as I too furely know,
That oft have felt a lover's pains and woe.

Τ'ωνδρος απο ςοματων παντ' εγενοντο χαμαι.
Ωπτημαι μεγαλη. τι μα δαιμονα εκ απο ρυσμε
Εἰκαζω, φωρος δ' ιχνια φωρ εμαθον.

> I burn, I burn, as when thro' ripen'd corn
> By driving winds the fpreading flames are born. Pope.

V. 4. And thrice the thirfty earth has drank the wine.] The young people of ancient Greece, and particularly of Athens, frequently amufed themfelves, at entertainments,
with a diverfion called Κοτταβος, Cottabus *. To which this verfe alludes. It was a fort
of Fortune telling, to know whether a lover could gain the affections of his miftrefs, and
they played it in the following manner. A piece of wood being erected, another was placed on the top of it, with two bafons hanging from each extremity in the manner of fcales;
beneath each bafon ftood a veffel full of water, in which was placed a ftatue of Brafs.
The young lover retired to fome diftance holding a phial full of wine in his hand. This
he endeavoured to throw into one of the Bafons, in fuch a way as to knock the veffel
againft the ftatue below, and yet not to fpill the wine. If he fucceeded, fo would his paffion; but if he failed, or if any part of the liquor fell to the ground, his Miftrefs was loft,
and his cafe defperate.

V. 8. That oft have felt a lovers pain and woe.] The original correfponds pretty
much with the common Englifh Proverb " fet a Thief to catch a Thief;" but however
agreeable this might have been in the days of Callimachus, I am afraid a modern reader
would think fuch a ludicrous conclufion rather unfuitable to fo ferious a beginning. For
the fame reafon Madam Dacier fuppofes the laft diftich to be a part of fome other poem.

* Potter's antiquit. Vol. II. p. 405. Suid. in verb. κοτταβιζειν.

By

XLIV.

By mighty Pan and Bacchus' greater name,
Beneath thefe embers lurks a fpreading flame.
Embrace me not ; tho' ftreams in filence fall,
They fap the bafis of the beft built wall :
Embrace me not ; left this invading fire
Should be but love, and fiercer flames infpire.

Εςι τι ναι τον πανα κεκρυμμενον, ἐςι τι ταυτῃ
  Ναι μα Διονυσον πυρ ὑπο τῃ σποδιῃ.
Οὐ θαρσεω, μη δη με περιπλεκε, πολλακι ληθει
  Τοιχον ὑποτρωγων ἡσυχιος ποταμος.
Τῳ και νυν δεδοικα μενε ξενε, μη με παρεισδυς
  Οὑτος ὁ σ', εἰ γ' ἀρνῃς, εἰς τον ερωτα βαλει.

Epigram XLV.] The laft part of this epigram explains the firft : a lover meets with
his quondam Miftrefs, but keeps her at a diftance left her embraces fhould rekindle the.
fparks of affection not yet entirely extinguifhed in his breaft.

When

XLVI.

When Archeftrata's charms I firft furvey'd,
By heav'n, faid he, this is no beanteous maid ;
Nor feem'd fhe fair, when view'd with carelefs eye:
But vengeful Nemefis ftood lift'ning by,
Cut fhort my fpeech, and fwift within my heart,
Infix'd, like fire from Jove, her fatal dart.
I burn, I burn ; fhall I the pow'r appeafe,
Or ftrive with blandifhments the fair to pleafe?
Could I, my fair, thy blooming charms enjoy,
The dart of Nemefis would prove a joy.

Των καλον ως ιδομαν αρχεςατον, ε μα τον ερμαν
  Ου καλον αυτον εφαν, ε γαρ αγαν εδοκει·
Ειπα, η α νεμεσις με συναρπασε, κ' ευθυς εκειμαν
  Εν πυρι, πας δ' εν εμοι Ζευς εκεραυνοϐολει
Τον παιδ' ιλασσομεσθ' α την θεον. αλλα θεϰ μοι
  Εςιν ο παις κρεισσων. χαιρετω α νεμεσις.

Epigram XLVI.] Dorvillius gives this epigram, as the production of fome unknown author, and Albertus only fufpects that it muft belong to Callimachus. Perhaps it was wrote by Phillipus the author of another epigram on Archeftrata, in the unpublifhed Anthologia. Dacier. 4

XLVII.

July the twentieth lately paſt,
This flying fair muſt yield at laſt,
I fondly ſaid; but e'er the ſun
Had half his courſe in Auguſt run,
She came all bright in blooming charms,
And ruſh'd ſpontaneous to my arms,
By Hermes led; O guardian pow'r
Thy ſacred name I ſtill adore,
And ſince that long expeſted day,
No more lament the ſhort delay.

Ληφθησῃ, περιφευγε Μενεκρατες, ειπα Πανημʊ
Εἰκαδι, ϰ̀ λωον τῃ τινι τῃ δεκαδῃ,
Ηλθεν ὁ βʊς ὑπ' ἀροτρον εκʊσιος εὐγ' ἐμος ἐρμας.
Εὐγ' ἐμος. ʊ παρα τας εἰκοσι μεμφομεθα.

Epigram XLVII.] The meaning of this epigram ſeems to be, that the lover, whoever he was, had long purſued his Miſtreſs in vain; that he laid a plan to entrap her on the twentieth day of the month Παnʊ́; or July; and that, although his firſt ſtratagem failed, ſhe had unexpectedly fallen into his power in the month Δωος, or Auguſt following. For we muſt obſerve that Hermes, the God of Cunning and Roguery was the protector of the lover; which ſhews that he had gained his Miſtreſs by ſtratagem, though the literal meaning be that ſhe yielded of her own accord. Nevertheleſs Madam Dacier with her uſual modeſty, ſuppoſes that theſe lines bear no relation to love, but to a creditor ſeizing the perſon of his debtor.

V. 6. And ruſh'd ſpontaneous to my arms.] The literal ſignification is " the Ox came

XLVIII.

Thus Giant Polyphemus fweetly fung,
While o'er the cliffs his goats untended hung;
The mufe to hopelefs love is ever kind;
The pow'r of wifdom heals a wounded mind,.
And meagre famine brings this only good,
It calms the pulfe, and cools the glowing blood.
Mifchievous boy, my thoughts no more fhall rove;
I'll clip, with thefe, the flutt'ring wings of love,
Defpife thy pow'r, fwift haften home, and there
With wifdom and the mufe difpel my care.

Ὡς ἀγαθαν Πολυφημος ἀνευρατο ταν ἐπαοιδαν,
   Τωῤῥα μενων αἰγαν ἠ καθημης ὁ Κυκλωψ.
Αἱ μυσαι τον ἐρωτα κατισχναινοντι. Φιλιππε,
   Η πανακει παντων φαρμακον ἡ σοφια.
Τυ δοκεω χ' ἁ λιμος ἐχει μονον ἐς τα πονηρα
   Τωγαθον. ἐκκοπτει ταν φιλοπαιδα νοσον.
Ἐσθ' ἡμιν χ'ἁ κασας ἀφειδεα προς τον ἐρωτα
   Τυτι, παι, κειρει το πτερα παιδαριον.
Οὐδ' ὑσον ἀλλ' ἀραγον σε δεδοικαμες· αἱ γαρ ἐπωδαι,
   Οικω τω χαλεπω τραυματος ἀμφοτεραι.

came of his own accord to the Plow," a proverb ufed to denote uncommon profperity
brought about by accident, and not by our own induftry. Bentley.

   Epigram XLVIII.] The firft diftich was publifhed by Madam Dacier; I have added
the reft from a manufcript. Bentley.

XLIX.

Loud fhouts from th' Acamantian choir proclaim,
At Bacchus' feaft, the joyful victors name ;
For him they weave the Dithyrambic crown ;
A wreath of rofes adds to his renown,
And, more to recompence his toil, they fhed
The facred unguents o'er the poet's head,
Who now victorious gives this lafting fign,
This golden tripod to the pow'r divine.
Antigenes inftructs the crouds beneath ;
But wife Arifto's ever tuneful breath

Πολλακι δη φυλης Ακαμαντιδος εν χοροισιν Ὡραι
Ανωλολυξαν κισσοφοροις επι διθυραμβοις
Αἱ Διονυσιαδες, μιτριασιτε και ῥοδων αωτοις
Σοφων αοιδων εσκιασαν λιπαραν εθειραν.
Οἱ τονδε τριποδα σφισι μαρτυρα βακχιων αεθλων
Θηκαντο. κεινες δ' Αντιγενης εδιδαξεν ανδρας.

V. 9. Defpife thy pow'r.] Ουδ ὁρον ατ]αραγον οι δαδικαμις " I value thee no more than
a cruft of bread;" an expreffion of the greateft contempt. Hefychius cites this paffage of
our poet to explain the word ατ]αραγος.

Epigram XLIX.] The fignification of thefe verfes is clear and perfpicuous. At the
feaft of Bacchus, when the tragic and comic poets recited fables to the Athenians, the victorious bard was Hipponicus of the tribe of Acamantis ; Antigenes recited the fable ; and
Arifto played on the Dorian pipe. This epigram was not wrote by Callimachus, but by
Bacchylis or Simonides   Bentley.

3   could

Could fweeter founds in Doric reeds infpire:
Hipponicus was leader of the choir,
Above the reft he fhone fuperior far,
The graces bore him in their airy car,
Obey'd the Mufes, and the Bard renown'd,
The Mufes with unfading Vi'lets crown'd.

L.

Efcap'd the horrors of a wat'ry grave,
To Samothracian Gods Eudemus gave
His little fkiff; and faid, ye mighty pow'rs,
Accept my gift; the votive gift is yours.

Εὖ δ' ἐτιθηνειτο γλυκεραν ὀπα Δωριοις Ἀριςων
Αργειος ἠδυ πνευμα χεων καθαροις ἐν αὐλοις.
Ῥων ἐχορηγησεν κυκλον μελιγηρυν Ἱππονικος
Στρϰθωνος υἱος, ἁρμασιν ἐν χαριτων φορηθεις.
Αἱ οἱ ἐπ' ἀνθρωποις ὀνομα κλυτον ἀγλααντε νικαν
Θηκαν, Θεαν ἰϛεφανων ἑκαδι Μοισαν.

Την ἁλιην Εὐδημος, ἐφ' ἡς ἁλα λιτος ἐπελθων
Χειμωνας μεγαλϰς ἐξεφυγεν δανεων.
Θηκε Θεοις Σαμοθραξι· λεγων ὁτι τηνδε κατ' εὐχην,
Ω λαοι, σωθεις ἐξ ἁλος ὡδ' ἐθετο.

Epigram L.] It has been mentioned in the notes on the XLth. Epigram, that the ancients frequently promifed an offering to fome Deity before undertaking a dangerous

enterprize;

LI.

As youthful Sinus gave me to the Nine,
He faid, Ye mufes grant me light divine;
And thefe accepting, like brave Glaucus, foon
For the fmall gift return'd a greater boon.

Εὐμαθιην ᾐτειτο διδὰς ἐμε Σιμος ὁ Μικκυ

Ταις Μυσαις· αἱ δε, Γλαυκος ὁκως, ἐδοσαν

enterprize; and that the vow was always paid upon their return. In like manner it was ufual to confecrate fome memorial of an efcape from battle, a fhipwreck, or other imminent danger in the temples of the Gods; as we learn from the XIth epigram of Anacreon, which I fhall give in Mr. Fawkes's tranflation;

> Minerva's Grove contains the favour'd fhield
> That guarded Python in the bloody field:

And likewife from the following paffage of Horace.

> Me tabula facer
> Votiva paries indicat uvida
> Sufpendiffe potenti
> Veftimenta maris deo *.

Of which I cannot prefent my readers with a more adequate tranflation than that by the great Milton.

> Me, in my fow'd
> Picture, the facred wall declares t'have hung
> My dank and dropping weeds
> To the ftern God of Sea.

Epigram LI.] Sinus, a young, but attentive fludent dedicates to the Mufes an image of Bacchus, which was erected oppofite to a figure of the letter ϒ ufually placed in the

---

But, with diſhevell'd locks, I ſtand and ſtare
Againſt the doubtful Samian letter there.
To me the boys addreſs their ardent pray'rs,
And cry, O Bacchus, ſacred be thy hairs ;
But I no more attend theſe idle themes,
Than if they told me laſt night's empty dreams.

Αντ' ολιγε μεγα δωρον. εγω δ' ανα την δε κεχηνως

  Κειμαι τε Σαμιε διπλοον, ο τραγικος

Παιδαριων Διονυσος επηκοος. οι δε λεγεσιν,

  Ιερος ο πλοκαμος, τεμον ονειαρ εμοι.

ſchools of antiquity, to denote the different roads leading to virtue and vice. This letter was called Samian, becauſe it was invented by Pythagoras a native of Samos. And the heads of Bacchus, which the boys invoked to inſpire them with learning, were always repreſented bearing long and diſhevelled hair : hence this deity had the names ἀβροκομης, and κισσοκομης. But the ſtatue, here mentioned, declares that the prayers of the boys were to no purpoſe; ſince, being inanimate, it could no more attend to them than to the relation of a dream. Bentley.

    Mr. Pope alludes to the Pythagorian letter in the following lines of his excellent Satire on modern Schoolmaſters.

        When reaſon doubtful, like the Samian letter

        Points us two ways, the narrower is the better *.

    But the note on this paſſage refers to Perſius and not to Callimachus ; although the little poem before us, contains the firſt mention of that letter in verſe.

    V. 3. And theſe accepting, like brave Glaucus, ſoon.] Bentley and Madam Dacier obſerve very juſtly, that Γλαυκος is the true reading, although it be γλικος in the manuſcript ; and that the poet refers to the exchange of armours betwixt Glaucus and Diomed mentioned by Homer.

Σ.6

LII.

S⟨tr⟩anger, would'ſt thou my ſtory know?
B⟨ehol⟩'d I ſtand a comic ſhow;
A⟨nd⟩ Pamphilus within this place
M⟨ay⟩ ⟨A⟩g'ranax's vict'ry grace:

Τη⟨ν⟩ ⟨πα⟩ραχυτατος με λεγε, ξενε, κωμικον οντως
Αγκε⟨ιτ⟩αι νικης μαρτυρα τυ Ροδιυ

'Ειθ αυτι Γλαυκω Κρονιδης φρινας ιξιλιτο Ζιυς,
'Ος προς Τυδιδην Διομηδια τυυχι αμιιβι,
Χρυσια χαλκιων ικατομβοι ινναβοιων †.
Brave Glaucus then each narrow thought reſign'd;
Jove warm'd his boſom and enlarg'd his mind:
For Diomed's braſs arms, of mean device,
For which nine oxen paid (a vulgar price)
He gave his own, of gold divinely wrought;
A hundred Beeves the ſhining purchaſe bought. Pope.

The preſent epigram may be ranked, if not among the beſt, at leaſt among the moſt uſeful of theſe wrote by our author; and contains an excellent leſſon for ſtudents and ſchool boys in all ages. The poet adviſes his young friends not to ſtand bawling to a deaf head of Bacchus (like the prieſts of Baal of old) but to give diligent application to their ſtudies, which is meant by invoking the Muſes; and that theſe Goddeſſes would not fail to recompenſe their labours ten fold, as they had already rewarded Simus the ſon of Micus.

Epigram LII.] Madam Dacier declares that ſhe cannot form a probable conjecture about the meaning of this epigram; but refers it to future commentators. And Bentley gives the following explication. Agoranax, a comic poet, in commemoration of his victory at the feſtival of Bacchus, conſecrates to that deity the ſtatue of a player named Pam-

† Hom. Il VI. v. 234.

Philus:

Altho' I feem not very fine,
Nor is the workmanfhip divine;
For half like fhrivell'd figs appears,
And half to foot refemblance bears.

LIII.

Thus Micus chofe to reimburfe
Old Phrygian Æfchra, once his nurfe;
Alive the dame on dainties fed;
He plac'd an image o'er her dead;
That late pofterity may know,
What kindnefs we to nurfes owe.

Παμφιλον, ἐκ ἐν ἐρωτι δεδαυμενον. ἡμισυ δ᾽ ὦπται
Ἰσχαδι κ̓ λυχνοις Ἰσιδος εἰδομενον.

Εἰς Αἰσχρην, τινα γυναικα ἐτω καλυμενην, την Μικκυ τροφον.
Την Φρυγινην Αἰσχρην, ἀγαθον γαλα, πασιν ἐν ἐσθλοις
Μικκος κ̓ ζωην ἐσαν ἐγηροκομει.
Και φθιμενην ἀνεθηκεν, ἐπ᾽ ἐσσομενοισιν ὁρασθαι
Ἡ γρηῢς μαθων ὡς ἀπεχει χαριτας.

philus; but a coarfe piece of workmanfhip, full of wrinkles, and black as foot, or as the lamp of Ifis, as the original expreffes it. Agoranax muft have been a poor poet indeed, otherwife he might have afforded, if not a richer, at leaft a more cleanly offering to his Protector.

Epigram LIII.] Though the meaning is fufficiently plain, Madam Dacier again pro-

feffes

LIV.

Four are the graces now; and all may see
Another added to the former three,
Yet wet with unguents, and but lately born;
Fair Berenice blooming as the morn,
So bright with charms, and such her beauteous face,
That robb'd of her the Graces lose their grace.

Εἰς την γυναικα Πτολεμαιȣ Βερενικην.
Τεσσαρες αἱ Χαριτες. ποτι γαρ μια ταις τρισι κειναις
Ἀρτι ποτ᾽ ἐπλασθη, κῆτι μυροισι νοτει,
Εὐαιων ἐν πασιν ἀριζηλος Βερενικα,
Ἁς ἀτερ ȣδ᾽ αὐται ται χαριτες χαριτες.

fesses ignorance, at which we need not be surprized; as the learned Lady seldom under-
stands a single verse, where a woman is concerned. Bentley observes that ἀγαθον γαλα, lac
bonum, is an elegant phrase for a good nurse; and Ernestus from Heringa that ἱπτσομɛɩοɩ
bears a very different import from ἱν᾽ ἱσομɩɩοɩσɩ, the former denoting *superstites*, *qui super-*
sunt; and the latter *apud futuros*. Were this observation true, the statue raised by Micus
must have been intended for the use of his cotemporaries only, and not for the benefit of
posterity. But I may venture to contradict it on the authority of Homer; the following
being the last verse but one of the third Iliad:

Ἢ τις ἱπɩσσɩμɛɩɩοɩσɩ μɩτ᾽ ἀ·θρɒποισι πɛλɛται

And age to age record the signal day. Pope.

Epigram LIV.] This Berenice was the daughter, and not the wife of Ptolemy Philadelphus. Dr. Dodd has it, she married her brother Ptolemy Euergetes, the successor of
Philadelphus; and soon after that marriage, Callimachus wrote the Coma Berenices, probably among the last of his performances.

V. 3. Yet wet with unguents, and but lately born.] The method of managing new
born

LV.

Theocritus looks black, 'tis true ;
But then his face is comely too :
If he hate me, your love is fuch
You hate him juft four times as much ;
But if he love, yon love him then
Beyond the love of mortal men.
And fuch, I fwear, O mighty Jove,
By facred Ganymede above,
The friendfhip once to him you bore,
And fuch the love ; I fpeak no more.

Τον το καλον μελανευντα Θεοκριτον, ει μεν εμ' εχθει,

Τετρακι μισοιης· ει δε φιλει, φιλεοις·

Ναιχι προς ευχαιτεω Γανυμηδεος, ερανιε Ζευ.

Και συ ποτ' ηρασθης. ἐκ ἐτι μακρα λεγω.

born infants among the Greeks has been already defcribed in the notes on v. 55. of Hymn 1. To which I fhall add from Madam Dacier that it was cuftomary to anoint the children of perfons of quality with fragrant oils.

Epigram LV.] Grævius has given this, and the fix following epigrams, upon the authority of Bentley, who tranfcribed them from a Manufcript then in poffeffion of the learned Edward Bernard. And he tells us that this was a copy of the ancient Heidelberg Manufcript preferved in the Vatican Library.

Lucina,

LVI.

Lucina, grant thy aid again,
Nor let Lycænis call in vain ;
To thee, propitious Pow'r, I bow,
And for a daughter thank thee now :
But if, bright Queen, a boy were mine,
A greater gift ſhould grace thy ſhrine.

Καὶ παλιν, Εἰλειθυια, Λυκαινιδος ἐλθε καλευσης,
  Εὐλοχος ὡδινων ὡδε συν εὐτοκιῃ·
Ὡς τοι νυν μεν, ἀνασσα, κορης ὑπερ ἀντι δε παιδος
  Τϛερον εὐωδης ἀλλο τι νηος ἐχοι.

Epigram LVI.] This epigram is very pretty; the thought being natural, well expreſſed, and intereſting particularly to the Ladies.

LVII.

What for Demodice was ow'd,
On Æſculapius is beſtow'd ;
Aceſon ow'd it for her charms, ,
Since firſt he revell'd in her arms. ·
And, ſays the picture, ſhould he chuſe ·
No more t' approach his lovely ſpouſe,
The fair would ſtill his praiſe deſerve,
Nor from the rules of virtue ſwerve.

Το χρεος ως απεχεις, Ασκληπιε, το προ γυναικος
Δημοδικης Ακεσων ωφελεν, αρξαμενος
Γινωσκειν. ην δ' αρα λαθη, κ̣ μη μιν απαιτης,
Φησι παρεξεσθαι παρθενιην ο πιναξ.

Epigram LVII.]   Aceſon, the lover of Demodice, had made a vow to dedicate her picture in the temple of Æſculapius, providing his Miſtreſs would conſent to marry him. After the celebration of the nuptial rites he performs his promiſe ; and the picture immediately praiſes Demodice for exemplary chaſtity.   The reader may have obſerved in the courſe of theſe epigrams that the moſt inanimate beings are frequently endowed by Callimachus with the faculty of ſpeech.   2

An

LVIII.

An ever-living lamp I fhine
To Canopifta, pow'r divine ;
With twenty matches I appear,
And Crita's daughter plac'd me here,
To pay what for her fon fhe ow'd,
What, for Appelles, late fhe vow'd :
And when my light you firft efpy,
You'd fwear the ftars had left the fky.

Τῳ με Κανωπιτᾳ Καλλιϛιον εἰκοσι μυξαις
Πλησιον ἡ Κριτιυ λυχνον ἐθηκε θεῳ,
Εὐξαμενα περι παιδος Απελλιδος· ἐς δ᾽ ἐμα φεγγη
Αθρησας φησεις· Ἑσπερε, πως ἐπεσες ;

Epigram LVIII.] Who the Godddefs Canopita or Canopifta was, I have not been
able to difcover, either from Voffius, Bryant, Banier or any other Mythologift. Suidas
quotes this epigram, but gives no account of the Deity *. I can only form a conjecture
from fimilarity of names. The princefs Arfinoe was worfhipped in the city of Canopus,
and might, from that circumftance, have received the name Canopifta.

* Suid. in verb μιξα.

M m   Eurnetus

LIX.

Euænetus declar'd that he,
For battles won, devoted me
A brazen cock, within this place
To Tyndaris' immortal race.
But Phædrus' fon I love and fear,
And, as my guardian God, revere.

Φησιν ὁ με ϛησας Εὐαινετος (ὐ γαρ ἐγωγε
  Γινωσκω) νικης ἀντι με της ἰδιης
Ἀγκεισθαι χαλκειον ἀλεκτορα Τυνδαριδησι.
  Πιϛευω φαιδρε παιδι Φιλοξενιδεω.

Epigram LIX.] Euænetus, whoever he was, having gained a victory dedicates a bra
zen Cock to the brother Warriors, Caftor and Pollux, who were called Tyndaridæ from
Tyndaris, another name for their mother Leda, the wife of Tyndaris, king of the Lacedæmonians. But the cock declares that he puts moft confidence in the fon of Phædrus,
the fon of Philoxenis; and of him we are entirely ignorant. Two folutions may be given;
either that the cock was part of the fpoils of war, and had been taken from the fon of
Phædrus, or that this perfonage was a Deity of equal rank with the Tyndaridæ.

Fair

LX.

Fair Æſchylis, from Thale ſprung,
In Iſis' fane an off'ring hung ;
And thus the vow her mother made,
Irene's vow is fully paid.

LXI.

Whoe'er thou art in tempeſts loſt
And driv'n aſhore by ſurges toſt,
Leontichus laments thy doom,
And lays thy body in this tomb ;

Ιναχιης ἑϛησεν ἐν Ισιδος ἡ Θαλεω ϖαις
Αἰσχυλις, Εἰρηνης μητρος ὑποσχεσιη.

Τις ξενος, ὠ ναυηγε ; Λεοντιχος ἐνθαδε νεκρον
Εὑρεν ἐπ' αἰγιαλοις, χωσε δε τῳδε τοφῳ.

Epigram LXI.] As the ancients imagined no misfortune ſo great as remaining
unburied after death, ſo no pious act was reckoned equal to that of beſtowing the rites of
Sepulture on a dead body when found by accident. Becauſe it was the common opinion
that the ſouls of the deceaſed were obliged to wander from place to place, upon the banks
of the river Styx, till their bodies had received the funeral rites ; as we find deſcribed at
large in the twenty third Iliad.

Thus

But mourns his own unhappy ſtate,
Expos'd, like thee, to certain fate ;
Expos'd to plow the wat'ry plain,
Or, like a ſea-mew, ſkim the main.

Δακρυσας ἐπικηρον ἑον βιον· ὑδε γαρ αὑτος
Ἡσυχον, αἰθυιης δ᾽ ἰσα θαλασσοπορει.

Θαπτε με ὁτ᾽ῖτ αχιςα πυλας Ἀϊδαω περησω·
Τηλε με ἑιργυσι ψυχαι, ἐιδωλα καμοντων.
Ὀυδε με πως μισγεσθαι ὑπερ ποταμοιο ἐωσιν·
Ἀλλ αὑτως ἀλαλημαι ἀν ἑυρυπυλες Ἀιδος δω.

Let my pale Corſe the rites of burial know,
And give me entrance in the realms below:
'Till then, the ſpirit finds no reſting place,
But here and there, th' unbody'd ſpectres chace
The vagrant dead around the dark abode,
Forbid to croſs th' irremeable Flood.   POPE.

Thus we have paſſed through theſe celebrated epigrams, to ſome of which no tranſlator
can do juſtice ; others are more eaſy, and ſome perhaps the reader may think would have
been as well omitted.   But it was judged neceſſary to give a compleat tranſlation, that
being the condition on which this book was offered to the Public.   And ſhould the reader
receive either inſtruction or amuſement from the peruſal of theſe and the preceding poems,
the tranſlator will think himſelf amply repaid for his labours.

THE END.   +

L I S T

S U B S C R I B E R S.

A

THE Vifcount of Arbuthnott, 5 copies
The Rev. John Aitken, St. Vigeans
George Aitken, Efq. London
Robert Allardice, Efq. of Memus
Alex. Abercrombie, Efq. Advocate
Robert Anderfon, M. D. Edinburgh
Thomas Adair, Efq. Writer to the Signet
Mr. Charles Abercrombie, Writer, Edinburgh
Mr. John Adam, Surgeon, Forfar
Mr. John Adamfon, Writer, Edinburgh

B

The Earl of Buchan
Sir John Wifhart Belches, of Fettercairn, Bart.
Robert Blair, Efq. Solicitor General
Alexander Burnet, Efq. of Strachan, Advocate

Charles Brown, Efq. of Coalfton, Advocate
William. M'Leod Bannatyne, Efq. Advocate
Mr. John Bennet, Surgeon to the Caftle of Edinburgh
The Rev. John Biffet, Brechin
The Rev. James Brown, Brechin
Mr. David Blair, Merchant, Dundee
Mifs Blair, Brechin
The Rev. Patrick Bryce, Carmyilie
Mr. Robert Baillie, Kincraig
John Brown Efq. at Mathers
Mr. Charles Black, Merch. Brechin
Mr. Wm. Black, Writer, Brechin
Mr. Robert Brown
Mifs Bryce, Carmyllie
Dr. Burn, New Norfolk Street
Lord Binning, Ham Common

C

Sir David Carnegie, of Southefk, Bart. 12 Copies

Patrick

Patrick Cruikſhank, Efq. of Straca-
thro, 10 Copies
James Cruikſhank, Efq. of Rich-
mond, Iſland of St. Vincent, 3
Copies
The Rev. Alexander Carlyle, D. D.
Inverefk
James Carnegie Arbuthnott, Efq. of
Balnamoon
Mrs. Carnegie, of Charleton
Patrick Chalmers, Efq. of Auld Bar,
2 Copies
The Rev. Alex. Chalmers, Cairnie
William Campbell, Efq. of Fairfield
Alex. Campbell, Efq. of Clathie,
Advocate
Alex. Chriſtie, Efq. of Townfield, 2
Copies
Daniel Cathcart, Efq. Advocate
James Clerk, Efq. Advocate
Jofeph Cauvin, Efq. W. S.
The Rev. Alex. Chaplin, Kinnell
Thomas Carnegy, Efq. of Craigo
Alex. Callendar, Efq. of Crichton,
M. P.
Miſs Carnegie, Southeſk

D

The Right Hon. Henry Dundas, one
of his Majeſty's principal Secre-
taries of State
Lord Dunſinnan
George Dempſter, Efq. of Dunni-
chen
Wm. Douglas, Efq. of Bridgetown
Sir Alex. Douglas, Bart. Dundee
Mr. Andrew Dalzell, Profeſſor of
Greek, Edinburgh
John Duncan, Efq. of Rofebank, 2
Copies

Alex. Duncan, Efq. Canton, 6 Copies
Mr. Alex. Dalmahoy, Merchant,
Edinburgh
Mr. James Douglas, Surgeon, Kir-
rilmuir
Mr. David Dakers, Merch. Brechin
Captain James Dick, Dundee
Captain Dempſter, Dunnichen

E

The Hon. Henry Erſkine, Dean of
the Faculty of Advocates
Sir William Erſkine, of Torry, Bart.
John Erſkine, Efq. of Dun
Wm. Elliot, Efq. Advocate

F

The Earl of Fife
Sir Wm. Forbes, Craigievar, Bart.
Sir Wm. Forbes, of Pitfligo, Bart.
Wm. Fergufon, Efq. of Raith
Rob. Fergufon, jun. Efq. of Raith
Alex. Fergufon, Efq. Craigdarroch
James Fergufon, Efq. Advocate
Alex. Ferrier, Efq. of Kintrockat,
4 Copies
Frederick Fotheringham, Efq. Writer
to the Signet
Colonel Alex. Forheringham O-
gilvy, of Powrie
James Ferguſſon, Efq. of Pilfour,
M. P.
George Fergufon, Efq. Advocate
Alex. Ferriar, Efq. Middleburgh,
Zealand

John

G

John Gillies, LL. D. and F. R. S.
Portman Street, 12 Copies
Lord Gardenfton, 7 Copies
Lord Adam Gordon
Major David Gardyne, Middleton
James Gregory, M. D. Profeffor of
the Practice of Medicine, Edinburgh
The Rev. Wm. Greenfield, Profeffor
of Rhetoric, Edinburgh
Charles Gray, Efq. of Carfe
Thomas Gillies, Efq. Balmakewan,
12 Copies
Colin Gillies, Efq. Merchant, Brechin,
3 Copies
William Gillies, Efq. London
Adam Gordon, Efq. Advocate
The Rev. John Gowans, Lunan
Major Cornelius Grant
Captain John Gray, late of 32 Reg.
Mr. Wm. Garden, Brackay Park
Charles Greenhill, Efq. Beauchamp
Charles Grant. Efq. Kinnard, 2 Copies
Alex. Gardiner, jun. Efq. Kirktenhill
Mr. Harry Guthrie, fen. Writer,
Edinburgh
Mr. Alex. Goodlet, Surgeon, Kirriemuir
Mr. David Guthrie, Merch. Brechin
Peter Gordon, Efq. Abergeldy
John Gordon, Efq. Advocate
Mr. Alex. Greig, Merch. Montrofe
Thomas Gordon, Efq. W. S.
The Rev. John Gillies, D.D. Glafgow
The Rev. Colin Gillies, Paifley
John Guthrie, Efq. of Guthrie
Robert Graham, Efq. Fintry
John Guthrie, jun. Efq. Guthrie

Lewis A. Grant, M. P.
Dr. Garthfhore, St. Martin's Lane,
2 Copies

H

Robert Heburn, jun. Efq. Clerkington
Colonel Alex. Hay, Ranas
Capt. Andrew Hay, Mount Blairy
Alex. Hay, M. D. London
Charles Hay, Efq. Faichfield, Advocate, 2 Copies
Wm. Honeyman, Efq. Advocate
Charles Hope, Efq. Advocate
John Hagart, Efq. Cairnmore, Adv.
M'Naughton Hunter, M. D. Montrofe
Mr. Robert Henderfon, Surgeon,
Cupar Angus
Mr. Charles Hay, Writer
Mr. Heavifide, No. 25, Somerfet St.
The Hon. Major John Hope, M. P.
The Hon. Capt. Char. Hope, M. P.

I

Capt. Imrie, Adjutant, Edinburgh
Major James Johnfton, Edinburgh
James Juftice, Efq. Juftice Hall
Charles Innes, Efq. W. S.

K

The Earl of Kintore, 2 Copies
Charles Keith, M. D. Morpeth
Patrick Key, M. D. Forfar

The

L

The Hon. Philip Leslie
Library of King's College, Aberdeen
Library of Montrose
Library of the Advocates, Edinburgh
Library of the Marischal College, Aberdeen
Col. Wm. Lindsay, Spynie
James Lindsay Carnegy, Efq. Kimblethmont
William Forbes Leith, Esq. Whitehaugh
Wm. Livingston, M. D. Aberdeen
Joseph Lowe, M. D. Brechin
Malcolm Laing, Esq. Advocate
Mr. Gilbett Laing, Edinburgh
David Lyell, Esq. Gallery
The Hon. Captain David Leslie, Melvill House
The Hon. Mrs. Leslie
The Hon. Colonel Colin Lindsay, Duchess Street, Portland Place

M

The Hon. Wm. Ramsay Maule, of Panmure, 12 Copies
Lord Monboddo
Sir Wm. Miller, Glenlee, Bart.
Wm. Montgomery, Esq. M. P.
James Montgomery, Esq. Advocate
Alex. Monro, M. D. Professor of Anatomy, Edinburgh
Allan M'Connochie, Esq. Advocate Professor of Law of Nature and Nations
The Rev. Joseph M'Cormick, D.D. for the University of St. Andrews, 2 Copies

John Hay Busby Maitland, Esq Advocate
John Miller, Esq. Advocate
James Wolfe Murray, Esq. Advoc.
John Mill, Esq. Fearn
George Mill, Esq. at Mill of Pert
Captain Hercules Mill
Capt. James Mylne, jun. of Mylnefield, 2 Copies
Allan M'Lean, Esq. Drimmin
Wm. M'Pherson, Esq. Inverishie
Thomas M'Donald, Esq. Barrister at Law, London
Bailie James Morison, Leith
Bailie Thomas Molison, Brechin
Mr. Alex. Mitchel, Morch. Brechin
Mr. John M'Gregor, 3 Copies
Major James Mercer, Sunny Bank
John Muie, M. D. Montrose
Mr. James M'Donald, Inglismaldie

N

Alex. Nairn, Esq. Drumkilbo
Mr. Wm. Nicsh, Unshank

O

The Hon. Walter Ogilvy, Clova
Wm. Ogilvy, Esq. Newton Mill
Robert Ouchterlony, Esq. Montrose
Mr. David Ogilvy, Surgeon, Brechin

P

The Earl of Peterborough
Mr. John Playfair, Professor of Mathematics, Edinburgh
Mr. Robert Playfair, Writer, Edinb.

The

The Rev. James Paton, Craig
Capt. Poplett, No. 8, New Norfolk Street, Grofvenor Square
Mr. Wm. Parfons, Efq. No. 143, New Bond Street

R

Sir Alex. Ramfay, Irvine, Balmaine, Bart.
Sir Wm. Ramfay, Banff, Bart.
Hercules Rofs, Efq. Roffie
Mrs. Rofs, Roffie
Charles Rofs, Efq. Advocate
John Rotheram, M. D. Edinburgh
Adam Rolland, Efq. Advocate
Francis Ruffel, Efq. Blackhall
Alex. Ruffel, jun. Efq. Moncoffer
George Robinfon, Efq. Gafk
Mr. James Robinfon, Surgeon, London
Colin Robertfon, M. D. Perth
Bailie James Ramfay, Perth
Capt. James Rutherford, 45 Reg.
Mr. Alex. Ritchie, Writer, Brechin
Mr. David Rickard, Merch. Brechin
Thomas Renny, Efq. W. S.
Wm Richardfon, Efq. the Ifland of St, Vincent

S

The Right Hon. Lord Salton
The Right Hon. James Sterling, Lord Provoft of Edinburgh
Lord Stonefield, 3 Copies
Sir John Sinclair, Bart. U.bfter, M.P.
George Skene, Efq. Skene, 12 Copies
Mr. Scott, Ancrum
Mifs Scott, Ancrum

George Robertfon Scott, Efq. Benholm, Advocate
Dughald Stuart, Efq. Profeffor of Moral Philofophy, Edinburgh
Charles Scott, Efq. Criggie
Alex. Scott, Efq.
George Skene, M. D. Aberdeen
Alex. Skene, Efq. Robiflaw
Robert Speid, Efq. Efq. Andovie
Mrs. Speid, Andovie
John Spence, Efq. Bearhill
Alex. Smith, Efq. Balmakelly
Walter Smith, Efq. Hedderwick
John Smith, Efq. Provoft of Brechin
James Smith, jun. Efq.
Mr. John Smith, jun. Poftmafter, Brechin, 2 Copies
The Rev. Robt. Small, D.D. Dundee
James Stormonth, Efq. Lidnathie
Mr. Robert Stuart, Surgeon, Dundee
Mr. James Spence, Writer, Edinb.
Mr. John Sievwright, Writer, Brechin
David Skene, Efq. London
Robert Stephen, Efq. Letham
Alex. Strachan, Efq. of Tarrie
Mr. John Speid, Merchant, Dundee
Mr. Stirling, Dundee

T

Lord Charles Townfhend
Wm. Tytler, Efq. Woodhoufelee
Alex. Frazer Tytler, Efq. Judge Advocate and Profeffor of Univerfal Hiftory, 2 Copies
Captain Tytler, 56th Regiment.
Crawford Tait, Efq. W. S.
Wm. Tait, Efq. Advocate
The Rev. John Taylor, Lethnot
John Taylor, Efq. W. S.
Major Alex. Turnbull, Ardo

The

LIST OF SUBSCRIBERS.

The Rev. Alex. Turnbull, Dilladies, L.L. D.
Hercules Tailyour, Efq. Montrofe
Robert Turing, Efq. Edinburgh
Mr. Dav. Taylor, Druggift, London
The Rev. Dr. Thomfon, Kenfington 2 Copies
John Turin, Efq. Middleburgh, Zealand

W

Col. Wm. Wemyfs, Wemyfs, M. P.
Mr. Williamfon, Monboddo
Alex. Watfon, Efq. Drimmie
The Rev. James Wilton, Maryton

Thomas Wilfon, Efq. Advocate
James Wilde, Efq. Advocate
James Whyte, Efq. Edinburgh
Mr. George Watfon, Writer, Edinb.
James Wyllie, Efq. Commiffary, Brechin
Mr. Thomas Wyllie
Mr. Patrick Wilfon, Bookfeller, Brechin
John Willifon, M. D. Dundee
Alex. Watfon, Turing

Y

James Yeaman, Efq. Murie
James Young, M. D. late of Antigua

www.ingramcontent.com/pod-product-compliance
Lightning Source LLC
Chambersburg PA
CBHW030343270326
41926CB00009B/946